An Unreal Estate

An Unreal Estate

SUSTAINABILITY & FREEDOM IN AN EVOLVING COMMUNITY

LUCINDA CARSPECKEN

INDIANA UNIVERSITY PRESS

BLOOMINGTON & INDIANAPOLIS

This book is a publication of

Indiana University Press
601 North Morton Street
Bloomington, Indiana
47404-3797 USA

iupress.indiana.edu

Telephone orders 800-842-6796
Fax orders 812-855-7931

Manufactured in the United States of
America

Library of Congress Cataloging-
in-Publication Data

Carspecken, Lucinda, [date]
  An unreal estate : sustainability and
freedom in an evolving community /
Lucinda Carspecken.
     p. cm.
  Includes bibliographical references and
index.
   ISBN 978-0-253-35681-9 (cloth : alk.
paper) — ISBN 978-0-253-22349-4 (pbk. :
alk. paper) 1. Sustainable living—
Indiana—Lothlorien Nature Sanctuary.
2. Self-reliant living—Indiana—
Lothlorien Nature Sanctuary. 3. Collective
settlements—Indiana—Lothlorien Nature
Sanctuary. 4. Communitarianism—
Indiana—Lothlorien Nature Sanctuary.
5. Lothlorien Nature Sanctuary (Ind.)—
Social life and customs. 6. Lothlorien
Nature Sanctuary (Ind.)—Environmental
conditions. I. Title.
  GE196.C37 2012
  304.209772'255—dc23

                               2011014341

1 2 3 4 5 17 16 15 14 13 12

For Phil, Sunil, and Roly

Contents

Acknowledgments

I am grateful to the dedicated people I met at Lothlorien, who accepted my presence and questions over a long stretch of time, and who made me feel welcome. They have been helpful beyond any conceivable call of duty, and have given me the sense of belonging to a large extended family. They are a group of idealists whose ideals are often different from one another's, sometimes stubbornly different, but it takes dreamers like this to maintain the place, and I continue to be amazed at the scale of volunteer work and creativity there. I owe a special debt to those who agreed to be interviewed, since their words—often humorous, insightful, and poetic—have added enormously to the book, even down to its title and chapter headings.

In the early stages of this study, Beverly Stoeltje provided wonderful scholarly advice. I received further helpful advice from Marvin Sterling, Sarah Phillips, and Rebecca Manring. Once the book was conceived, I was very well supported by the good people at Indiana University Press—Linda Oblack, Peter Froehlich, Nancy Lightfoot, and June Silay. Candace McNulty was an exceptionally thorough copyeditor. And thanks to Deleska Crockett, Roly Carspecken, and Sunil Carspecken for transcribing interviews.

My husband, Phil, encouraged me and acted as a sounding board throughout the fieldwork and writing process. My sons, Sunil and Roly, inspired me with their originality and self-motivation and made me laugh when I needed it. All three of you have provided a wonderful, loving home base. Thank you so much.

A Note on Names

In most cases the research participants in this book gave me permission to refer to them by their first names or by their commonly used chosen names. I used one pseudonym, by request. Where more than one person shared the same first name I added an initial.

An Unreal Estate

The creek running through the
woods at Lothlorien.

Courtesy of Jason Wadsworth

1

"That Dose of Unreality"

An Introduction to Lothlorien Nature Sanctuary

It's a strange thing that so many people just love that
little piece of dirt so much. And it's not really much
different than any other hundred acres.

Jef, 2006

Lothlorien is unreal estate.

Tuna, 2006

Andrea, who has been a Council member at Lothlorien Nature Sanctuary, once
attempted to convey the experience of her first festival there in an essay for an
undergraduate English class. Her assignment was to write a detailed factual
description of a person, place, or object. Usually a good student, in this case
she was considered to have failed to obey the directions and received a D–. The
instructor refused to believe that the place was real.

When I read Andrea's paper I found the teacher's skepticism understandable.
Lothlorien provides such a marked contrast to its surroundings that a description of it could stretch anyone's imagination. Two themes in particular stand out
for me in her writing, themes that have come up again and again in interviews,
conversations, and survey responses about this piece of land, especially when
people describe their first impressions. One is a kind of visual enchantment,
including, for example,

> the candles, tea-lights, and tiki torches that line every path, that light up
> this heavenly body called Lothlorien, like the Milky Way. All this light
> converges in a pinnacle of flame at Thunder shrine . . . At night it is a
> magical space, lit with an immense fire. (Andrea Chesak, 2005)

The other is the unusual degree of *communitas* and openness she found among festival-goers based on an ethic of tolerance:

> You will find kinship flourishing in a multitude of topics, with common or differing opinions, but it is an environment where you can agree to disagree. (Ibid., 2005)

Communities that come to be described as "utopian," like works of utopian fiction, stretch credibility almost by definition. Thomas More, who popularized the term by using it as the title of his fantasy society, chose a spelling that implied both "good place," from the Greek word "eutopia," and "no place," from the Greek "outopia." This was apt because, first, it is easy to assume that existing and "common sense" social forms in any given time or place exhaust the possibilities for human organization and, second, ideals tend to keep expanding or changing when put into practice—which means that perfection is never actually reached. Since 1987, Lothlorien participants have been consciously trying to refute common sense, maintaining a space that is unlike the world around it. Organization, land stewardship, community, and ritual have been reenvisioned in a number of ways. Andrea's impressions are fairly typical of visitors' initial responses. One participant described people's first year of experiences at Lothlorien as their "year of enchantment." The enchantment often wears off over time. But Tuna, another Lothlorien volunteer with a gift for words, describes the site as "unreal estate." The land and community seem unreal in comparison with the world outside their gates both because they take so much influence from fantasy literature and because they defy mainstream expectations about the ways things can or should work in North America.

Lothlorien embodies a patchwork of alternative visions inspired partly by environmentalism, partly by Neo-Paganism, partly by fictions of various kinds. It plays several different roles. It combines a festival site, a nonprofit organization, a residential community, and a nature sanctuary. Each of these roles has unique features. The organization runs on a high level of volunteer commitment and individual motivation. The land and buildings are collectively owned. The festival site is characterized by ideals of freedom in religion, creativity, lifestyle, and worldview; the residences and other structures employ innovative ecological design; and relationships between people and land involve to a greater than usual degree, respect for, and conscious reenchantment (through ornaments, shrines, rituals, lighting, and symbolism) of, the natural world. Lothlorien, then, is deliberately unusual economically, politically, and culturally.

Raymond Williams (1977) describes the pervasive cultural and economic assumptions of a given time—their particular vantage points—as "hegemonies."

An Unreal Estate

These tend to reinforce existing power relations, although they are always in process, reinventing themselves and diffusing or expropriating alternative or opposing norms. Williams points out that hegemonies may be powerful but they are not total. They include remnants of previous social institutions or value systems, pockets of resistance, and seeds of possible future change. Utopian novels, religious visions, and experimental communities fall into these categories. Without the benefit of hindsight it can be difficult to tell which will prove ephemeral or retrograde and which will prefigure changes in the wider world. But, like mutations in a gene, they open up possible avenues for new formations and directions.

In this book I will describe some of the unique features of Lothlorien Nature Sanctuary, pointing out how they work (to the extent that they do.) I will argue that just as Lothlorien itself took concrete form partly through imaginative models in fiction—from *The Lord of the Rings* (Tolkien 1954), which inspired its name, to science fiction and fairy stories—the place itself, like other experimental communities, embodies some new examples of what is possible, "natural" and real for the rest of us. I will argue, further, that grassroots utopianism, whether in fiction or in social experiments, can be a valuable force for change, one that is often treated warily by academics. The unreal, in literature and film, and the exceptional and seemingly unlikely, in alternative living arrangements, are forces that can shape and pull what we normally consider "real" in social life. Lacan originated the term "social imaginary" in 1936, in his psychoanalytic theory, and the idea has been taken up in social philosophy by Castoriadis (1975) and Taylor (2007, 2004), among others, to describe clusters of imaginative symbols along with values, rules, and norms that are woven, invisibly but powerfully, into the social world. In utopianism, imagination is drawn on explicitly and with a greater degree of conscious choice or agency than is usual in social life.

I define utopianism here as a pull toward new possibilities and forms of decision making rather than as the advocacy of a blueprint, and I am referring to grassroots experimentation in spite of state ideals and laws, and as a way of circumventing these, rather than to top-down state impositions.[1] Also, while a substantial number of utopian fictions or experiments have been based on fixed social designs created by charismatic visionaries and theorists, or rooted in religious belief systems, many others have been more concerned with alternative processes than with end results. Lucy Sargisson (1996: 9–38) distinguishes "form based" from "content based" approaches to Utopia in contemporary women's fiction, noting that the worlds described in the former utopian fantasies tend to be fluid rather than static. The two approaches she describes have coexisted for

"That Dose of Unreality"

a long time in experimental communities as well as in fiction, as, for example, in the difference between the rigidity of Harmony under the Pietists and the chaos and shifts in the community that followed it at New Harmony (Arndt: 57–88, in Pitzer, ed., 1997; Pitzer, ed., 1997: 88–53). But increasingly, particularly since the mid–twentieth century, it is common for utopianism to incorporate an expectation of change, negotiation, and conflict rather than a fixed end point. This is certainly true at Lothlorien, where ideals and priorities are continuously contended, sometimes fiercely.

One of my aims in writing this book is to look at the power of grassroots experimentation and utopian imagination both in the conception and maintenance of Lothlorien and in the impact of Lothlorien's existence on those who visit it and learn about it. My other aim is to convey, as much and as vividly as possible, the experience of being at Lothlorien, at least from my own perspective and through the words of community members. For every phenomenon that fits a general rule, like the role of social experiments within mainstream societies, there are features that escape it. Lothlorien is not easy to define. Perhaps no place is. Tuna considered this study a long shot at best. "You're trying to pin down what can't be pinned down," he said. "Lothlorien is beyond description."

Lothlorien, as he maintains, is unclassifiable on some level. It is a place with a particular landscape, a particular configuration of oak and beech, clay soil, limestone, geodes, hills, nettles, and bird song. It is a place where black and yellow butterflies dodge each other over the creek in summer while the pollen floats down on it like snow. It is a place where mosquitoes nibble at you and the humidity frizzes your hair when you work in the forest or the garden so that the heat and the irritation of the bites meld into an overall *gestalt*. Radiance Hall or the Long Hall, the largest community structure, has a particular smell that I cannot describe; a cocktail of damp, mold, old cooking, over-chlorinated tap water, tobacco and wood smoke, which brings up memories every time I step into it.

This is also surely the only place in the world where a giant tuna hangs from a four-story-high geodesic dome in the middle of the woods. This is the place with campsites called Upper Boom, Bag End, and Scientists' Circle. This is the place where you can go to a vendor's tent called Jake's Greasy Spoon and be offered homemade peanut butter and jelly liquor, which tastes exactly like an alcoholic peanut butter and jelly sandwich in liquid form. This is the place where a group of teenagers call themselves the Feral Land Children and a place that regularly hosts fire dancers. This is the place where you can play Elf Chess (which has no rules) on a Trollbar, and be understood if you say, "I love you in a Charlton Heston kind of way." This is a place where a woman called Acorn

The back of Radiance Hall in winter.
Courtesy of Scott Martin

sometimes plays the violin against the backdrop of drums after dark around a fire. This is a place where you may walk through forest trails and come upon a face carved in a tree stump, or walk through campsites and see paper snowflakes hanging in tree branches and painted statues of fairies, gnomes, and deities among the plants.

A net of words wide enough or precise enough to throw over any community, place, or passage of time and capture it perfectly has yet to be found, at Lothlorien or elsewhere. Besides this challenge for researchers, being defined can be, and often has been, an uncomfortable experience for those being researched. Conney, one of Lothlorien's founders, says, for example, "I tend to run from labels . . . so I don't know what I am. It's safer that way." I experienced my efforts to put Lothlorien into words as confounding in my first few months there. I would seize on some angle through which to interpret what I was seeing or talking about during the day and do background research on it at home only, frequently, to be told by somebody that I had been wasting my time on the research, that Lothlorien was not a part of whatever tradition or classification I

"That Dose of Unreality"

had been attempting to fit it into. The tradition of intentional communities was one of the first frameworks I tried. Neo-Paganism was another. In both cases, participants told me that these were inaccurate labels.

Some people refer to Lothlorien as a Neo-Pagan site and some do not. Lothlorien was conceived in part as a sanctuary for people as well as nature, people whose religious practices did not fit comfortably with the mainstream. Consequently visitors or members with any degree of involvement and any religious affiliation are free to conduct ceremonies, prayers, or rituals and also, within certain limits, create or add to shrines and tree art. Most promotion is done through Pagan Pride processions or Pagan websites, which suggests at least a strong link to Neo-Paganism. But recognition of many paths and divinities is a part of this movement's core definition and its many shrines may hold Madonnas, symbols of the elements, crucifixes, mirrors, Buddhas, skulls, saints, children's toys, gods, fairies, and humorous items side by side. Officially Lothlorien is ecumenical, welcoming all paths. If there is a common element to the varied religious visions on the land, it is care for the environment. Lyn, who used to work on legal and financial issues for the organization says,

> Lothlorien was . . . brought about by the environment, and our care of the environment. That's how it started. It started with a focus on nature. Thus, "Lothlorien, Nature Sanctuary." And, what it's progressed into, with getting the 501(c)(3), and reincorporating, the entire structure reincorporated. We reincorporated it under a religious ecumenical organization. And it's not so much that now we've become religious, it's just that now what we've stated is that our religion is the religion of nature. (Lyn, 2006)

On an individual level, many Lothlorien participants do not describe themselves as Pagans, or even fit easily under the umbrella of nature worship. Some wish to remove themselves from fundamentalist perspectives, to spend time in a culture of religious, philosophical, and behavioral openness. Bonedaddy, who has been living on the site much of the time since 1993, expresses this point of view eloquently. His father was a Christian minister and much of his childhood was spent in a Christian summer camp. While he loves and respects his parents, he appreciates the chance to be among people with less fixed beliefs:

> When you start believing in organized religion, you stop searching. I have a bad opinion of any religion or idea system that says, "We're right and you're wrong." I freely admit that I don't have the slightest idea where we came from or where we're going. I'm one of those people

who requires proof. I believe in the earth because I'm standing on it. I believe in my friends and the people I love. I believe in my emotions . . . I have no absolute truth. I'm still searching for the absolute truth and I won't stop until I'm dead. (Bonedaddy, 2006)

The religious affiliations, in fact, of many of the active volunteers I interviewed or talked to were at least as difficult to pin down or categorize as Lothlorien itself. Paul, for example, described himself as an "alternative theologian," while Laura said she was a "scholastic theologian, reading too many books, not practicing enough." Bonedaddy called himself "an agnostic forest freak." Scott used the phrase "non-denominational Taoist" to describe his religious leanings, while Braze said he was a "pantheistic Taoist with hedonistic tendencies." I have also met Wiccans, Goths, Christians, Buddhists, Sufis, ceremonial magicians, agnostics, atheists, and combinations of all of these on the land. The most succinct description I have heard so far about Lothlorien's religious links is Conney's: "It's Pagan, but not exclusively."

Whatever else I do with this portrait, then, I want to avoid flattening out the individuals, landmarks, and events in overly general statements about utopianism, intentional communities, festival sites, or Neo-Pagans. Describing Lothlorien and its role as a utopian example involves putting it, at least loosely, into a category or combination of categories. But as I do so I want to keep in mind that it fits in unique rather than predictable ways.

Beginnings

Lothlorien was conceived in 1983 during an overnight conversation and a Tarot card reading between two friends, Michael Posthuma and Terry Kok. "Elf" (standing for Elf Lore Family) was a name and concept for the original organization that came to Terry's and Michael's minds at almost precisely the same moment. They envisioned a nature sanctuary, education center, camping ground, and festival site. Michael felt that they had hooked into the inspiration rather than created it:

Elf was just this brainchild that kind of got a hold of us and said, "Hey, we need you silly-ass humans to pay attention for long enough." (Michael, 2006)

The organization later changed its name, since "ELF" had also been adopted by an ecoactivist group originating in Britain that used property damage as a tactic. (In the British group, the acronym stands for Earth Liberation Front.)

The current name for the organization that runs Lothlorien is Elvin HOME, with the letters standing for Holy Order Mother Earth. Participants sometimes refer to themselves as "elves."

Promotional literature produced by Terry in 1985 articulates his ideal for the land:

> *LOTHLÓRIEN* will be: a **NATURE SANCTUARY** for all gentle animals, brilliant flowers, verdant green . . . a **SURVIVAL EDUCATION CENTER** teaching the woodland living arts, star magicks, and Elf-lore . . . a **WOODLAND MEETING GROUNDS** for all "friends of the **ELF**," a **CRAFT** contax point and camping grounds, seasonal rites & festival site, an **ELF** council center.
>
> *LOTHLÓRIEN* will be located in the beautiful hills and fertile valleys of Southern Indiana near the HOOSIER NATIONAL FOREST and Bloomington, IN . . . we're looking at 80 acres minimum and are setting our wish at 200 or more . . . enough space for SILENCE and MAGICAL PLAY!
>
> *LOTHLÓRIEN* will have three simple rules:
> 1) no violation of the land or its inhabitants through needless killing or pollution: chemical, mechanical, radiative, or otherwise. . . .
> 2) no violence towards private property (that which is not permanently attached to the ground)—in all ways respecting the owner's stated wishes. . . .
> 3) PERFECT LOVE & PERFECT TRUST
>
> (Terry Kok, Elf Lights, 1985)

For the first few years Terry and Michael held festivals in public parks to raise money, with the help of their wives, Conney Freese and Nora Liell. Then in 1987, Conney found a piece of land near where her family lived in Lawrence County, and they bought it, along with the friends and volunteers who were involved in the Elflore Family. The property covers 109 acres. Part of it used to be cornfields. A creek runs through it. About ten acres of the cornfield area was adapted into a campsite, while most of the land was left to revert to forest. Conney describes some of her first impressions along with the group's plans for the place:

> This is what this new piece of ground was meant to be, a place where the earth is treated with respect. We wanted to create a green haven, a place for people to escape from the cities, a place to practice healing, renewal, and restoration, of the land and of ourselves. We called it Lothlorien, after the last wooded haven of the elves in *Lord of the Rings*. It was meant to be an outpost of nature, a blow for the wild against the spread of pavement and subdivisions. We harbored no illusions about this being forest primeval. The decreasing size of the trees in the deep

floodplain along the creek showed where farmers had gradually given up. The uphill fields were overgrown with greenbriar and multiflora. The only large trees grew on the ridges that had been too steep to plow and in a rocky valley between the upper fields. (Conney, 2008, www .elvinhome.org)

As is clear from Conney's words, Lothlorien defines itself in part through the contrast with its surroundings, "a blow for the wild against the spread of pavement and subdivisions," an escape from what some participants call "Mundania," the "real" world. My introduction to the site, then, includes a brief description of the area outside Lothlorien's borders.

The Surrounding Community: Southern Indiana and Lawrence County

Southern Indiana was one of the first areas of the Northwest Territories to be settled by people of European origin (Nation 2005; Rafert 1996.) The Native Americans preferred the flat, uninterrupted landscapes of central and northern Indiana because they farmed collectively, in large tracts. The Europeans preferred the hill country of Southern Indiana because it reminded them of home (the southern uplands of the United States in many cases, or hilly parts of Europe—Germany, Ireland, Scotland, Belgium, Switzerland, and France) and because it was well suited to individual family farm-holdings, the land being demarcated by its hills and valleys. These settlers regarded farming collectively as "uncivilized," whereas their own separate and stratified family units constituted evidence of their superior rights to the land. By 1834, they had removed the last of the Miami Indians from Indiana through a combination of warfare and legal manipulations. Among the new settlers a tradition of distrust for peoples of non-European origins continued until at least the end of the nineteenth century and in some cases beyond. In 1850 Indiana established a state constitution that forbade African Americans to live in the state. This was overruled by the federal government in 1866.

Among themselves, however, the first farming families in the area were unusually egalitarian. Many small farms were developed and owned by many landowners, as opposed to a few large ones with a surplus class of landless people. There were few servants or farm hands, and while people were stratified *within* families by gender and age, the class system was minimal.

Nation, in his detailed study of Southern Indiana in the nineteenth century (2005), describes the settlers as extremely religious. Churches served congre-

"That Dose of Unreality"

gations of Catholics (usually from Germany), Methodists, Presbyterians, and Baptists, with the Baptists being the most populous. The tone of the churches was conservative and exclusive. For example, missionary activity was considered futile by many of the Baptist churches. In their view, God's salvation was predestined. Only a few were chosen, and a person not born into a Christian community was probably not one of these few. The most extreme version of this doctrine was Parkerism, which held that there were "two seeds" populating the human race; one from God and one from Satan. This doctrine fed easily into racism, and also distrust and avoidance of any type of outsider. "Original sin" was also a common focus among the churches, so that humans (presumably even the ones that came from God's seed) needed a great deal of supervision, correction, and oversight.

Southern Indianans in the nineteenth century tended to have much more trust in the local community than in any outside institution, including government or markets. This was partly because only the immediate community could provide the kind of close-range supervision they felt that people needed. Trials and public confessions were often held in church, for example. Clusters of related families tended to farm near each other, and local loyalty was much stronger than that of nation, state, or any other affiliation (Nation 2005).

Lawrence County, where Lothlorien is situated, is in the center of Southern Indiana. It was formed and settled in 1818. It developed in large part because of the limestone industry in Indiana's Stone Belt, which extends from about ten miles north of Bloomington to a few miles south of Bedford. Commercial quarries were in place by the 1830s and grew in importance over the next hundred years. Land in Southern Indiana became less and less profitable to farm after World War I, but Lawrence County has had a well established limestone industry until the last two decades (Ferrucci 2004). The limestone is said to be the best in the world.

At present, Lawrence County as a whole has a population that is almost 98 percent white, and Oolitic, the nearest town to Lothlorien that I could find statistics for, is almost 99 percent white. Bedford, the nearest mid-sized town, has one African American family. The county is somewhat different from other parts of the area because it has a tradition of labor and of unions as well as of agriculture. Besides these factors, Indiana University in Bloomington to the north has made an impression as a source both of employment and of new residents.

Overall, Southern Indiana (apart from Bloomington) remains a socially and politically conservative place, with a strong Christian presence. Yet it has also attracted a surprisingly large number of alternative communities. In the early

An Unreal Estate

nineteenth century it was frontier land, a place where idealists could try to live out social experiments, the best known of which was New Harmony. Currently Padanaram (a patriarchal religious commune), May Creek (a semi-communal housing subdivision and nature preserve), Ourhaven, (a privately owned Pagan community), Amish communities, a Tibetan monastery, and a nudist colony are all within the area. It is possible that a continuing ethic of localism protects such communities from extreme forms of neighborly interference, while relatively low land prices make them feasible.

The contrast between Lothlorien's founders and their neighbors has sometimes resulted in tension, however, especially in the early days. When, in 1985, they held one of their first festivals near Bloomington, in Yellowwood State Park, a local newspaper called *The Brown County Democrat* ran an article titled "Satanic Rites Held at Yellowwood Forest," based on interviews with two police officers (Guinee 1987; Pike 2001), describing the community as devil-worshippers. The officers told the newspaper that they saw "emblems that have been connected with devil worship." Several officers had prowled through the festival throughout the weekend with or without their vehicles, sometimes shining headlights into tents. One of Lothlorien's Stewards, Uncle Dan, told me that the police had been searching through the campfires for bones. They frequently asked festival attendees if they were about to sacrifice a goat. (Blood sacrifice is not a Neo-Pagan practice, but is associated with Satanism in the popular imagination.) Nobody was arrested, no goats were sacrificed, no bones were found, and no laws were observed to be broken. According to Glacier, another Steward, a local church, the Bean Blossom Baptist Church, also found out about the gathering, and the congregation brought anti-Satanic leaflets, which they spread among the participants.

This kind of tension was one of the factors that motivated Lothlorien's founders to acquire their own land rather than hold festivals in public spaces. When the purchase was finally made, however, neighbors still resented Lothlorien's presence, partly because they had previously used the land for hunting—its owner had been absent much of the time—and partly because of its owners and visitors living such a different lifestyle. Both communalism and Neo-Pagan practice remain suspect in the eyes of the public, especially in conservative and fundamentalist Christian areas (such as much of Southern Indiana.) Jerry Falwell, for example, in his much quoted speech about the attack in New York on September 11, began by condemning the influence of "the pagans and the abortionists and the feminists."[2] Conney and Michael both told me that vandals came right before the first festival based on the land. Then, soon after the community had moved to Lothlorien, local teenagers drove around the land at four

"That Dose of Unreality"

o'clock in the morning, shouting obscenities and trying to run over a resident in the driveway, who had come out to see what was happening. Although the tensions have died down in recent years, less extreme reenactments of this scene have recurred frequently, according to Michael, with teenagers from the neighborhood pulling into the front entrance, yelling insults, and pulling out again.

Sarah Pike, in her work on Neo-Pagan festivals, *Earthly Bodies, Magical Selves* (2001: 19), describes the North American festival gathering as "a place apart." Even outside of festival times the contrast between Lothlorien and its immediate neighborhood is stark.

Coming to Lothlorien

It was Lothlorien's associations with Paganism as well as its socially experimental nature that first drew me there. A friend had suggested Wicca as a dissertation topic because she knew of my desire to find a community or place that could offer examples of unusual, preferably progressive, social configurations. Contemporary Wicca, she thought, was one of the few religious movements she had directly experienced that fit that description, with female as well as male deities and leadership or figureheads that again included women as well as men. I was then lucky enough to find a graduate student at Indiana University, Denise, who had been involved in Wicca and Neo-Paganism. It was she who told me about Lothlorien, thinking perhaps, that this was a tangent.

When I heard the name Lothlorien, I was immediately intrigued; I had loved *The Lord of the Rings* as a child. Also I had an academic interest in the relationships between fiction and the social world. Further, I had been curious about communal and cooperative organizations since a month-long working visit in my teens to an Israeli kibbutz. This curiosity had been bolstered during this same period in my life by reading utopian novels such as Richard Adams' *Watership Down* (1972). I had fantasized about starting my own community someday, which, predictably, never happened. Lothlorien, then, reignited several long standing interests.

I liked Lothlorien tentatively, cautiously, on my two very brief visits to festivals in 2005. Denise took me into the wild part of Lothlorien first, and we sat and talked on a stretch of pebbles by a creek among the acres of tall trees. I remember greenness, quiet, the sense of being able to breathe freely, away from roads and buildings, and I remember seeing a snake swimming with its head above the water. Later, among the campsites I found the combination of scruffy ornaments and shrines with greenery intriguing; but, although I felt welcome, the large gathering of unfamiliar people was a little overwhelming.

Many community members, however, told me that they had had immediate, visceral responses when they first arrived, something akin to "love at first sight." The reasons they gave for this included the land itself, the aesthetics of the campsites, the environmental ideals expressed there, and the community spirit visitors experienced.

Janie describes the way she was struck by the creative touches added to the land, along with her experiences with other people:

> I just had an absolutely fabulous time. I really had a good time. I think it was more of that festive atmosphere I think that first really got me . . . It was Elf Fest. That was my first festival. I guess that was in . . . '93 . . . I like to camp anyway. But it was the way they camped, you know. It wasn't just a tent in the middle of the woods, but it was the festivities of hanging up additional tapestries, that made it kind of colorful, or setting up camp with the lighting in the evening, the lighting was so wonderful. All the different little elements—seeing the shrines lit up. (Janie, 2007)

Stew had a serendipitous experience when he first came to Bloomington to search for Lothlorien in the early 1990s. The first person he asked for directions turned out to be Terry, one of the founders of Elflore family. When he arrived, the land had an immediate effect on him:

> I remember the first time that I stepped into Lothlorien's forest; these magical elfin woodlands; and I felt an immediate sense of "HOME." (. . . HOOOOOOMMME . . .) There was obviously something to that as, even though I did continue on Grateful Dead tour and other various mystical travels, I wound up back here and here is where I've mostly been ever since. I've always believed in our collective vision . . . (Glorfindel/Stew, from *Lothlorien Leaf*, January 2008)

Bonedaddy, who had already been living in the woods in Brown County, appreciated finding a group of like-minded people with similar ethics to his own; Paul F. shared that appreciation, although the two express this in different terms:

> I wanted to find more people that were open minded . . . [At Lothlorien] I didn't feel so alone. I found people cared about the planet. I found that not all people felt that way, but it's a better way to live life than "Consume, consume, gimme, gimme, greed, greed . . ." Society teaches respect but it doesn't teach respect for the environment. Not enough, yet. (Bonedaddy, 2006)

> I kept finding people like me who seemed to be willing to question authority, themselves, their environment, spirituality. (Paul, 2009)

Others expressed not so much the appeal of finding *like*-minded people but of finding people who were accepting and welcoming. (This very common theme in the interviews is a topic of discussion in chapter 5.) Jef, for example, first visited Lothlorien in the late 1980s:

> I started to do other festivals, and they were okay, but still I never found any place that was like Lothlorien. Everybody just accepted you. If someone is obnoxious and rude you don't get accepted. But I mean if you just a little bit show like you really cared and you want to learn and want to just be part of the Lothlorien scene if you want to call it that, people would just accept you. And back then they just accepted us, because the first time we went there we had no idea what was going on, what we were going to have to come into. We pulled in on Friday night at Wild Magick,[3] so it was in full bloom—the festival was just kicking by the time we got there, on a full moon, and it just overwhelmed me. We didn't even know where we were supposed to park, or camp. We ended up camping down on the field parking lot . . . We had no idea where we were supposed to be and nobody gave us crap, they didn't make us move . . . they just said it was okay. (Jef, 2006)

Lyn, similarly, felt immediately welcome on her arrival at Lothlorien in 1994:

> Out of the Trollbooth, which is where you first come in and sign in, out pop, as I put it, "Larry, Moe, and Curly"; and what it was was the trolls,[4] because the trolls used to actually man the booth, most of the time, . . . one guy in a skirt, two guys in pantaloon pants, and you know, no shirts or vests, and tans, and long hair halfway down their backs. And I'm going, "I have just stepped in to another dimension." I get out of the vehicle, and the smell of patchouli almost made me fall over. But the thing that was so special was . . . the feel of the land, even at the Trollbooth, and when I did get out of the car I was met with "Welcome home," and a huge hug.
>
> . . . And I didn't realize how big of another place it was until all of a sudden I've got one of these guys sitting on the hood of my rented car, my rental car. I'm driving down to the festival field, with this guy on the hood of my car. He helps us offload, and then goes, "Can I park your car?" And I didn't hesitate to flip him my keys. That's not normal, somebody you don't even know you're giving your keys to; especially on a rental car. And it was like, I just felt, "I don't have any worries; I don't have to worry about it." (Lyn, 2006)

An Unreal Estate

Braze's original reasons for being attracted to Lothlorien involved ideals—in his case, the ideals of freedom and contribution as well as environmentalism:

> To become a part of something that was larger than myself as a whole and to contribute (in a way) that not necessarily ensured a legacy, but made a profound contribution to my people, whoever in the hell that is, another big question there. And to enable the resistance, you know. Always been a freedom fighter, always been a rebel, the underdog and whichever teams looks like it's going to lose I'm there pulling for them . . . And so this was an opportunity to do all those things. (Braze, 2006)

And for Sarah too, the original draw of Lothlorien had a lot to do with environmental ideals, with the desire to set an example, and with her disillusion with materialism:

> So I came and I instantaneously fell in love with the place. It just reminded me that there is still good in the world. And not all of it has McDonalds on it. And shopping malls . . . This is what life is supposed to be like on my path, I guess . . . and this is just like a perfect place for me to learn how to be more conscious of my environment, of what I'm putting into it, what I'm taking out of it, different ways of doing things . . . There's just so many things that we're doing that I don't understand why we do them that way when there's other ways to do them, and so instead of just keep on doing the same-old, same-old I decided to come live like this, and do these things to live by example. Maybe if other people see that I can do this, then they can see that they can do this. (Sarah, 2006)

Joe took a down-to-earth approach to the site and was drawn by the camping, friendship, and music "all in the same place," as were several of his friends. A college mate of his had read a flyer about the place and suggested they take a look. She said, "I don't know if I believe in elves, but I believe in land." Joe remembers being

> completely shell-shocked by the ritual part of it. And that was true until the last time I was there—only because I think you'd describe me as a recovering Catholic . . . I've always been that way about religion. I was the first kid in my family that left religion before I left home . . . I just had no interest in that part of it. . . . For me it was more about camping . . . We went on hikes, went down to Faerie,[5] went to the little waterfall. (Joe, 2010)

"That Dose of Unreality"

For Brooks, on the other hand, Lothlorien fitted into a mystical worldview, following some of his unusual experiences in early life with dreams and visions. He found out about Lothlorien by chance one night when he was spending the night at a friend's trailer that happened to be nearby in Lawrence County.

> About 3 o'clock I went outside . . . and I heard drums. I think our forefathers killed anyone who played drums a long time ago. So I imagined it must have been a mystical Brigadoon[6] community of Indians. . . . A mystical community that wanders out of the mist every one hundred years . . . So the next morning I wake up, "I heard drums last night." He goes, "Oh that's the elves." That intrigued me. (Brooks, 2010)

He visited later on a quiet, off-festival day in 1996:

> Nothing but trees—beautiful. I loved it, I could feel it immediately. I was walking around in circles. Beautiful sensations. I could feel what's been ensconced there. So many people having so much good times. It just seemed like a very special ground. I didn't want to leave . . . People have worshipped there, you could tell. It felt like a church. The whole woods felt like an outdoor church. (Brooks, 2010)

Among those who were coming regularly to Lothlorien from 2006 to 2010, then, a strikingly good first impression and the pull of idealism (from a wide range of viewpoints) were common themes. The group of people I interviewed, however, consisted mainly of people who had decided to continue spending time at Lothlorien after arrival and who were thus not necessarily typical. Those who had come once and never returned might have had negative impressions to share, and I did not have access to these. Larry, who had lived on the land for a few years, expressed his memories in more skeptical tones than any of the other interviewees, suggesting that, for some people at least, the enthusiasm may be temporary:

> Yeah, it was typical—prima donna enchantment for the first year. Everything's all hunky dory, everybody loves each other . . . Prima donna attitude is what we have interpreted around here as basically your first year, your greenhorn year, your rookie year, and you still have the notion that you are in a community, that everyone gets along, everyone gets together, and we all have at least one common goal throughout the whole thing: that my life is going to get better because I'm finally starting to find focus and I'm with nature and I like being outside and I like getting my hands dirty and I'm going to sleep in a tent for a year and

An Unreal Estate

really rough it; and all that fun stuff that most city dwellers love to do. Which is why most country people move into the city, 'cause they don't want to do that work anymore. (Larry, 2006)

Whether or not they withstand the test of time in every case, these first impressions and the varied desires and ideals they reflect—environmentalism, community, fun, beauty, mystical experience, tolerance—have inspired a group of volunteers to create and maintain an unusual range of structures and events at Lothlorien since 1987, and to do this with collective ownership, volunteer labor, and a minimum of rules, rewards, or sanctions; in a way, in other words, that often defies the common sense notions of how things work in the industrialized world. While I enjoyed the physical beauty of the place, it was these features that came to "enchant" me over time. Lothlorien's appeal to me grew as I came to see and respect the dedication, camaraderie, disagreements, and messy democratic processes that went into running it.

"A Jane Goodall Moment": Insiders and Outsiders in Ethnography

From March of 2006 onward I began spending time at Lothlorien on a regular basis. The governing Council formally voted to accept my request to do research there and for the first year I took a Staff (part-time volunteer) contract as a way of giving something back as I did research, as well as a way of learning more about the way the site was managed. In 2006, a lot of my time was spent in the community garden or participating in other maintenance projects. I also attended all the festivals and most of the meetings. Since I lived only half an hour's drive away, in Bloomington, I went home at night to sleep, with the exception of a few nights during festivals. From November 2006 until the present (in 2010) my visits have been less frequent, although I still attend monthly Council meetings, and some festivals.

Interviews were an essential part of the research. My original plan was to interview people at as many levels of engagement with Lothlorien as possible; to catch the flavor of the organization and community in the past as well as the present, and to include experiences of the land through past and present visitors and past and present volunteers. Early on it became obvious that this was overly ambitious. About a thousand people come to Lothlorien over the course of a year, the festival site has been running in its current location since 1987, and the original organization formed in 1983. Although I did conduct a range of interviews, I decided after a while to concentrate mainly on the present and

"That Dose of Unreality"

on the core group of regular volunteers. Some had recently arrived, others had been there for a long time. But running Elvin HOME's festivals, maintaining the land and structures, handling the finances and promotion, were group efforts, and I wanted to try to convey the sense of this whole group and their work over the relatively short span of time of my involvement.

In the end I conducted forty-one interviews, most with Council members, residents, and active volunteers and a few with regular festival participants or former regular participants. My interviews were open ended, starting with a question about what had first drawn the person to Lothlorien and taking the interviewee's lead as much as possible from that point onward. The time of each interview ranged from twenty minutes to three and a half hours. Most people I asked seemed comfortable with being interviewed and were articulate and insightful. To add a slightly broader perspective on Lothlorien I distributed an open-ended survey in the autumn of 2009. Fewer people returned these than had given me interviews, so my attempt at more breadth failed. The survey did, however, provide a few people with the opportunity to comment on Lothlorien anonymously, and thus complemented the interviews.

Whether we acknowledge this or not, ethnographers are being observed as well as observing. In the first month or so of coming to Lothlorien I was un-comfortably conscious of this fact, with the question, "How does it feel to have an anthropologist hanging around?" never far from my mind. This, coupled with a tendency to shyness, motivated me to work in the garden more often at that time than to ask for interviews or to sit and socialize. I knew that I was an object of study too. One day when I was pulling up nettles and clumps of grass behind a trellis, Scott played explicitly with the observer/ observed relation-ship, saying, "I'm having a Jane Goodall moment—watching the anthropologist among the weeds."

At Elf Fest (a large spring festival) in 2007, I was washing breakfast dishes in Radiance Hall; my fellow dishwasher, Dan V. said that he did not believe I was really studying Lothlorien. "You're really one of us and you're just pretending to be an observer," he said. "That's what everybody says." I felt honored by this comment. Time at Lothlorien has given me a strong sense of belonging and identity with the place and the people, and since I live only about twenty-five miles away, this will be sustained for the foreseeable future. At festivals I like to keep track of the registration counts not just for data, but also because I want to know how "we" are doing. I want Lothlorien to thrive, financially and otherwise, on the same prerational level that makes me want England (my coun-try of birth) to win the World Cup in soccer. When I first formally presented a research proposal to the Council, in May of 2006, after volunteering for a month or so, Braze was prophetic: "You're in danger of becoming one of the monkeys," he said.

This sense of belonging has affected the writing of this ethnography. For one thing, I have tended to keep the community at Lothlorien in my mind as an audience or readership while I write. This makes me conscious of being fair to the various members of the group, and has made me try (probably unsuccessfully) to keep a balance among all the different points of view, especially among all the participants whom I had most contact with at the time of my research. I have worried about the interviewees whose words I didn't cite as frequently as others, and I regret the absence of interviews I did not conduct. Community readers were mostly positive about the dissertation, although Braze felt that I had skirted around what he sees as Lothlorien's key defining factor—shamanic experience. Conney and Braze both helped by checking for factual inaccuracies.

To complicate a common ethnographic problem further, at Lothlorien and within Neo-Pagan communities, insider and outsider status are both matters of choice and difficult to define. First of all, anyone of any ethnicity, age, class, gender, or affiliation could come to Lothlorien. Second, "belonging" there is a very fluid thing. Many combinations of religious or cultural identity are possible, and tolerance of a range of beliefs and lifestyles is a strongly held value.

As for being an insider to the Pagan elements of the festival site, several people I have met or interviewed at Lothlorien said that before they had heard of Neo-Paganism, "I was a Pagan all my life without realizing it." The symbolism common in Neo-Pagan ritual and ornament is pervasive in Euro-American culture, especially in its stories, and the themes resonate with many people because they are familiar. This has been true for me. I was brought up in the south of England as a Christian and later adopted a yoga practice for a few years. But I had been a bookish child in a bookish family, with an interest in fairy tales, Robin Hood, King Arthur, *The Lord of the Rings,* Greek gods and goddesses, *The Wind in the Willows* (Grahame 1995 [1908]) and, later in life, Romantic poetry. (As I will show in chapter 2, literature has been a major influence both on Neo-Paganism and on intentional communities). I am an insider, then, in the sense that many of the symbolic reference points in Neo-Paganism are already a part of my imaginative landscape. And while I was not a member of the Lothlorien community, or a Neo-Pagan, before I began my research, I have since spent enough time there to want to continue attending festivals and helping on the land when the study is over, and enough time to consider many people there my friends.

An insider position cannot be equated with an uncritical view. First, there is a lot of variety in perspective within Lothlorien itself, and one would be hard put to find an active participant who did not have criticisms of the way festivals are run, of other participants' ethics and belief systems, of the process of decision making or of the stewardship of the land. Second, one of the central roles of anthropology is to attempt to make explicit the implicit aspects of cultures, a process requiring both an understanding of meanings from an emic point of view and the capacity to reflect on them. A completely relativistic view is not possible, for me, for any social researcher, or even for any human being involved in social interactions, since the selection of topics and even the words I use will involve my value judgments. The potential for critique *and* shared understanding of meaning are both implied and essential aspects of communication and description, written or otherwise.

While there is no such thing as an essential insider, then, to some extent taking an insider position is a choice. I see this in the differences between Greenwood's (2000) and Luhrmann's (1989) works on magicians in London. Both were participants, both similar to those they were studying in class, age, and ethnicity, both native language speakers, and neither of them were magicians or Neo-Pagans when they set out on their research, yet Greenwood seems to make a choice to take an emic perspective in a way that Luhrmann does not. A more emic perspective is also held, to a large extent, by the other Neo-Pagan scholars who have written since the 1990s, notably Sabina Magliocco (2004) and Jone Salomonsen (2002). Magliocco talks about making a choice to be willing to change and about compassion as a method. She argues that her sincere participation in ritual gave her a much deeper level of understanding of the movement:

> I was aesthetically pleased and genuinely moved by some of the rituals I attended, and as a result of these experiences I changed in significant ways. Because I decided to remain open and vulnerable during rituals, I gained access to imaginative experiences I had banished from my consciousness since reaching adulthood. These were crucial in helping me understand the essence of the culture I was studying; had I *not* had them, I would have failed to grasp the importance of religious ecstasy in the Neo-Pagan experience. (Magliocco 2004: 12)

She also notes, eloquently, the frequent psychological shifts involved in researching Neo-Paganism—shifts from scholar to participant and back—and points to the misleading essentialism involved in categorizing oneself as insider or outsider.

When Magliocco talks about "absorption" (2004: 15), when Greenwood says that she was choosing to be an insider, and when Salomonsen, citing Behar (1997), talks about being a "vulnerable observer," willing to be transformed, these are ethical statements as much as identity claims. They reflect a choice

An Unreal Estate

to empathize with as well as study a community. All three of these authors, along with Berger (1999), Pike (2001), and Orion (1995), describe, often movingly, rituals and social interactions in which they were involved and through which their worldviews shifted. In the sense of being willing to be changed by conversations, rituals, and working experiences at Lothlorien, and in aiming to express participants' perspectives as much as possible on their own varied terms, I also made the ethical choice to be more "insider" than "outsider" as an ethnographer. In retrospect what I have found most transformative has not been the element of ritual (although ritual has provided moments of joy) but the varied network of relationships I developed, and the sense of family that I felt and feel still through having worked and socialized with the community.

Before describing Lothlorien in depth, I will provide some context for its culture(s) in chapter 2, while looking more generally at aspects of the power of imagination over social life. This will entail a discussion of the literary roots of Neo-Paganism, particularly in Romantic literature; a few historical examples of utopian communities in the United States; and a preliminary discussion of utopianism and "human nature." Then, beginning with chapter 3, I will take four broad areas—land, organization, community, and ritual—to explore ways in which these are reimagined and reconstructed at Lothlorien. While it is impossible to argue with any certainty for the impact, or lack of impact, of social experimentation like this on wide-scale social change, I can explore on a small scale ways in which involvement in Lothlorien acts on the lives and worldviews of some of its participants and, more speculatively, the possibility of using aspects of life there as models for new social forms, new realities.

Pike notes a variety of ways in which the word "real" is used at festivals (2001: 19–26). Sometimes it is used to describe the outside world, the daily mundanity of work and routine. At other times "reality" is used to refer to festival space *itself*, because participants may experience heightened sensory awareness and freedom to be themselves. Thirdly, festival space may be a deliberately created reality, one which is more congruent with participants' worldviews than is everyday life: "Neopagans make an effort to create, for a week, reality as they think it should be, a world that heals body and soul and encourages interaction with nature" (23).

Jason describes his memory of a sense of unreality and shift the first time he came to a festival on the land. He brings these memories to life through references to scents and sounds:

> The smell of the place, the wood smoke, the incense—you smelled
> incense everywhere. And the sounds of the woods, the people, and just

"That Dose of Unreality"

the sounds of distant people talking and laughing, maybe a little bit of drumming or a flute playing in the distance. I felt like I'd stepped back in time or stepped back into a completely different dimension. And it was . . . nothing like I'd ever experienced ever before. (Jason, 2008)

Between festivals too, volunteers, organizers, residents, and visitors at Lothlorien try to create an alternate reality, even in their approaches to the less glamorous features of life: decision making, composting, finances, building, kitchen work, record keeping, gardening, road maintenance, festival promotion, and trash collection. I shall explore some of these in the chapters ahead.

Lothlorien and other alternative communities invite both resistance and change because they seem to defy common conceptions of reality in any given time and context. Frank expresses this idea:

Once you get that punch in the face, so to speak, that dose of unreality, then all of a sudden you begin to rethink where you are and what your priorities are. (Frank, 2009)

Setting up an alternative community of any kind entails being involved—sometimes inadvertently, sometimes consciously, and sometimes in seemingly day-to-day details—in ideological battles over what social reality *is*, what human beings really *are*. Woven through the history of utopianism, and through accounts of Lothlorien as well, these struggles are in evidence as people carve out new spaces for themselves, looking for chances to expand beyond current limits and expectations around how they interact with one another and with the natural world, who they are and who they have the right to be.

An Unreal Estate

2

"Dream Flowers"

*Fiction and Utopian Imagination in Neo-Paganism
and Alternative Communities*

"Taste every word, Meggie," whispered Mo's voice inside her,
"Savor it on your tongue. Do you taste the colors?
Do you taste the wind and the night? The fear and the joy?
And the love. Taste them, Meggie,
and everything will come to life."

Cornelia Funke, Inkheart

The first time I went to the Bag End campsite at Lothlorien, to stack firewood, I had the impression of being immersed in one of the Tolkien stories I had grown up with. It was a cool day with intermittent clouds, there were elm and oak trees around me and it felt like English weather. As a teenager, I had especially enjoyed the descriptions of Bag End, which is Bilbo and Frodo's house in the Shire in *The Lord of the Rings*. The Shire is a kind of idealized England; not much like the real thing, but rather what many of its inhabitants wished it was. The associations stirred up by the name Bag End were evocative of this fictional world.

In the Tolkien novel, the forest of Lothlorien and the elvin community there are described in impressionistic rather than specific ways. There is a Council, presided over by Queen Galadriel and Lord Elrond. There are song lyrics, descriptions of music and food and of the natural surroundings and structures, but little detail as to how things work. What the reader comes to know of it is that it is a hidden oasis of beauty and goodness and that it is a magical place where no evil can come. It is the last earthly home of the elves, who protect and are protected by the trees. It is a sanctuary. The novel also describes a small fellowship of diverse beings—an elf, a dwarf, a wizard, several humans, and several hobbits—who are closely bonded in a common goal.

Inspiration from Tolkien's work was a part, at least indirectly, of the vision for the original Elflore Family and the land they wanted to find:

> That's where a lot of these original ideas came from, because those books were so instrumental in our thinking, and of course we had read those years before we ever dreamed of an idea like this. (Michael, 2006)

Laura, a regular festival visitor who had grown up reading fantasy literature, including Tolkien, told me that she had been both delighted and amazed, in 2005, to discover a place called Lothlorien. She notes the way aspects of Tolkien's symbolic world weave through the real life community and land, and the way it acts as a source of inspiration (rather than a blueprint) for sustainability and ritual:

> It figures really hugely into the history and . . . the developed mythology of the people down there on the land too . . . They named the land itself after an elvin space, a space of magic in a set of really in-depth fantasy novels . . .
>
> They did it in such a way that it wasn't just kind of cheesy and campy like a science fiction convention in a hotel somewhere. They delved more deeply into the natural side of it and connecting with the trees and the plants and trying to find sustainable ways of dealing with things. And a lot of people really do believe in transformation through magical means and ritual means and things like that, and I think that's really important. (Laura, 2010)

Vic told me that the example of community among the characters in *The Lord of the Rings* had particularly inspired her, and she related that to her experiences in the real life community in Indiana:

> I really enjoyed the way they thought, and taking care of each other—community—I liked that. I liked the sense of community. And that's what I'm trying to get; like there's not that many people you could say—you wouldn't see them for a long, long time, and if you showed up on their doorstep at 3:30 in the morning and woke them up, would they just let you in or just say, "Go away?" And I've got several people like that since I moved over here. I know that if I have troubles there's people that I could go to, and I would do the same for them. So that's a really good feeling to know that, that you could go to them and they'll do whatever they can to help you. That's a good thing. So if you ever need help, knock on the door and we're here. (Vic, 2006)

Similarly, Denise said that one of the things that struck her and inspired her in reading *The Lord of the Rings* as a teenager was the bond between the characters. She found herself

> reflecting on this whole notion of how these different fictional peoples within Middle Earth were caring about each other and taking care of each other, and that notion of what I call "chosen family . . ." I was already finding that attractive. (Denise, 2006)

"Lothlorien" translates in Tolkien's invented language as "dream flower" or "the place of the dream flower." The name suggests dreams made manifest, imagination made into reality. Conney says that she thinks of the flower as a lotus, and that for her it conjures

> [an] image I have of something that just keeps opening and it has more and more layers and it changes, and it's not quite finished blooming ever but it's always in some stage of change. And, I mean, some days it would be kind of nice if everything stayed the same for a while. Something that's constantly changing, constantly evolving, there's always something new to do or new that's good or new that's bad. There's always new people coming and going. (Conney, 2006)

Braze expanded on the "dream flower" theme to explain the way work gets completed on the land. He said that each person tended to bring their own seed and cultivate their own flower, their own dream. I asked whether Lothlorien should be called "dream flowers" in this case. He thought it should remain "dream flower" but (jokingly) suggested that people get coloring book copies of the flower, and fill these in according to their own preferences.

The influence of other kinds of fiction besides Tolkien is also palpable at Lothlorien. Many of the objects and place names refer to stories. An unusual ambience has developed there that is steeped in a variety of fictions. In the trees, on the ground, in shrines, or within the structures there are visual symbols from folk stories involving magic, elves, and fairies, from ancient Greek, Norse, or Celtic mythology, from the legends of King Arthur, from pirate stories, and from science fiction. Reminders of literary or movie fantasy are everywhere, not only in images but also in rituals, religious ideas, and social organization. These fantasies are not fixed; they change over time, as Conney said, and reflect the imagination of different people at different times, as Braze implied in his "coloring book" analogy, rather than one singular vision.

Cornelia Funke's children's book, *Inkheart* (2003), quoted at the opening of this chapter, tells the story of a man with the power of bringing stories to life

"Dream Flowers"

Pan, painted in bronze, gold, and
green, by the garden pond.
Courtesy of Laura Dolloff

by reading aloud, dissolving the boundaries between fiction and reality. The idea is perhaps not as far-fetched as it seems. For, as I will argue, social realities have often originated in fiction, through literature, film, or other imaginative expressions. Stories have power. This is evident at Lothlorien, and it is also evident in the histories of Neo-Paganism and of social experimentation in the United States, since both these traditions have taken a great deal of inspiration from literature.

In European and North American academic writing and political thinking, it is common that social change is seen as a process of people recognizing problems, experiencing dissatisfaction, voicing their criticisms, and finally taking action. In the social sciences the desire for change, for justice, for a more equitable world is usually associated with critique. Although ideals and examples are inevitably implied in critique, they tend to receive less explicit attention, and in academia for the last few decades the potential latent in countercultural groups or communes and in the fictions that inspired them has been largely neglected as a progressive force. In this chapter then, and in the book as a whole, I want to highlight the pull of imagination, particularly utopian imagination—the power of new possibilities and examples. As Krishan Kumar says, "Utopia challenges by supplying alternatives," (1991: 87).

While Lothlorien is neither an exclusively Pagan community nor exactly an intentional community, it shares with the latter a pattern of seeking alternatives to mainstream institutions and with the former a specific cluster of social ideals and ideals around interacting with nature. Both of these groupings also draw a surprising amount of inspiration from fiction, including utopian fiction, as I will show. I shall provide some context for the community, then, through a discussion of these broader influences. I will conclude the chapter with a more theoretical discussion of the crisscrossing relationships between fiction, social theory, utopian imagination, utopian experiments, and social change.

Twenty-First Century Neo-Paganism: A Rough Definition

To distill the essential elements of Neo-Paganism, with its broad range of people, groups, and interpretations, is a challenge. For more detailed accounts I refer the reader to Ronald Hutton (1999, 2003), who is the seminal historian of Neo-Paganism, and also to Adler (1979), Berger (1999), Clifton (2006), Harvey (1997), Magliocco (2004), Pike (2004, 2001), and Salomonsen (2002). But since the movement is both relatively new and frequently misrepresented or misunderstood by the media and general public, it requires at least a brief definition before I discuss its ties to literature, a definition that attempts to summarize the main points of these same authors.

The following principles are central to Neo-Paganism:

- The divine is immanent in nature, living beings (including humans), and the elements. The natural world should therefore be treated with reverence and care, and the elements—earth, fire, water, and air—are often referred to explicitly in ritual.
- God, or divinity, however this is understood, is both female and male. This idea may or may not assume a fixed delineation of masculinity and femininity. And it may or may not see divinity personified as one or more male or one or more female beings, the Lord and the Lady, for example, or a pantheon from one or more traditions or an immanent pansexual divinity. It also may or may not see divinities as symbols. But there is an explicit inclusion of femininity in divinity.

"Dream Flowers"

- There is an emphasis on self transformation through ritual. Magliocco (2004: 152–181) uses the word "ecstasy" to describe the goal here, and Hutton (1999: 389–390) talks about invoking inner divinity.
- Hutton distinguishes Neo-Paganism from other religions that share the preceding features by adding that Pagans "turn for symbolism, kinship and inspiration to the pre-Christian religions of Europe and the Near East" (1999: 390). This (usually) includes a common observance of what are considered to be pre-Christian holy days; eight *Sabbats,* corresponding to the seasons and the relationship of the sun to the earth, namely Samhain or Hallowe'en; Yule or Winter Solstice; Candlemas or Imbolc; the Spring Equinox; Beltane or May Day; Summer Solstice; Lammas; and the Autumn Equinox. *Esbats,* or full moons, are also celebrated. It also includes imagery from European folk and fairy tales, and rituals and symbolism from Norse, Tuscan, Greek, Roman, Cabbalic, Egyptian, Druidic, Celtic, and other traditions.
- Neo-Paganism does not subscribe to rules set by an external authority or book. Books of Shadows are sometimes used, as compilations of rituals, but they are continually subject to adaptation and addition. Divinity is more often seen as internal rather than external. Experience is the ultimate touchstone. The one rule that Neo-Pagans accept, which is known as the Wiccan Rede, is "Do what you will but harm no one," which is often expressed in more archaic English, "An' it harm none, do as ye will."

I include a further idea, which is implied by those above and which is common, if not universal, in Neo-Paganism:

- Human nature, including instinct, emotion, intuition, and will, is trustworthy rather than suspect, closer to original innocence than "original sin." Hence, pleasure, joy and sexuality, are good rather than bad, with the caveat (see the fifth bullet above) that one should avoid harming others or the natural world.

This last feature, which resonates strongly with some strands of Romanticism (as well as some strands of Enlightenment thinking), is sometimes in tension with a competing idea, implicit in some Neo-Pagan writings and conversation, that humans have damaged the earth and their connection with it, and that they have shown themselves to be less trustworthy than its other inhabitants.

Whether in spite of or because of the last two points, many Pagans with whom I have been in contact have a strong ethical sense, although these ethics are not always in line with mainstream Christian or secular principles. For ex-

An Unreal Estate

ample, sustainable lifestyles are emphasized, with a corresponding disapproval of waste and consumerism, while there is an acceptance of homosexuality and approaches to monogamy are more variable. At least at Lothlorien, honesty is highly valued. I will give two anecdotal examples of this latter point. One is the high level of trust I and many others have developed around personal property at festivals. I often leave my purse on one part of the land while I wander off to another, and vendors often leave their stalls and tills unattended for periods of time. The other example came up in a conversation I had recently with a woman attending a Lothlorien festival, who was talking about the need for maintaining honesty and openness in her life. "I'm a witch!" was her way of making and emphasizing this point. For her, witchcraft and integrity were synonymous.

The range of traditions within Neo-Paganism includes Wicca, which is the original organized form of the religion from 1940s England, now referred to as Gardnerian Wicca to distinguish it from the many forms of Wicca that have developed since. Strega, from Italy, and Celtic Wicca, for example, adapt Wicca to remnants of Tuscan and Celtic cultures respectively. While Gardnerian Wicca follows fairly set guidelines for rituals and originally had male and female priest figures as well as stages of initiation, other forms are more eclectic and may or may not have an inner hierarchy.

Besides Wicca and its offshoots, the movement also includes a large number of Reconstructionists, who attempt to revive ancient ritual practices from one or other part of the world, often one that its participants have family links to. Examples of these include Druids (in Britain), Asatru (a Norse revival group), Hellenismos (Greek revivalism), and aficionados of Slavic, Baltic, Celtic, or Egyptian mythology and ritual. There are also groups that have taken some or all of their inspiration from science fiction, such as the Church of All Worlds, which was based in Robert Heinlein's *Stranger in a Strange Land* (1961), and the Discordians, whose anarchic philosophy of chaos and nothingness was popularized by the novelists Robert Shea and Robert Anton Wilson in their *Illuminatus!* trilogy in 1975. The New Reformed Order of the Golden Dawn grew out of a college assignment to design a ritual. There are ceremonial magicians who have an interest in Aleister Crowley's works or other traditions of ceremonial magic. Reclaiming and Dianic witches are more explicitly feminist than most Pagans, and there are the Radical Faeries, a nonhierarchical group of mostly gay men with feministic, nature-friendly beliefs.

Within some groups, covens take on their own ideologies and styles and particular ritual practices, and these can be quite idiosyncratic. In Indiana, for example, there is a coven of car-loving Pagans called the Motorhead Circle. Within each grouping also, there are many iconoclasts with their own take on rituals, beliefs, or lifestyles. New divinities are discovered, revived, or even invented—for example, Asphalta, the goddess of cars and travelers. New combinations with existing religions or traditions are made; there are Christian Pagans and Cabbalic Pagans, for example. Besides this, there is a great range of degrees and types of faith, with some participants seeing their practices as symbolic or therapeutic, others taking spells or rituals or worship more literally, some focusing on magic, others taking Neo-Paganism as a diffuse worldview. There are also, of course, lapsed Pagans and even self-described dissident Pagans. (The latter are quite rare, since Neo-Paganism is not dominant or pervasive enough in most environments to create a tangible pressure to buck).

As Isaac Bonewits points out,[1] it is very difficult to gather statistics about Neo-Pagans, or even to assess how many exist. This is partly a problem of unclear definitions and self definitions (compounded by the fact that Neo-Paganism does not always involve faith or exclusivity), and partly a problem resulting from the fear of legal or social repercussions if one is open about one's association (see chapter 6).

Romantic Literature, Romantic Thought, and Neo-Paganism

Hutton traces the emergence of modern Paganism in Britain through language, ceremonial traditions of magic in guilds and secret societies, literature, anthropology, folklore, and a few seminal authors across these traditions. While all these areas overlap, I shall focus on literary influences primarily, beginning with a focus on British Romantic authors, since it was often through literature that ideas from anthropology and other disciplines made their way into the popular imagination.

Barbara Jane Davy (2006), Magliocco (2004), and other authors point to the elements that the movement has in common with the Romantic ideas that sprang up in Europe and the United States from the late eighteenth century onward. They argue that in many ways Neo-Paganism is a continuation of Romanticism. Although the term "Romanticism" is slippery and, at least in the popular use of the term, somewhat misleading—grouping together authors who differed deeply in their time—some of its ideals, preoccupations, and sets of symbols have been adopted and reconstructed by Neo-Pagans.

Commentators such as Isaiah Berlin (1998) have had a tendency to emphasize the distinction between Enlightenment and Romantic thinkers from the same time period, but such a sharp delineation is not useful when it comes to the Romantic authors whose ideas had the strongest influence on what eventually became the Neo-Pagan movement. For one thing, these particular strains of Romanticism, as I will argue, contained Enlightenment precepts at their core, although their emphases were different. I will focus on populist writing and art, especially that which was influential in Britain, where Neo-Paganism originated. According to Marilyn Butler (1985), there were three broad phases of the original literary and aesthetic movement that later came to be referred to as Romantic.

The first phase, ranging roughly from the mid–eighteenth century until the early 1790s, included, among others, the German poet Goethe, the English poet and engraver William Blake, the Scottish poets Robert Burns and James McPherson, the Swiss painter Henry Fuseli, and the young English poets William Wordsworth and Robert Southey. Although this group was internally quite disparate, there were a few consistent themes. One was a respect for human nature in its "primitive" uncorrupted form, which often led them to idealize peoples from the past or from societies not touched by industrialization. The Goths, the Ancient Hebrews, the Scots, the Celts, the rural British, the Polynesians, the American Indians, the early Christians, and the pre-Christian Anglo-Saxons all served as early Romantic reference points in various works. A second theme was populism, which included sympathy for the nascent American Revolution and for the beginnings of the French Revolution. A third—closely related to the second—was individual freedom, seen in contrast to the authorities of church, state and aristocracy. And a fourth theme was an emphasis on "sensibility," intuition, and emotion (Butler: 9–68).

Blake provides a representative example of the early phase of Romanticism. He was an iconoclast, was influenced to some extent by Swedenborg, an eighteenth-century Swedish mystic, and developed his own form of dissident Christianity (Ackroyd 1995). The Dissenters, a group into which Blake could be loosely categorized, formed a large and influential movement at that time in England and were struggling for legal recognition and protection. Like others in a long tradition dating back to the thirteenth century through the Brethren, the Diggers, and others, Blake believed in personal religious revelation without the intervention of priests, in the inner divinity of all human beings, including women and people of non-European races, and in individual freedom, including the emancipation of slaves and of women. He also saw matter and sexuality as acceptable, even holy. This last point put him at odds with mainstream Christianity at that time, and also with a few other populist Dissident groups like the Shakers. But in most of his ideas there was compatibility with those of his contemporaries who are usually associated with the Enlightenment, or at least its more radical wing, and Blake was in communication with atheists

"Dream Flowers"

and revolutionaries like Mary Wollstonecraft, William Godwin, and Tom Paine. Early Romantics and some Enlightenment thinkers of the late eighteenth century shared many ideals, including sympathy for the American Revolution and for early or pre-revolutionary French populism (Butler 1985; St. Clair 1989).

A second phase of Romanticism, covering the last years of the eighteenth century and the first years of the nineteenth, included the poets Wordsworth, Southey, and Coleridge in their older years, all of whom became more conservative than their youthful selves or their predecessors. From the mid 1790s onward, following Britain's war with France and a gradual disillusion with the French Revolution among Britain's radicals, dissident thinkers like Blake and Godwin were either driven underground or developed a more pessimistic outlook on human potential. The Germans continued to turn to folk culture as a form of psychological resistance to French expansion. But both primitivism and populism became suspect in Britain, because of their association with the French. Once war had begun, the British government treated French, or "Jacobin," sympathies as treasonous.

Wordsworth had been an early supporter of the French Revolution and had traveled to France, but was disturbed by the violence and the betrayal of its original ideals. Like all the Romantics, he revered nature and idealized people who lived close to nature, but his poetry came to reflect an image of the natural world that was a manifestation of God's power rather than a backdrop for unfettered human expression. Human beings, in Wordsworth's later landscapes, tend to be small, solitary, and powerless, rather than the divinely inspired beings who populated Blake's poetry. Wordsworth, Southey, and Coleridge came to adopt a more conventional religious stance than either earlier and later Romantics, and their gradual acceptance of the monarchy went along with this respect for religious authority and for British traditions. All three, however, were interested in the new scientific breakthroughs of their times and in regular communication with their mutual friend, Humphrey Davy, who was a rising star in the sciences as well as a poet (Holmes 2010: 235–304).

The third phase of Romanticism, from the early 1800s until about 1830, included at its core Percy Bysshe Shelley, Mary Shelley, John Keats, George Byron, Thomas Love Peacock, Leigh Hunt, and William Hazlitt. (Butler calls this "the Marlow group," since all of them had ties to Marlow, in southern England.) Like Blake, they were very much to the left of the political scene of their time, espousing individual freedoms like abolition and the franchise. However, they were forced by their government and by popular suspicion of "Jacobism" during the wars with France to be more guarded in their expressions than had authors from before the war.

An Unreal Estate

This third group tended toward skepticism about Christianity. As an undergraduate, Shelley was expelled from Oxford for writing a pamphlet espousing atheism. Also, excavations in Greece, Egypt, and Italy around the turn of the century threw up new examples of ancient art and architecture, some of which were displayed in the British Museum and which enhanced public interest in these cultures. Archaeologists were beginning to talk about common elements of religious mythology in the Mediterranean and in other parts of the world—mythology based in fertility and natural cycles, with gods and goddesses associated with the sun and with the earth. Among others, Richard Payne Knight and Erasmus Darwin (Charles Darwin's grandfather), saw procreation as the key to creation and the various religions as ways of paying symbolic homage to it. Drawing partly on these influences, the Marlow group thought of Christianity as one of many nature religions. Aesthetically and ideologically they were more drawn to polytheism, where the various gods and goddesses were easier to see as symbols—poetic, human-made symbols of various aspects of nature, of fertility, of the mind, and of the libidinous energy they regarded as the real driving force behind creation (Butler 1985: 113–137).

Leigh Hunt, although he has now been largely forgotten, was a popular poet in the early nineteenth century and a pivotal figure in this group as well as in British populism. He published Keats, Shelley, and Byron in the *Examiner*—a liberal newspaper he and his brother ran for many years—and was instrumental in bringing these authors into the public eye. He wrote a weekly column, which occasionally took up themes that sound distinctly Pagan. One of his editorials, for example, was dedicated to the Green Man, his conception of the wild nature deity behind the heads surrounded by foliage often found in West European churches (Holden 2005; Hutton 1999; Roe 2005). He was also one of the best-known radicals and reformers of his day, and the majority of his columns dealt with politics. Hunt spent some time in prison for criticizing the prince regent, as Blake had been arrested a decade or so earlier for "treasonous" words about the king. Hunt's prison cell and later the house he and his family shared with the Shelleys in Marlow were two of the centers of the Romantic network.

Like Blake, but unlike the Lake poets, this group accepted and even revered sexuality and the material world. Also like Blake, Godwin, Goethe, and others of the first wave of Romanticism, they espoused greater freedom in sensual relationships, for women as well as for men. Shelley included these lines in his poem "Epipsychidion" in 1821:

> True love, in this differs from gold or clay
> That to divide is not to take away.

In this time period, Romantic authors created and popularized a variety of new symbolic landscapes, many of which also pervade present day Neo-Paganism. Butler describes an incident where Keats recited an ode to Pan—a god of wilderness and libido—to Wordsworth and was rebuffed with the comment, "A very pretty piece of Paganism" (Butler 1985: 136). Besides highlighting what they saw as a more humane alternative to orthodox Christianity, the Marlow group's use of Greek and Roman symbolism allowed them to express radical themes indirectly, and therefore with less fear of government retribution. It was safer to write about Greek struggles with Rome than about populist struggles in England, and safer to write an ode to Pan than to write overtly about the church. They expressed reverence, but the reverence was not for an overarching, authoritative, inaccessible being or institution, like the monarchy or the Anglican God and priesthood; rather, it was on the one hand for the more accessible gods and goddesses who reflected the human psyche and who acted out human fantasies and foibles, on the other for human freedom fighters whose struggles were expediently transposed in their poems to faraway places and times.

This fascination with Greece and Rome, and also Egypt and other ancient civilizations, was shared by many Enlightenment thinkers such as Diderot and Voltaire, to the extent that one Enlightenment historian, Peter Gay, entitled the first part of his trilogy "The Enlightenment: The Rise of Modern Paganism" (Gay 1966). By "Pagan," here, he meant pre-Christian or non-Christian, since Enlightenment intellectuals turned to Roman and Greek works for alternatives to Christianity. The information they had about these civilizations was sparse, leaving them free to speculate about idealized versions and to draw on them for ideas of new social forms.

Romantic and Enlightenment thinkers, then, while their mediums of expression were different, often informed one another's work, shared sources of inspiration, and took the same radical positions. Romantics also had many close personal and family ties with such Enlightenment thinkers as the radical and atheistic William Godwin and his wife, the early feminist Mary Wollstonecraft. The Shelley and Godwin families were related by both blood and marriage, since Mary, Godwin's and Wollstonecraft's daughter, married Percy Shelley. And like Southey and his friends, Byron, Keats, and the Shelleys took an interest in Davy and other scientific innovators (Holmes 2010: 325–326, 350). Mary Shelley's *Frankenstein*, written in 1818, explored some of the new scientific debates and possibilities of the time.

Enlightenment thinkers, like Romantic thinkers, have always had more than one trajectory. "Reason" could on the one hand be used as a rationale for imposing European social organization on less powerful countries and for

An Unreal Estate

marginalizing and belittling folk traditions and non-European religions, as did nineteenth-century social theorists and anthropologists such as Herbert Spencer, Lewis Henry Morgan, and Edward Burnett Tylor. On the other hand, as in the works of Tom Paine, Mary Wollstonecraft, and John Stuart Mill, it had the potential to be a basis of *critique* of the inequalities within the European powers and between these powers and the countries they colonized, and it could also be used to critique accepted social mores and mainstream, rather than folk, religious beliefs. The starkest division in early nineteenth-century Britain was not, then, between Romanticism and the Enlightenment but between advocates from both these camps of established hierarchies—the church, the aristocracy, and the monarchy and patriarchal family forms on the one hand—and advocates of populist, liberal positions on the other, the latter groups sometimes drawing on pre-Christian peoples or thinkers for inspiration.

Keats, Shelley, and Byron all died young, but they and other Romantics lingered in the public imagination throughout the nineteenth century and into the twentieth, along with Pan, Venus, the Goths, nature, fairies, and other assorted Romantic symbols that had pervaded their writings. Nature meant something different to the Lake poets than to the Romantics who preceded and followed them, but the distinctions came to be blurred over time, so that Romanticism as a whole was associated with a reverence for nature that seemed to offer an alternative to the problems stemming from the Industrial Revolution and urbanization: the new levels and forms of poverty, crime, pollution, inequality, and disease.

Romanticism's more radical social perspectives cropped up at intervals through the nineteenth century, along with its nostalgic ones. Algernon Charles Swinburne was against both hierarchy and the mores of his time, seeing Christianity as the enemy of nature and beauty. According to Hutton (1999: 23–24), his works caused a stir verging on an insurgency in nineteenth-century British universities, with students marching around Oxford and Cambridge arm in arm, chanting excerpts from the poems.

Hutton traces references to Greek or Norse gods and goddesses, to fairy tales and to nature spirits in English literature up until Neo-Paganism's first organized emergence in the twentieth century. Pan in particular took on great popularity in the nineteenth and early twentieth century, which peaked in the years before World War I. Somerset Maugham wrote of Edwardian England that "God went out, oddly enough with cricket and beer, and Pan came in. In a hundred novels his cloven hoof left its imprint on the sward" (Maugham, quoted in Hutton 1999: 48). A nature goddess increasingly became another familiar feature of popular culture over the course of the nineteenth and early twentieth

"Dream Flowers"

centuries. Examples of descriptions of a recognizably Pagan (or Neo-Pagan) god and goddess can be found in *The Wind in the Willows,* by Kenneth Grahame (1908), which eulogizes Pan, and *The White Goddess,* by Robert Graves (1948).

As for other aspects of modern Neo-Paganism, fairy and folk tales like those revived by the German Grimm brothers, the poems of Yeats, and parts of *Puck of Pook's Hill* (1906) by Rudyard Kipling, kept images of elves, fairies, witches, and magic alive. Such folk tales as the story of Robin Hood or the tales of King Arthur—tales with long histories and many variants—were a part of this tradition, and some of the early Wiccans looked to them for clues about a pre-Christian worldview (see, for example, Valiente and Jones 1990).

As Hutton points out, there are records of pockets of people in Britain who acted very much like Neo-Pagans before the movement had any official or organized existence, and these were often people with ties to literature:

> Before I commenced my research, I had been aware of Rider Haggard as a novelist . . . I had not thought of him as somebody who habitually bowed to the moon as the image of the goddess Isis and honored Thor and Odin. To me Kenneth Grahame had been the author of "The Wind in the Willows." I had always recognized that this latter work contained one of the most striking manifestations of Pan in English literature, but had not known that Grahame's first book had been called "Pagan Papers," and that on the morning of their wedding his wife Elspeth rolled in dew and wove herself a chain of flowers to symbolise the closeness of her relationship to the natural world. Yeats was of course familiar as a poet, and also as somebody with a personal mysticism rich in occult symbolism. I had not realized that at one point of his life, he had hailed the return of the pagan deities to Ireland. (Hutton 2003; 268–269)

Meanwhile in the United States, alternative religions combined with Romanticism in North American literature. Sarah Pike, in *New Age and Neopagan Religions in America* (2004), traces the progress from the eighteenth to the twentieth century of alternative North American religions, many of which promoted beliefs now common in Neo-Paganism. The Shakers, for example, saw god as both female and male, went into trances, and engaged in ecstatic ritual dances. Swedenborg inspired the Spiritualists and Transcendentalists in the United States, including Ralph Waldo Emerson and Henry David Thoreau. Swedenborg believed in communion with angels and spirits and a universal soul—the "oversoul."

Emerson, Thoreau, and Ernest Thompson Seton helped put words to and give shape to a love of and reverence for nature in the popular psyche, and Walt Whitman can be seen both as a child of Romanticism and as another forefather of Neo-Paganism in his tendency to write about sensuality as an essential part of spirituality rather than an obstacle to it. In "Song of Myself" (1891), for example, he writes, "I am the poet of the body / And I am the poet of the soul."

An Unreal Estate

Like his British predecessors in the Romantic tradition, Whitman expressed ideas that incorporated strands of left-leaning Enlightenment thought as well. Martha Nussbaum (2001: 645–678) highlights the democratic ideals that are embedded in Whitman's poetry, and he was a staunch populist, committed to abolition, to universal suffrage, to sexual freedom, and to women's liberation.

Anthropology, Literature, and Early Neo-Paganism

In the nineteenth and early twentieth centuries, speculation about gods and goddesses from anthropology and folklore often spilled over into literature. As noted above, the later English Romantics—Keats, the Shelleys, Hunt, Hazlitt, Love Peacock, Erasmus Darwin, and others (including thinkers usually associated with the Enlightenment)—were influenced both by new archaeological discoveries in Greece and by theories of fertility as a universal underpinning to mythologies and religions around the world. As the nineteenth century progressed, anthropological interest in ancient religion and ritual spread in Europe and the United States in the context, on the one hand, of widespread colonialism on both sides of the Atlantic and, on the other hand, of a new approach to natural history, Charles Darwin's evolutionary scheme. The earliest anthropologists, Tylor and Morgan, along with other thinkers of their century such as Spencer, Bachofen, Marx, and Engels, transposed (in one form or another) the idea of evolution to human societies as well as natural species. This fit well with the contemporary justifications for colonization—of the settler or administrative variety—through a view of the supposedly more "evolved" condition of the European races, especially of peoples from areas that had well-developed industry and extensive military power. Tylor (1871) both worked within and gave expression to the new scheme, influencing Darwin in his turn. These anthropological theories reinforced the idea that there were clues to earlier societies in folk tales or myths. This was a view also held by Morgan (1877).

Morgan, Tylor, Bachofen, Marx, and Engels postulated prehistoric matriarchal societies, which had given way, in time, to patriarchies. They considered the step from matriarchy to patriarchy as a sign of evolutionary progress. The archaeological discoveries and description of female figurines at the end of the century were seen as providing evidence for this idea. These figurines dated from Stone Age and Copper Age sites from the Balkans, the Levant, Greece, and Crete and were interpreted as images of a goddess, reflecting a time of goddess worship that had preceded recorded history. The idea of ancient matriarchies persisted into the late twentieth century, and although by the 1970s it was no longer the dominant view in academic circles, the existence of egalitarian or

"Dream Flowers"

matrifocal societies is still being contested and discussed by archaeologists and cultural anthropologists.[2]

Hierarchies both of race and of gender were assumed and implied by the nineteenth-century matriarchy-to-patriarchy scheme, but they proved double-edged. While on the one hand the scheme was used by empire builders and conservatives in ways that legitimized colonialism and gender inequalities, it was also seized on for different reasons by early women's liberationists like Matilda Joslyn Gage, who both read Morgan's work on remnants of matriarchy among the Haudenosaunee (Iroquois) and spent time with her contemporaries within this nation, receiving adoption into the Wolf Clan. And in 1899, the folklorist Charles Leland's influential work *Aradia, or the Gospel of the Witches,* documented his conversations with an Italian witch who claimed to be part of a long line of traditional witches. The popular acceptance, then, of a history of folk traditions in which females had positions of power inadvertently opened up the possibilities, first, that there might be pockets of such traditions remaining and, second, that women might be entitled to, and capable of, holding power again.

In the early twentieth century, one of the most important figures in the foundation of Neo-Paganism began publishing some anthropological texts on witchcraft. She was Margaret Murray—a British folklorist and Egyptian scholar who wrote *The Witch Cult in Western Europe* (1921) and later *The God of the Witches* (1933) after publishing several articles for the Royal Anthropological Institute in England. Her thesis, like Leland's, was that a religion predating Christianity had persisted through the centuries in Europe. Her main focus was Britain, especially Scotland. Part of her method was to treat the "confessions" of witches at their trials as ethnographic data. She was interested in why there was so much consistency in their descriptions in a time before mass communications. She did not think this consistency could be adequately explained by the stereotyped view of witchcraft held by the Christian clergy or shown in such texts as the medieval *Malleus Malificarum.* The latter text was first published in Germany in 1487 by Kramer and Sprenger as a handbook for identifying and destroying witches and was republished thirteen times in the late fifteenth and early sixteenth centuries. The title translates as "the hammer of the witches." Murray also studied the laws against practitioners of religions other than Christianity from the time of the conversion of the monarchs until the witch trials that began in full force in the fifteenth century.

While it is a reasonable assumption that there were conflicts and tensions between old and new religious and ritual traditions, it is difficult to establish with any certainty what *kinds* of practices were in place before Christianity; and, given the difficulties of communication, a wide diversity among these

An Unreal Estate

seems likely. Evidence from witch trial confessions is suspect, because even in cases when these were not made under torture, they were all produced in an atmosphere of fear and coercion and at a time long after the introduction of Christianity.

In spite of these problems, Murray's thesis was accepted fairly commonly until the 1970s, when several historians, led by Keith Thomas and Norman Cohn (see Hutton 1999: 362) questioned her use of sources. She was accused of being selective in her examples and also of taking quotations out of context. She tended to generalize, taking isolated examples to postulate a religion with a single nature God, the Horned God, worship of whom, she claimed, had spanned centuries and nations. Hutton restates the argument that there is not enough historical evidence to back up Murray's thesis. Written records of the kind of ritual or religion Murray argues for are few and far between, and while her hypothesis of a continuing nature religion and its suppression as "witchcraft" cannot be ruled out entirely, there are too many historical blind spots for it to be understood as a consistent body of thought. However, in the mid–twentieth century, versions of the ideas of Murray, Leland, Bachofen, Morgan, and others about a historical shift from matriarchy to patriarchy, and about witchcraft as the remnants of an ancient nature- and female-centered religious tradition, were widely held and further reinforced and disseminated through literature.

While Murray's hypothesis was inadequately supported, another magical and ritual tradition can be traced back to ancient Greek Neo-Platonic and Hebrew Cabbalic writings. Both of these persisted in various parts of Europe through the Middle Ages, enjoyed a revival in Renaissance Europe, and had a strong influence on the Freemasons, the Rosicrucians, and other guilds and secret societies. The Victorian author and magician Aleister Crowley drew on the rituals of these societies in his writings on magic, which in turn influenced Gerald Gardner. Dafo, another strong influence on Gardner and Wicca, was a Rosicrucian (Hutton 1999: 177–180; Hutton 2003: 137–192; Magliocco 2004: 33–34). Several aspects of this body of thought are present in Neo-Paganism—the emphasis on self-transformation and ritual, the invocation of divinity, the blurred lines between religion and magic, a nuanced acceptance of polytheism, and, importantly, some of the central symbolism and ritual practices, such as calling to the elements from the four compass points and "casting a circle" of magical space. As Magliocco points out, the guilds and secret societies combined practices that tend to be associated with the Enlightenment—for example, democratic egalitarianism—with rituals, reverence, and links to an ancient past that tend to be associated with Romanticism.

"Dream Flowers"

As noted above, Romanticism and the Enlightenment overlapped in many ways. In the late twentieth and early twenty-first centuries, Neo-Paganism and secular liberalism overlap also, and the movement encompasses a great variety of degrees of faith, including agnosticism. Rather than the fault lines between Neo-Paganism and the rest of the world involving a contrast between Romanticism and the Enlightenment, between "irrationality" and "rationality" (Luhrmann 1989), between science and secularism on the one hand and faith or superstition on the other, the strongest opposition both *toward* Neo-Paganism and *from* Neo-Pagans toward others usually involves institutions of authority, including fundamentalist churches. Although it includes a range of degrees and types of faith, Neo-Paganism is closer to secular liberalism than are its most vocal opponents, who are much more likely to be conservative and exclusively Christian (Pike 2001; Victor 1993). And according to the research on Neo-Pagan attitudes carried out by Berger, Leach, and Schaffer (2003), participants more frequently express distrust of institutions and of hierarchies than of science, and the movement tends to attract "nerds." Science and rationality, as noted above, take on different trajectories and different boundaries as they are informed by different sets of values or interests.

All the currents of thought that have fed into Neo-Paganism converge and overlap in places. Religion and folklore involve a great deal of fiction and literature, of moral tales, creation stories, popular fables, and songs, so that it is less easy than the categorizations above suggest to distinguish one area of influence from another. But whatever the social forces involved, by the time Wicca developed in the 1940s and 1950s, many of the ideas behind it had long been current in the popular imagination, from literary, religious, magical, and anthropological sources. Neo-Paganism brought them together, drawing on their common themes. In this sense, while it might be difficult to trace the content of an ancient heritage for the movement, it has roots that are both long and deep. It draws on a populist, reflective, and anarchic, rather than traditional or faith-based, strand of Romanticism, and has often been informed by literature.[3]

Gerald Gardner and Starhawk

Neo-Paganism first developed a recognizable and organized form through a self-trained (and self-described) anthropologist *and* fiction writer named Gerald Gardner. He became involved with a group in Hampshire in the South of England in the 1940s, which he believed to be a continuation of an ancient tradition of witchcraft (Hutton 1999: 205–240). Echoing Murray, he saw this as a tradition predating Christianity that had persisted underground, in spite of the

An Unreal Estate

repression that had reached its climax in the medieval witch trials. In Gardner's view, this tradition had honored femininity as well as masculinity, honored the earth and the animal kingdom, and honored sensuality, while European Christianity had come to repudiate all these aspects of life. Witchcraft was illegal in England until 1951, so Gardner's first book after coming into contact with the tradition, *High Magic's Aid* (1949), was written as fiction. Once the law changed, Gardner put together and wrote about a set of practices and incantations related to this tradition, called Wicca, which he presented in *Witchcraft Today* in 1954.

Gardner described himself as a student and observer of rituals he had learned from a witch, who had in turn inherited the teachings from her family and from associating with her *coven* (a small group for collective ceremonies). But whatever these influences were, Gardner's writings in the early days also echoed ceremonies from guilds and secret societies and the works of Aleister Crowley, who had developed his own obscure magical and ritual system with many elements in common with these secret societies.

Gardner acknowledged in *Witchcraft Today* that the coven may have been influenced by the Freemasons, Rosicrucians, and other ceremonial practitioners of magic, but maintained that it was also maintaining a more ancient tradition of witchcraft. He wrote several versions of a "Book of Shadows" to encapsulate the rituals and prayers, claiming that he was recording what he had heard and seen in rituals or copied from magical texts. This claim, especially the second part of it, is controversial; it is still not clear whether Gardner was recording or helping to invent a set of religious practices, or something between the two (Heselton 2003; Hutton 1999: 205–240; Hutton 2003: 282; Magliocci 2004: 51–54).

Another figure who helped shape Wicca was Doreen Valiente. She attended the group, and became its high priestess from 1951 to 1953, adding much to it herself. She wrote large sections of the final version of Gardner's particular Wiccan Book of Shadows in 1954 (many versions have been written since by other covens and groups) and designed rituals. She replaced the parts she felt were too much influenced by Crowley with more poetic, literary writings. In 1959, she broke away from Gardner, who she considered had become chauvinistic and arrogant following the publication and popularity of his books. She became widely read in her own right as an authority on witchcraft and took a more egalitarian approach to ritual than he did.

Valiente, especially in her later writings, also expresses a greater degree of ambivalence than Gardner about the persistence of a tradition of witchcraft through the centuries. She accepts the idea on the whole, but admits she can have no certainty about the content of the tradition, as in this statement in *Witchcraft: A Tradition Renewed*, written with Evan John Jones:

What is known of the faith was written by its enemies; and through a long catalogue of pain and suffering meted out to those who dared think differently there are glimpses of the faith they died for. Unfortunately there is not enough to form a sound basis to build upon. Instead, whether as a group or as individuals, each of us must find our own way or path to the portals of the castle . . . It works for us, and what more can you ask than that? (Valiente and Jones 1990)

After Gardner and Valiente, others began establishing covens, Books of Shadows, and ritual traditions of their own around the British Isles, each with slight differences.

Literature on Wicca and related forms of Neo-Paganism began to attract interest in the United States in the early 1960s. Loosed from its moorings in Britain, the movement took many new forms. Its development coincided with the growing popular movements for racial and gender equality. Women and men looking for nonpatriarchal forms of religion embraced it and formed groups that were more politically conscious and more overtly feminist than the original Wicca. Neo-Paganism also offered people a chance to find ethnic roots and a folklore that were not associated with imperialism, racial, and gender hierarchies or with what they saw as repressive aspects of organized Christianity. And it appealed, as in Britain, to people with environmental concerns, people who were disillusioned with industrial capitalism and who wanted to restore a link with the natural world either individually or collectively.

In the United States, Starhawk is Neo-Paganism's best known figurehead and has remained so from the late 1970s until the present day. Like Gardner, she is an author of fiction as well as a disseminator of Pagan ritual. Her book *The Spiral Dance,* published in 1979 and reprinted many times since, is the most widely read publication among Neo-Pagans, and her tone is quite different from Gardner's or Valiente's. She has an explicit political commitment to environmentalism, pacifism, racial equality, gay rights, and feminism—issues they had dealt with more implicitly if at all. She helped found a branch of Paganism called Reclaiming Witchcraft, which has a strong commitment to social justice.

Jone Salomonsen describes Starhawk as a "utopian" witch. This utopianism involves both looking to a lost golden age and to possibilities for the future. Starhawk, like Murray, draws on the distant past for clues to pre-Christian religious traditions, but her emphases are different. Citing Maria Gimbutas (1982) and Sumerian texts, among other sources, she postulates an ancient world where worship of a goddess or goddesses alongside a (slightly less important) god or gods was the norm.

Starhawk also looks to the future. She has written a science fiction work called *The Fifth Sacred Thing* (1993), which envisions a community based on

An Unreal Estate

environmental, egalitarian, pacifist, polyamorous, and anarchistic ideals.[4] This community also exemplifies religious tolerance. It is suffused with varied forms of collective ritual and magic, some but not all of which are reminiscent of contemporary Pagan practice. And a third sense in which Salomonsen sees Starhawk as a utopian is in her political activism. This is typical of many within the Reclaiming tradition, and to a slightly lesser extent, of Pagans as a whole, "Pagans and Witches have accrued a proud record of involvement in feminist issues, gay liberation, and antinuclear, antiwar and environmental concerns. Personally I stopped counting my arrests in direct action when they numbered something like two dozen" (Starhawk 1999 [1979]: 7).

Salomonsen notes, however, that even among the Reclaiming witches (only one of many Neo-Pagan groupings) there are a variety of perspectives, some of which she describes as "utopian" because of their sense of political mission, and some of which she describes as "generic," taking their association with Paganism as one personal choice among many rather than a commitment to changing the world. Lothlorien tends to attract people with the latter rather than the former orientation.

More and more since Murray came under fire in the 1970s, the scouring of the past for something better, as well as the reinvention of the gods mentioned above, have become conscious choices rather than assumptions about the way things were or attempts to legitimate the movement.

Neo-Paganism as a Narrative Embedded in Time

The preceding histories of fiction, anthropology, and this newly formed religious movement show a continual juggling between conceptions of the past and conceptions of the present. In "Ethnography as Narrative," Edward Bruner (1986) shows how ways of seeing of the past and the future, which are themselves subject to change over time, shape perceptions of the present. Similarly, Pike shows how Neo-Pagans use the past, and sometimes the future, to construct a counternarrative for the present in a time of disillusion. "If the present was bankrupt, then past cultures and future worlds were the best sources of inspiration for new communities . . . Neopagans looked optimistically to the past as a source of constructing a better future" (Pike 2004: 78).

The past under consideration here in most cases is not the recorded past, not the chronology of battles and rulers within easy access of historians, but an ancient, unwritten past, of which there are glimpses—through Maypole dancing or female figurines or Greek or Norse myths or songs or circles of stones—but enough unanswered questions to allow for creativity and speculation in filling

"Dream Flowers"

in the gaps. Current desires for change, current sensibilities, color this imagined past. So the gods and rituals can be in a way reinvented.

Some Neo-Pagan rituals may also evoke a sense of wholeness that has been missing from lives lived at desks, through screens, and in houses, cars, and offices. Dancing and drumming around a fire, for example, are whole body experiences. Such experiences can feel like a visceral reconnection with something lost, either with an unknown past or with a core part of oneself. Jason suggests something like this in his description of drumming around the central fire at Lothlorien, and it will be referred to again in chapter 6:

> Some people have said that your body can actually remember things . . . I don't know about the truth or the validity of that, but I do know that when I'm down there (drumming in Thunder Shrine), when I'm experiencing that, it does feel like something that has been going on for millennia; thousands and thousands of years . . . that we as humans used to do. And it just seems part of our nature—part of our nature that maybe for centuries and centuries of time we've been trying to grow out of for various reasons. (Jason, 2008)

On a more ideological level, Neo-Paganism among white people can also reflect an attempt to find an authentic Euro-American culture that is less oppressive than the options available in the mainstream (Magliocco 2004: 205–237). The movement explores real or perceived preindustrial roots for cultural elements that were respectful of nature, of women, of rural people, and of all races. It reaches for a way to be a white American or European without the association with capitalism and colonialism, a way of looking back to find something better to identify with. Magliocco notes that there is an element of "folklore reclamation" of the past in Neo-Pagan practice.

> Reclamation differs from other forms of cultural revival in that it presupposes a relationship of power imbalance between a dominant culture (sometimes, but not always, a colonizing culture) and a marginalized, silenced or subdominant folk group. Reclamation focuses on exactly those traditions, elements, even words, that the dominant culture considers emblematic of the subdominant group's inferiority. By reclaiming them, groups give these elements a new and illustrious context in which they function as important symbols of pride and identity—a reconstructed identity consciously opposed to the one portrayed by the dominant culture. (Magliocco 2004: 8)

Examples of this are the embrace of the word "witch" by Wiccans and bumper stickers like "My other car is a broomstick." Starhawk's "remembering" of goddess traditions is also an aspect of reclamation.

To sum up, Neo-Paganism has been partly a product of the selected memories, social realities, and futuristic dreams of its times, drawing on the past, the present, and the future. It developed a recognizable and organized form in the mid–twentieth century as a continuation of Romantic preoccupations, of folklore and of traditions of ceremonial magic, defining itself in contrast to the backdrop of the industrialized world, and attempting to heal perceived rifts between humans and nature, reason and instinct, and to restore the sacred to everyday life. From the 1960s and 1970s on it fused these ideas with a more explicit political consciousness honed by the civil rights movements and by feminism and environmentalism. And Berger and Magliocco both describe the most recent forms of Neo-Paganism as "late modern" in their sensibilities, in Anthony Giddens' sense of this term, as reflexive. There is certainly a great deal of self-reflection, humor, and irony expressed in its rituals and shrines. This was also noted by Hutton (1999), Luhrmann (1989), and Pike (2001).

I shall now turn to another tradition of which Lothlorien is a part, again loosely, a tradition looking more to the future than the past for inspiration. This is the long history of utopian experiments in the United States.

Utopian Experiments in the United States: A Brief History

Before I begin this second overview, I should make at least one of my key terms clear. I am defining the term "intentional community" here as a social grouping that involves a degree of conscious choice. For example, in recent American Indian history, Alcatraz and Wounded Knee—two pieces of land that Native people chose to occupy as part of political protests—were sites of intentional community in a sense that reservations, originally defined by a powerful foreign nation with little or no input from the residents, were not. Sometimes the individuals involved in an intentional community are choosing to remove themselves from the cultural contexts in which they have grown up and to find a different kind of social structure. In many cases this involves taking on an unusual degree of agency in designing or helping to design a social world on a small scale. In other cases the shift involves choosing to *give up* a degree of choice in order to focus more fully on some other value, as in the decision to join a religious order.

Lothlorien is not an intentional community in the strict sense of this term, since very few active participants live there full time. Most come in and out for work and festivals. It is, however, experimental in many ways. In her announcement for a July 4 celebration, on Elvin HOME's website, Conney links Lothlorien to the utopian spirit of the American Revolution:

"Dream Flowers"

America was created by a bunch of idealistic dreamers, people seeking a place to follow beliefs other than the prescribed ones, quirky individualists, people willing to dedicate their lives to an idea and people who saw and appreciated the bounty and beauty of the land around them. So Lothlorien is certainly a great place to celebrate America's Independence Day. (Conney, July 2, 2007, www.elvinHOME.org)

North America has long had an appeal as a place to try out new visions of social life. These have encompassed both the "pull" of a utopian ideal and a "push" away from the mainstream, the need in many cases to find spaces apart from oppressive social relationships and structures. Intentional and experimental communities involve dual motivations, a movement toward a mode of living and a movement away from a mode of living, a critique, as Brown (2002: 153–179) puts it, and a new direction at the same time.

In the following sections I use the terms "utopian communes" and "alternative communities" synonymously with "intentional communities." I shall draw heavily on the considerable scholarly contributions of Miller (1999, 1998) and Pitzer (in Pitzer, ed., 1997).

Often, especially in the early years of colonization, European motivations for communal living in North America have focused around participation in minority religions (Durnbaugh 1997; Pitzer 1997). In the 1620s and '30s, some of the first Old World settlers, Calvinists and Puritans, collectivized their property. The Puritans considered their community a "Bible Commonwealth." Dutch Mennonites also formed a commonwealth in 1663 (which was cut short by the British capture of their settlement). A community of Calvinists made another attempt in Pennsylvania in the 1680s, followed by Seventh Day Baptists and the Moravian Brethren in the eighteenth century.

In keeping with this trend, in 1774, one of the most famous and long lived North American intentional communities came into being under the guidance of Mother Anne Lee (Brewer 1997; Kitch 1989). Anne Lee started her life as a poor and illiterate woman, a factory worker, from Manchester in the North of England. She bore four children, all of whom died. She joined a group of "Shaking Quakers," dissident Christians who acquired their name because they used dance as a form of religious upliftment. One day, during a sojourn in jail (one of many) for breaking the Sabbath, Lee had a vision of Christ, which inspired her to preach and to collect disciples. She followed what she considered to be the spirit of Bible teachings rather than the taking the Bible literally. She saw God as being both male and female, and she encouraged female as well as male leadership in her religious organization. After attracting considerable notice in England, she crossed the Atlantic in order to start a rural community where her ideals could be lived out more fully. She died in 1784, but her vision was already taking shape.

By the 1830s there were four thousand Shaker members in sixty celibate clusters called "families." These were spread out from Maine to Indiana. They farmed, built houses, made furniture, clothes, and edible goods, with a great attention to detail and perfection, believing that work was a form of worship, and until the Industrial Revolution took hold they thrived financially, since their name was a byword for quality in the goods they traded. They espoused racial and gender equality and took in African American members on equal terms. Each cluster of "brothers" and "sisters" were supervised by an Elder and Eldress respectively. They were also the first conscientious objectors, and were granted Lincoln's permission to stay out of the Civil War. One community still remains at Sabbathday Lake, Maine. Because they thrived for a long time, the Shakers provided an example that inspired others to attempt communal living.

From the beginning of the nineteenth century, the communal movement burgeoned, along with Romanticism and the optimism inspired by the recent American Revolution. And because the Midwest was frontier land at this time in North American history, this area, including Indiana, attracted a significant number of dreamers and planners.

Many of the utopian communities continued to be Christian—for example, Harmony and Economy, in Indiana and Pennsylvania respectively, which were established by German Pietists. Swedish Pietists settled in Illinois in 1846. The Amana villages in Iowa, set up by "inspirationalists," lasted as communes for about a hundred years before adopting private property. The common element to these particular religious groups was that they believed human life and human nature to be redeemable and perfectible, although this might require considerable effort and self-abnegation. In this sense they were more optimistic than many of the mainstream Christian organizations of their time. Mormons and Jews also experimented with communal living in their first years of settlement. In these groups (as was sometimes the case with minority Christian groups), communal living was often a bulwark against minority religious status and the resulting oppression or discrimination either in the country of origin or in the United States (May; Bartelt; both in Pitzer, ed., 1997).

Other communes were secular and had political ideals. In 1825, a Scotswoman called Frances Wright bought a tract of land near Memphis, on which slaves could work their way to freedom (Rexroth 1974). Wright was horrified by slavery and espoused racial equality, along with socialism, women's rights, sexual freedom, and universal education. But racial equality failed to materialize at Nashoba, and the African Americans still ended up doing most of the hard

"Dream Flowers"

physical labor while the ten white Americans did administrative kinds of work. There were also reports of harsh treatment of the African Americans by at least one of the white residents of Nashoba when Wright was absent. Nashoba attracted enormous criticism and notoriety from outsiders, not, unfortunately, because of this continuation of inequality, but because the laws preventing marriage between races were ignored. Wright eventually freed the slaves at Nashoba, transported them to Haiti, and found them work there. Although Nashoba itself was not the example of equality it set out to be, it inspired a number of similar communities where slaves could work for their freedom and train for employment outside. Somewhere between three and five thousand slaves were freed through intentional communities like Nashoba before the Civil War.

Oneida, in New York State, was a group that followed a Christian philosophy called "perfectionism," which held that humans could become perfect (Foster, in Pitzer, ed., 1997). This was a view shared by some of the Pietists and inspirationalists, but a preacher named John Henry Noyes took it a step further, saying that once humans found perfection they would be subject to heavenly rather than earthly rules. They practiced birth control and "complex" marriage (where everyone in the commune was considered married to everyone else) for twenty years during the mid-1800s, and lived communally for thirty, usually with a fairly stable membership of around two hundred people. Women were involved at all levels of decision making, work, and public life, so that, although Noyes believed in male superiority as a general principle, they were more influential and had fuller lives than they would have had access to in the world outside. All the members engaged regularly in theatrical and musical productions and celebrations.

Noyes's charisma and leadership was crucial to this particular group, and when he aged, it lost its focus. His experiments with eugenics in the later years, which allowed certain chosen people to have children together but prevented this possibility for the majority, was one of the factors that caused resentments and dissatisfaction. But Oneida was always economically successful, and in 1881 the group abandoned communalism and became a commercial company, which still exists.

On the site of Harmony, in Southern Indiana, where the Pietist George Rapp and his group of Harmonists had lived, a Scotsman named Robert Owen and others started a short-lived and chaotic experimental community called New Harmony (Pitzer, in Pitzer, ed., 1997). This embodied a kind of paternalistic socialism. And from the 1840s on, followers of Charles Fourier formed "phalanxes"—communities similar to New Harmony but based ideally in elaborately planned architectural structures (which proved impracticable in real life). One

An Unreal Estate

of the communities based on Fourier's ideas was Brook Farm, where Nathaniel Hawthorne lived for a time (Delano 2004).

In the late 1840s, various "Icaren" communities sprang up in response to a work of fiction called *Voyage en Icarie,* written by Etienne Cabet. These ranged from Texas to Illinois, Missouri, Iowa, and California, and also involved elaborate planning along socialist lines. Cabet's ideas concerning equality were extremely exacting. In his novel he advocated every family eating identical foods at their predetermined mealtimes and wearing clothes cut from identical patterns. Although ostensibly a secular group, this was one of the most rigid of all the utopian experiments. Breakaway groups emerged as some members tried out more flexible versions of Cabet's blueprint (Sutton, in Pitzer, ed., 1997).

Timothy Miller traced communes in the United States from the beginning to the middle of the twentieth century in his book *The Quest for Utopia* (1998), noting that during this period they tended to be smaller, more democratic, less isolated, less regulated, and more low-key than they had been in the nineteenth century. The last feature was to some extent a necessity in a climate of national distrust of anything that smacked of "red" influence.

One unusual commune he discussed that had persisted from the late nineteenth century was the Women's Commonwealth, or Sanctificationist group, which was a Christian community of celibate people, most of whom were women, in Belton, Texas (Kitch 1989; Miller 1998). This was formed by Martha McWhirter, a married woman who had been inspired to a life of celibacy and prayer through a vision of Christ. She also believed in sexual equality. A group of women formed around her, leaving (or being left by) their husbands and living communally. They eventually prospered in business and bought land in Maryland. A few men joined the Belton group, but these so enraged the neighbors of the commune that they were taken from their rooms at night, whipped severely, and committed to an insane asylum. They were released after promising never to return to Belton County. More minor incidents of violence and vandalism persisted over the years, especially from relatives or former husbands of the women, but the community kept going until 1946.

The first two decades of the century saw the birth of a number of Christian communities. There was also at least one Swedenborgian community, in Pennsylvania, and a few secular ones, including some long-lived communities of artists, such as Roycroft, Rose Valley, Yaddo, and Quarry Hill. Then the 1930s saw a growth in more economically focused communitarianism as people tried to cope with the challenges of the Depression. The Roosevelt administration set up about twenty-five cooperative farms between 1937 and 1939, and these had varying degrees of success; but they were vigorously opposed by more conserva-

"Dream Flowers"

tive members of government, who associated the venture with socialism. After this short time span they were sold off. Quakers, socialists, Catholic Workers, and several other groups also began cooperative enterprises or living arrangements to offset the hardships of the time (Miller 1998).

Father Divine's Peace Missions, a predominantly African American religious and communal movement, effectively shielded many of its members from economic catastrophe throughout the 1930s (Weisbrot, in Pitzer, ed., 1997). Father Divine was both a charismatic Christian preacher and a dedicated social activist who had been inspired to promote human equality along racial and gender lines by the Biblical words from Corinthians, "The spirit of God dwells within you." His was one of the largest cooperative and communal ventures ever to have been established in the United States. Its home bases were in New York and New Jersey. For a few years the Peace Mission was the largest property owner in Harlem. By the late 1930s there were 150 communal houses scattered throughout the country with property held in common and at least 10,000 active participants. From the 1940s, however, Divine became preoccupied with various lawsuits, and the focus of the organization moved away from communalism, becoming more conservative and emphasizing its religious aims over its activist ones.

In the war years of the 1940s and into the 1950s, communal living reached a low ebb. But the Quakers, as pacifists and outsiders in a wartime and then cold war atmosphere, put energy into the creation of the Fellowship of Intentional Communities. One of its best known member communities was Koinonia Farm—an interracial community in Georgia, founded in 1942 (Miller 1998). Koinonia Farm attracted great hostility from its neighbors, including boycotts and even bombings, but it has persisted until the present day. Some of its members originated Habitat for Humanity.

In the 1960s, another period of communal burgeoning began. Miller (1999), who has done a second huge survey of communal utopias in the 1960s and 1970s, estimated that there were somewhere between one and ten thousand such experiments from 1960 to 1975, most of which were short-lived. He divided these into three rough categories.

First were religious communes of all kinds. These included many Christian groups, from Anabaptists to evangelical Protestants to the activist and reform-minded Catholic Workers. Some Asian groups, Buddhists, Hindus, and Sikhs, set up communes and ashrams after 1967 (immigration laws were eased in 1965). There were also a few Jewish groups, a few groups with Islamic roots such as the Sufis and the followers of Gurdjieff, and some with independent spiritual teachers—for example, Love Israel's group, the One World Family, and Padanaram.

An Unreal Estate

Second were urban, secular communes with a political or reform or service agenda. One of the best known of these was the Keristans, who practiced group marriage in family groups containing between six and eighteen members. They lived communally, sharing all resources, from 1971 to 1991.

Third, and least common, were the countercultural "hippie" communes in rural areas. Two long-lived and well-known examples of this trend were the Farm and Twin Oaks. The Farm, in Tennessee, has been going since it formed as the outgrowth of a college class, led by Steven Gaskin, in 1970. Gaskin was charismatic, and especially in the early years took the role of spiritual as well as ideological leader. Recently leadership has been more diffuse. It has also developed a world-renowned midwife program led by Ina May Gaskin, Steven's wife, and some charitable activities in Central America, as well as growing its own food (Fike 1998). Since 1983, however it has shifted from strict communalism to a more cooperative group living situation, with families taking responsibility for providing their own incomes.

Twin Oaks formed in 1967 in response to B. F. Skinner's behaviorist utopian novel, *Walden II* (1948). It has since dropped the behaviorist aspects of this work while keeping the communal economic structure of "labor credits": giving one labor credit for one hour of work, and including housework and childcare in this as well as what has normally been considered "productive work" since the Industrial Revolution (Kinkade 1994; Kuhlmann 2005). It has maintained a population of about eighty people and inspired at least two spinoffs, East Wind and Acorn, which are also thriving.

Miller writes that hundreds of the communes from this era are still going in the twenty-first century, and that hundreds more have started on "1960s principles." But religious groups remain the most numerous intentional communities still, especially Christian or Asian religious groups.

To Miller's list I would add two communities that sprang up as Native protest movements—Alcatraz and Wounded Knee. Both involved the occupation of pieces of land that the American Indian Movement (AIM) felt were rightfully theirs. They also involved cooperative living arrangements and a resurgence of hope. Richard Oakes describes the shoring up of a sense of community during the nineteen-month stay on Alcatraz:

> We did a lot of singing in those days. I remember the fires at nighttime, the cold of the night, the singing around the campfire of the songs that aren't shared by the white people . . . the songs of friendship, the songs of understanding. We did a lot of singing. We sang into the early hours of the morning. It was beautiful to behold and beautiful to listen to. (Richard Oakes, 1972, quoted in Mankiller and Wallis 1993: 195)

— 51 —

Miller's last compilation included no Neo-Pagan communes, possibly because the movement had not had much time to take hold before 1975. (These may be included his next book, which will cover the years from 1975 to the present). While there are other collectively owned Pagan-friendly communities in the United States—Wildheart, for example, in northern Indiana, and Compost in California are two that I have heard or read about—Lothlorien is one of the longest-lived of these, having survived in one form or another since 1983 and, as a land-based community, since the spring of 1987.

Intention and Inevitability:
Utopian Communes and Diverse Cultures as
(Contested) Testing Grounds for Human Nature

Utopian or experimental communes have varied enormously, from the extremely hierarchical to the extremely egalitarian, from anarchy to rigidity, from reactionary to radical, and from secular to religious. But in several ways they offer potential challenges to the norms of mainstream North America through their mere existence. One kind of challenge arises when a group removes itself from a situation in which they have had to depend on another group for survival, for approval, or for permission on a regular basis; that is, where groups are in constant contact on an unequal basis of power. Hence, for example, Father Divine's Peace Mission offered a space for both African Americans and women during the Depression where they could make a living away from the discriminatory climate of the society at large, and the Women's Commonwealth enabled a group of women to live independently of husbands, fathers, or other male authority figures.

Karl Mannheim (1936) contrasts utopianism with ideology, defining the former as the impulse for change, the latter as the entrenched ideas of a given time and order. Across the board, the existence of each intentional community, even the most conservative, the most rigid, the most faith-bound, offers the statement, "Yours is not the only way to live." Experimental communities tend to be unsettling rather than stabilizing to the societies beyond them for this reason. This is a different challenge from that offered by examples of varied kinds of society in cultural anthropology, in that the members of an intentional community have made a conscious choice to live differently. The two categories overlap, however, when a minority community occupying some of the same land as a dominant state or community chooses oppositional identities and lifestyles in line with their traditions, as at Alcatraz.

An Unreal Estate

Potentially more challenging still is what the existence of an intentional community can say regarding whatever beliefs about "human nature" are prevalent at the time. Hence, for example, at Koinonia Farm in the Southern United States during segregation, the existence and persistence of a community of African Americans and white Americans living on equal terms flew in the face of contemporary local ideas about biological racial difference. As in this case, the member of an intentional community potentially says, "I am not willing to accept the explanations you give about who I am as a man or a woman of a particular age or race or class. I am not willing to accept the inevitability of the life and work and types of relationships you have laid out for me." Intentional communities provide one kind of strategy for expressing this challenge and reinforcing a new, chosen sense of self. Wilma Mankiller describes the impact of the Alcatraz occupation on her life:

> The Alcatraz experience nurtured a sense among us that anything was possible—even, perhaps, justice for Native people . . . I . . . would become totally engulfed by the Native American movement, largely because of the impact that the Alcatraz occupation made on me. Ironically, the occupation of Alcatraz—a former prison—was extremely liberating for me. (Mankiller and Wallis 1993: 192)

Ideas of human nature can serve either to bolster or to undermine existing types of social formation, and usually the "common sense" assumptions in any given time bolster them. They can also either help to expand or to contract the parameters of acceptable behavior. Intentional communities often become bones of contention because they tend to expand, by example, possibilities for human nature and human relationships.

Fiction, Ethnography, and Utopia

Geertz (1973) and other anthropologists (Clifford, in Clifford and Marcus 1986; Wolf 1992) have written over the last three or four decades of the role of ethnographers as authors as well as observers (see also Stoeltje, Fox, and Olbrys 1999). Geertz used the term "fiction" to describe what ethnographers make when they write. Here, it is important to stress, he did not mean that ethnographic writing should or does contain falsehoods or fantasy, but that it is constructed as a genre of writing by a human being, that it has its own particular way of constructing a narrative out of the world, and that it a created entity, like all pieces of writing. Geertz's points about authorship make for more, not less, accurate and complete observations in anthropology, as

"Dream Flowers"

the writer him or herself, along with his or her role, position in relation to those studied, biases, expectations, and writing style become legitimate objects of scrutiny.

Writing is an ethical project. It is not a only an act of recording what is seen and heard, although it should strive to do this as faithfully as possible. On the one hand it inevitably involves a process of selection: what area or phenomena to study, which hypotheses to explore, where to focus for examples, how to word descriptions. On the other hand, writing also *acts* on the world, justifying colonialism, as Tylor (1871) did by dividing up human groups into "savage," "primitive," or "civilized," creating religious traditions (Judaism, Christianity, Islam, Hinduism, Sikhism, Buddhism, Neo-Paganism), inspiring the formation of communities and providing impetus for social change.

Religious texts, for example, have been a major source of inspiration for social change and in the development of communes, just as in other contexts they have provided justifications for resisting change. Most religions have an element of utopianism, whether it addresses a world after death or during life. The Hebrew Bible has inspired *kibbutzim* in Israel, while the New Testament, and writings about the early Christians, have played significant roles in inspiring communes, monasteries, and convents for two millennia. The early Christian communalists also drew, in many cases, on the writings of the church father Tertullian. Neo-Paganism itself has diverse utopian leanings, as I noted above, looking toward both the past and the future. It has been influenced by portrayals of pre-Christian divinities and ideals, first through their portrayals in Romantic literature, then in Murray's and Frazier's works, and later in Gimbutas's and Starhawk's, among others, and it has produced its own visualizations, songs, and fictional writings with an eye to the future, like Starhawk's *The Fifth Sacred Thing*.

There is a continual interaction between the world and the written word in secular fiction also, as new ideas spark new social forms that facilitate new ideas, and so on. A number of the communes discussed above were either inspired by literature or begun by people who had written utopian fiction. Nashoba's Frances Wright wrote, among other works, *A Few Days in Athens*, in 1822, which idealized ideals of democracy, friendship, and equality among the Greeks. *Voyage en Icarie*, as mentioned earlier, gave rise to several Icaren communes. Edward Bellamy's utopian novel *Looking Backward* (1888) was a best-seller in its time and was the spark for the creation of several communities. A German novel called *Freeland* was the basis for a community of the same name in 1899 and another in 1905. J. William Lloyd both wrote utopian novels and started an anarchist community, sometime between 1908 and 1913, called Freedom

An Unreal Estate

Hill. His daughter also printed the works of William Morris, who had written another popular futuristic novel called *News from Nowhere* (1891).

In the early twentieth century there was also a range of anticolonial and antiracist utopian writing. African Americans from the United States wrote some classic works of utopian fiction. Pauline Hopkins envisioned an ideal underground city in Ethiopia in *Of One Blood* (1903), and W. E. B. DuBois wrote first about a collective agrarian community of African Americans in the Southern United States in *The Quest of the Silver Fleece* (1911) and later about an international community of nonwhite people in *Dark Princess* (1928).

Later in the twentieth century, B. F. Skinner's utopian novel, *Walden II* (1948), was extremely influential in the communitarian movement, although the communities it inspired ended up looking very different from his original vision. It inspired about thirty-six intentional communities from the 1960s onward, including some successful ones that are still going, such as Twin Oaks, mentioned above. Hilke Kuhlmann has written an excellent study of these called *Living Walden II* (2005).

Science fiction may or may not be utopian, but it has also been influential among communards because it often explores "what if?" questions. What if we were taken over by machines as in the *Terminator* and *Matrix* movies? What if we lived without laws, as in Ursula Le Guin's novel *The Dispossessed*? Intentional communities can give concrete shape to such questions. What if we prayed for six hours a day, for example, or raised children collectively, or eschewed private property? A relationship with possible futures through science fiction is quite common at Lothlorien. The library at Lothlorien also has a huge selection of science fiction, and science fiction provides a way to explore alternative futures. Jef and Vic, two Eldars on the Council, told me that they had originally become interested in Neo-Paganism—which led them to Lothlorien—through science fiction. Vic describes how this genre of writing impacted her as a child:

> We moved around so much that I always read a lot. I always could find a library, you know, being a little girl in school, and I got into science fiction at an early age. And that was my first exposure to alternative thinking, different viewpoints and all that, and it made me think—and it really ly opened up my ideas, "Wow, I never even considered that!" (Vic, 2006)

Miller points out the role of imagination in setting up communes, even in cases where nothing is written down or enacted: "To a very large degree, the world of utopian communities is a world of dreams—including a good many that never reach any kind of actuality" (Miller 1999: xxiii). Imagination, drawing on either the past or the future, is also a necessity in instigating any social

"Dream Flowers"

change. The first feminists, abolitionists, trade unionists, and civil rights activists had, in a sense, to be capable of creating fictions, to be able to envision something very different from the way they lived. Martin Luther King's best remembered speech was framed by a series of images prefaced by the words "I have a dream." An example of how a change might look, how a different kind of society might look, can be powerful and subversive whether in concrete form, in imagination or on paper. This beautiful passage by Richard Oakes describes the impact the Alcatraz occupation had on some of its participants:

> Alcatraz was symbolic to a lot of people and it meant something real to a lot of people. There are many old prophecies that speak of the younger people rising up and finding a way for the People to live . . .
> There was one old man who came to the island. He must have been eighty or ninety years old. When he stepped up on the dock he was overjoyed. He stood there for a minute and then said, "At last I am free."
> Alcatraz was a place where thousands of people had been imprisoned, some of them Indians. We sensed the spirits of the prisoners. At times it was spooky, but mostly the spirit of mercy was in the air. The spirits were free. They mingled with the spirits of the Indians that came on the island and hoped for a better future. (Oakes, 1972, quoted in Mankiller and Wallis 1993: 194)

The power of experiences like this, the power of stepping outside of the mainstream, explains in part why some of the communal experiments described above attracted such intense hostility as well as intense idealism. They were real threats and they were resisted as such.

Krishan Kumar (Kumar and Bann 1993), Philip Wegner (2002), and other scholars of utopian writing note the role of utopian and dystopian fiction writers as social analysts, critics, and activists as well as authors. But while every vision implies a critique, and every critique implies a new possibility, the positive end of this continuum, the presentation of possibility, has tended in recent years to be treated more warily by academics and by the reading public than the critical end of the continuum. The word "utopian" in Marxist thought was a synonym for "unrealistic" or "unscientific." Novels that present not utopia but dystopia, like *Brave New World* (Huxley 1932), *Animal Farm* (Orwell 1945), *1984* (Orwell 1949), and *We* (Zamyatin 1924) have commanded respectful reviews, while, as Kumar (Kumar and Bann 1993) points out, the word "utopia" conjures cynical reactions in, for example, the works of Isaiah Berlin (1990), Karl Popper (1962), Milan Simecka (1984), and others, especially since the collapse of the Soviet Empire. But Kumar argues for the importance of utopian thinking: "Our historical condition—one in which life itself is threatened with insupportable damage, perhaps even extinction—is unprecedented. There is nothing to guarantee that we will find our way out of this mess. But at the very least we can think about,

An Unreal Estate

we must think about, alternatives to the system that has got us into it" (Kumar, in Kumar and Bann 1993: 80).

I have also noticed a tendency in anthropological and historical academic treatments of utopian communities to pair the word "utopia" with something sinister, as in *Utopia and Its Discontents* (Charles 2010; Pilon 2007; Rothstein 2003; Slacek and Turnsek 2010; Spiro 2004)—there are *five* articles sharing this name, which is telling in itself—*Purgatory and Utopia* (Iwanska 1971), and *Brook Farm: The Dark Side of Utopia* (Delano 2004). The last of these referred to a nineteenth-century community that came across as a cheerful place with nothing "dark" about it other than a chronic shortage of money and an accidental fire. It is as if a utopian imagining brings with it almost automatically the expectation of a dire and sinister result.

This association, I think, arises partly because utopias *do* threaten change and shake up assumptions about human relationships and possibilities, but also partly from memories of times when utopian visions have been seen as final rather than as temporary. Among the worst features of the large-scale social nightmares of the twentieth century, involved in life under Stalinism, Maoism, and Nazism, were their denials of any need for improvement or change. But, as noted in chapter 1, utopia is "no place" as well as "good place" in Greek. Even Thomas More, the creator of the original fictional *Utopia* (1516), thought it would be desirable for its inhabitants to change religious beliefs if they were to find better ones, which was quite a radical statement for his time. By this definition, then, utopia can never be arrived at finally, only headed toward.

Ethnography has often played a role similar to utopian fiction and science fiction by expanding imaginative boundaries, bringing to light alternative possibilities from cultures around the world—whether experiments in living from within the industrialized world, like Lothlorien, or social structures and forms that have developed outside it. This applies to less formal kinds of exposure to other cultures also. In his book *1491*, about the Americas before Columbus, Charles Mann (2005) argues that the examples set by the Iroquois, Cherokees, and Algonkians inspired American revolutionaries in their establishment of a democracy. Ethnography has at times actively looked for examples of difference and opened up possibilities of learning something about approaches to age, for example, from Bengal (Lamb 2000), to birth, from Holland and Yucatan (Jordan 1978), or to democracy, gender equality, and sexuality from Native American communities (Jacobs, Thomas, and Lang 1997; Lang 1998; Mankiller and Wallis 1993). At the very least, ethnography has the potential to throw into question rigid expectations about gender, age, race, class, sexuality, economics, religion, and a myriad of other issues. Raising questions about assumptions and

"Dream Flowers"

stratifications within their own society was part of the agenda of some of the early American cultural anthropologists such as Boas, Mead, Benedict, and Hurston, all outsiders in their time and professions, and this phenomenon was noted and explored by George Marcus and Michael Fischer in *Anthropology as Cultural Critique* (1986).

Susan Brown applies a similar idea to intentional communities, coining the phrase "critiquing with one's feet" (2002: 158) to describe the resistance involved in forming or joining such a community, and pointing out that while the former critique is the prerogative of scholars or those with access to the public ear, the latter is "a nonelitist form of critique available to the privileged and unprivileged alike" (158).

In reading utopian fiction, ethnographies, *and* descriptions of intentional communities, I often recognize these same motivations in myself—critiques of what already exists and the desire to see concrete examples of happier, more just ways for humans to organize ourselves. While this desire is rarely met in an unequivocal way, there can be a certain relief in realizing, through some of the readings, that aspects of our lives that we tend to take as given are not, after all, universal, that a variety of possibilities exist, that there is always something new to learn about social configurations, always hope.

Besides aspiring to provide an example, Lothlorien clearly takes much of its own inspiration from stories of all kinds. These stories often take up Romantic themes of wildness and magic; there are many of them, rather than one dominant story; and they situate spirituality within rather than outside the natural world and its inhabitants. Laura here explores what she finds appealing at Lothlorien in ways that tie together stories, magic and nature. It is interesting that while she does not identify as a Pagan or Wiccan, she relates positively to Pagan symbolism and some of its underlying ideas because of the fantasy literature she read as a child:

> I'm fairly agnostic and I just appreciate theology in general and the mythologies behind it . . . And how it's all interconnected and how it all tells stories about how we live . . . The Pagan thing has always appealed to me because I read fantasy books as a kid and I think that's an extension of something that I've been looking for for a long time— the idea of regrouping with nature and not being in a box all day long. There's a lot of spirituality in that . . .
>
> Nobody's making fireballs here, on this plane of existence, and nobody's summoning dragons or anything like that, but there seems to be

An Unreal Estate

something to the idea of people being connected and there being energy and there being kind of a network. To be able to find people who also see that and feel that is—it's really important. And I guess it's an extension of everything I ever read that was fantastic as a kid. (Laura, 2010)

Lothlorien, like Neo-Paganism, draws on traditions and stories whose origins are often uncertain. This is the case with festival rituals based in Wicca, with folk traditions like the Maypole dance, with fairy tales and fantasies, or with the veneration of ancient gods and goddesses. Because of this uncertainty people are free to take the images or vestiges that remain and invest them with their own meanings. And because there is so little that is fixed or certain in the traditions Neo-Paganism draws on, they can be idealized. They seem free (whether or not they remain so once they are revived) of the baggage of sexism, racism, religious repression, and capitalism that comes with much of Euro-American history. Past, present, and future meet here. For ancient worlds and imaginary future worlds, the worlds of science fiction and fantasy, have much in common. They are malleable, they are worlds of imagination, and it is understandable that they should be juxtaposed.

Lothlorien occupies an unusual position in time, then, ideologically unmoored from the present and from the recent past. Its festivals and land stewardship draw on preindustrial symbols and on Neo-Paganism, and they are also future oriented, not only in the pervasive influence of science fiction but in their provision of examples of a different way to live. They offer a small taste of a possible future on a broader scale. Hence the community is heir to North American utopian experimentation as well as to the influence of Neo-Paganism. This is reflected in the interactions between humans and the natural world, in the material culture, in organization, in community relationships, and in rituals. In the chapters that follow I will look at each of these in turn.

An elemental cross among "snowflakes" at one of the campsites.
The spokes represent the four elements—earth, fire, water, and
air—and the circumference represents infinity.

Photo by Lucinda Carspecken

3

Faerie and Avalon

Reimagining Nature

> I know that nature is not just plants and animals, nature includes rocks
> and dirt and us. Nature is a force that works and moves through everything.
> It is possible to walk in the forest or along a beach and become submerged
> in nature with no more effort than breath. People are at the core animals;
> the same force that tells geese when to fly south or tells spiders how to spin
> can guide us if we allow it. This force is at the green heart of every forest.
>
> *Conney, 2008, www.elvinhome.org*

> This land could be watched over by anybody. Not necessarily me or Conney or
> Lyn or all the other people who have come and gone, it could be anybody, but
> it is the land. This land, I think, has a consciousness of its own . . . I think we
> give it a name so we can recognize it, so we can focus on it, so we can get it.
>
> *Michael, 2006*

Bonedaddy shared an experience that he said had been instrumental in keeping
him living and working at Lothlorien. One July night he went walking through
Faerie, Lothlorien's woods, at two o'clock in the morning after a heavy storm.
The valley was flooded, and because of the summer warmth it was full of mist.
The clouds had cleared, a full moon shone through the tall trees, and fireflies
were everywhere, their smaller lights also penetrating the mist, creating lumi-
nescent spheres. The firefly lights and the moonlight both reflected in the water.

The relationship between the community at Lothlorien and the natural surroundings is unusual in many respects. Two broad areas of difference stand
out in the context of Southern Indiana—collective stewardship and (varying
degrees of) reverence toward nature. The organizational aspects of the former
will be discussed more fully in the next chapter. In this chapter I will look at

the impact that collective stewardship has on human interactions with the land and artifacts, and at influences from Neo-Paganism and from compatible earth-centered and alternative worldviews. These are reflected both in common perceptions of the forest and gardens and in the imaginative themes that pervade ornaments, structures, rituals, place names, and conversation.

There is a distinctive aesthetic identity infused in the material culture at Lothlorien, although it is composed of a disparate jumble of components, and much of this identity self-consciously presents an alternative to mainstream worldviews. Images of the genders differ from those in much of the United States, since women and men are both portrayed as divine. A number of symbols—the Tree of Life or Heart Tree, the Pentagram, the Celtic Cross, the Green Man—associate divinity further with the elements and with nature. Sensuality is included in the sacred, as are mundane objects and mirrors. Symbols and humor related to science fiction and pirate stories are also present in the material culture. From a more practical standpoint, energy conservation and environmental protection are essential parts of the rationale and design involved in building, gardening, and letting alone in various parts of the land. Limited funds lead to a makeshift feel to many of the artifacts; bathtubs to encase altars, ancient couches in Radiance Hall, colored glass bottles built into its walls.

An alternative ethic pervades the broader movement of Neo-Paganism also, and although many participants do not identify themselves as Neo-Pagans, it is largely due to this influence at Lothlorien that objects and structures on the land and attitudes toward the land often blur or turn upside-down "common sense" categories—sacred and profane, divine and humorous, mundane and otherworldly, human and nonhuman (Magliocco 2004; Pike 2001; Salomonsen 2002).

Magliocco argues that partly as a result of Pagans experiencing mistrust and discrimination based on their religious worldview, and partly because their worldview itself is out of sync with mainstream culture, they embrace oppositional identities, taking these into their own hands rather than accepting other people's interpretations of them. Hence, for example, Pagans have reclaimed the word "witch" and slogans like "Never Again the Burning Times."[1] Magliocci notes that marginalized groups within larger, more powerful societies often find creative ways of asserting their value:

Usually, one side of the symbolic continuum is accorded higher status than the other, which is coded as negative, taboo, dangerous or ambiguous, therefore justifying social disparity. However, this less valued side emerges regularly in

An Unreal Estate

numerous forms of expressive culture—such as ritual, drama, parody, satire, and play—that reverse or invert the established social order, valuing, however temporarily, the very emblems that are devalued by the dominant system. (Magliocco 2004: 185)

The approach to land expressed in interviews and conversations by regular volunteers and visitors at Lothlorien was implicitly critical of the instrumentalist and disenchanted strand of Euro-american culture described by Weber (1904). From a Neo-Pagan vantage point, the divine is immanent in all things, and it is especially evident in those aspects of the world that are in their natural state. Many active participants see the land, and all nature, as sacred, and their attitude toward it has religious elements.

Those who do not give themselves the label of "Neo-Pagans" may still share this view. This latter group tends to see the land more from an environmentalist perspective, stressing the need for sustainable approaches to forestry, gardening, and energy use. Environmentalism among interview participants at Lothlorien, however, does not usually draw on the instrumentalist discourse commonly associated with it in industrialized countries; instead, it incorporates greater than usual degrees of reverence, especially when it comes to dealing with the forest. The closest I can come to labels for this cluster of perspectives or discourses are "reverent agnosticism" or "reverent environmentalism." There are also a number of people who espouse a combination of Christianity and Paganism or Taoism and Paganism. But participants in all these groups usually present their affiliation as a choice of individual perspective rather than a fixed belief system about the way things are, which means that the various worldviews are not mutually exclusive or in opposition but overlap and blur into one another. Any one of these disparate perspectives encourages great caution and care about the land. This is in evidence in the building work, forest maintenance, and gardening. In a sense, the land *is* a part of the community.

A distinction must be made here between the active volunteers and the sporadic festival goers. The festival goers are much the larger group of people, although they are at Lothlorien for less of the time. While they must be at least comfortable around both non-Christian ritual and nudity—a qualification that rules out a sizable percentage of the local population—and while most have environmentalist ideals, there is a great deal of variety in people's reasons for attending festivals, and not all can be assumed to share this respectful attitude to nature. Some festival attendees are brought in by friends or relatives, and a few have just come looking for a party of one kind or another. There are often complaints after festivals by volunteers, especially long-time volunteers, about the amount of trash left on the land or about waste of water and firewood:

> My cynical side really agrees with Stewy's little phrase, which is "the festival is great except for the campers." I mean, they're messy, they leave all kinds of trash around. They expect this to be like a KOA camp with all the suburban amenities. (Chris, 2006)

However the vast majority of regular attendees and of volunteers and members do have an unusual degree of respect for land. They also live between (at least) two worlds: the festival site and the Midwest. They are familiar with modernist environmental discourses and share many mainstream environmentalist aims but want to create an alternative to the administrative top-down approach. Elvin HOME—the nonprofit organization that maintains Lothlorien—makes its own rules, works with the land directly rather than through planners and hired labor, and regards commitment to the ecosystem as central to their organization. As I will show, most active participants also use language about the land that makes less distinction between human and nonhuman species.

In this chapter, I will begin by discussing the forested part of Lothlorien, Faerie, noting the relationships between people and wild land as I go. I will follow this with a description of a few parts of Avalon, where festivals are held and where community members garden, build, and in some cases live. These landmarks will serve as lenses through which to look at the human footprint at Lothlorien, exploring Neo-Pagan influences and other points of difference between the approach to land stewardship and artifacts there and in mainstream North America. I shall discuss these differences in terms of the implied critique and the alternative possibilities they present to more prevalent modes of relationship between humans and their environment.

Faerie

Lothlorien covers 109 acres. It is rolling land that was missed by the glaciers that flattened much of the Midwestern United States. Ninety of these acres are forested, with oak, hickory, elm, maple, and beech trees predominating. They include low-lying areas, or bottomland, and here there are also box elders, sycamore, poplar, and cottonwoods among an abundance of tall grasses and stinging nettles. On the better drained top lands the trees include black

An Unreal Estate

cherry, black locust, ash, buckeye, and walking sticks. One area to the north has pines. A creek winds through the forest, and people swim there in summer. The northwest part of the land is stony and has the rarest types of trees, such as blue ash, because it has not been cultivated for the last fifty years.

The forest, called Faerie, is left mostly undisturbed by community members, except for cleared pathways for walks and the occasional shrine among the trees. In the early years of land ownership, members were reluctant to cut any trees at all, but this has changed. Uncle Dan told me that certain species of tree, for example oak and hickory, need cleared spaces in which to grow when they are small. He thought that to prioritize these hardwood trees over more common species like box elder required, in his words, "selective harvesting" of the latter at times. It is rare to see a tree cut in Faerie but occasionally they are felled in the camping or residential areas if they are dead or dying or to make way for a new structure. Conney describes the broad approach to forest stewardship thus:

> In the years since we became stewards of the land, we have tried to work with the needs of the land as well as the needs of the group. Letting nature have its way is not simply a matter of "leaving it alone." When we cleared away the greenbriar and old weed stalks, twiggy saplings grew quickly into young shade trees. As a group we have worked for this balance. We cut and trim trees as little as possible, usually when dead limbs are dangerous, or when scrub trees are blocking the light from young oaks and maples. We constantly refine and relocate paths, because rainwater tends to find these cleared spaces on hill-sides the easiest way down, and where water goes topsoil is sure to follow. We have large brushy areas of wildlife cover. There are areas we rarely go which we have left as nearly alone as possible, to let nature rebuild in its own course and time; we have marked special spots as shrines to those aspects of nature they seem to represent.
>
> All the work on Lothlorien has been done by volunteers out of love and a common desire to see the earth regreened wherever possible. Everyone who comes here has to find their own way of working with the land. (Conney, 2008, www.elvinhome.org)

The word *Faerie* denotes both the small supernatural beings from folk tales and fairy tales, and an immanent divinity in nature itself. This is an archaic spelling of *fairy*, popularized by the Irish poet W. B. Yeats, and the use of the word to denote a piece of nature or wild land is fairly common in Neo-Pagan circles, as in this definition from a Pagan website: "Faerie represents the prana or life source of the plant life of our mother earth. Faerie is the spirit of the plant, stone, water, and aroma. Faeries are the angels of nature and the natural elements. Faerie is energy" (Lisa Steinke, www.thefaeriegathering.com). Terry,

Faerie and Avalon

one of Lothlorien's originators, offers his own definition, expressed in his idiosyncratic style, in *Faerie Wyzdry* (1985b). This was written two years before the land had been found, and as part of a package of writings to promote participation:

> FAERIE is a LIVING REALITY which is bounded by the limitless potentials of NATURE. It is formed from the collective consciousness of the ANIMAL and the PLANT: blood & sap. It is the land of ever-changing birth, growth, death, and decay . . . FAERIE, as potential, exists everywhere between heaven and earth.
> (Terry Kok, 1985)

Calling the forest "Faerie" is a reminder of its essentially sacred nature. It may also be seen as a state of mind induced by the natural world. In this sense Faerie is the symbolic heart of Lothlorien. Being in the forest or in other wild places is being in the presence of a divine presence or divine beings who may want to communicate with humans who are open to this idea. In some cases these beings are personified as elves or faeries in the plural, in others as the forest itself, as this particular piece of land, or as trees or other living beings.

Michael expresses his sense of relationship and communication with Lothlorien as a whole:

> This land has its own power. If it wants to talk to you . . . you can't really ignore it. (Michael, 2006)

and Braze recounts some concrete experiences of communication:

> I believe if I have religion at all, it's Faerie . . . It's those stories of the land on the other side of twilight, and I've had experiences here . . . that were Faerie . . . (There's) the elation of realizing that trees do talk to each other. They have a very slow way about them, just like old Tree-beard. That's a collective that's in the forest, it's very real . . . Those entities are the best teachers.
>
> I remember one time feeling very upset and angry and distraught about the political situation that was going on (in the Lothlorien community). And I went to a place that I call the Grandfather Maple. And it's this maple tree down in Faerie that's got a six-foot-diameter trunk, that stands a hundred foot tall and dominates a canopy of a hundred and fifty feet around it. It's like walking into a cathedral when the leaves are out, because it dominates the space. So I sat with this tree one day and out loud I told him everything that I was really upset and pissed off about, and sitting there listening to myself speak there—the point was illustrated quite silently by my friend, that in his perspective

An Unreal Estate

these things are very trivial and the forest has this inertia and it just—
it grows and it builds its soil. So you know, there was a perspective
thing that happened there, and that's an example of how the forest
can teach you.

In my first year here I was feeling kind of antisocial and depressed
and . . . I heard this voice that was low and dark . . . and I remember
there, sitting here, in the dome, shaking, going, "Oh motherfucking
sweet Jesus Christ, this is like really real." And I realized that there is
a—a power as Faerie—you know, there's a magic in Faerie, and it's not
so much to be commanded as to be interacted with . . . It'll come up
and sit right down to you and say, "Hey, let's talk." And you've got
to go, "Eek, that's really real. Oh shit. Um, god, magic is real and this is
real." And well—either that or I'm crazy, but it's okay. In a way it's real,
because I'm perceiving it. (Braze, 2006)

Several other active volunteers at Lothlorien describe the land as having a
will and consciousness of its own. This idea involves a combination of the will
of wild places in general, like Faerie, and the will of Lothlorien in particular
as a center for festivals and rituals.

Sometimes Lothlorien has a way of calling people to it . . . when it
needs them. And it called me to it and I'm here and I'm not sure how
long it's going to need me, but . . . when the path changes then I'll
know it's time to go and if it doesn't then I'll know that I need to stay.
(Sarah, 2006)

If you miss time the land is going to be understanding, if you have to
miss time because of work. The land is going to understand if you miss
time because the kid is sick, or if you don't have gas money to get out.
(Larry, 2006)

I've always had the feeling that this place had a sort of separate energy to itself that . . . drew people to it. (Lunis, 2006)

Bonedaddy, agnostic though he is, expresses this in terms of the universe or
a higher power working through Lothlorien:

It seems to me that it resists a lot of types of control. It's almost as if the
universe uses people to prevent that happening. I'm not saying I believe
in that, but it seems like the universe controls the land. Something put
this idea in Terry's mind. Something draws the people here. (Bonedaddy, 2006)

The power of Faerie, or the power of Lothlorien, are talked about at times as related to or even in a sense created by the people who have come to the land over the years, either indirectly, by letting the wild land be undisturbed—

I've been to a couple of the borders here, and what's amazing is, is you see the clear cut, how they clear cut the trees around this area, and Lothlorien is a sea of green. And, you know, with very little around her. And civilization is pressing in on our borders, but we remain, we remain strong, and we are, we are, there is a heartbeat here. (Lyn, 2006)

—or directly, through rituals, intentions and thought:

The people try to hold on to some of that magic, even if it seems totally ridiculous or totally outlandish. If you can think it, then it you've kind of created that existence with your own mind, because perception is reality in a sense. And if you have enough people pulling energy into one idea or thought or place, then it becomes a lot more real, because a lot more people are thinking it. And I just—it's great that people want to keep magic and things like that alive, because there's not enough of it in the world. There's just commercialism and industry and you know, G.E. and Nike and Abercrombie & Fitch and all those things. (Sarah, 2006)

At the same time, several people see Lothlorien, especially Faerie, giving more to the people who come to it than the other way around:

The forest continues. It has an inertia that is of its own, and the elf lore family sometimes pretends like the forest depends on us to survive, but I think that there's a symbiotic relationship there that we don't get. The forest, in a lot of ways, actually is a buffer and a veil and a guard. (Braze, 2006)

In some interviews Lothlorien's gifts were expressed in terms of the psychological effect the land has on the people who come to it. Michael sees this psychological impact as what has been most valuable to him about the land in the last twenty years:

Truly, truly, this was a saving grace thing for me. This has become that thing for so many other people. I see it in their faces when they're here . . . You could go away with some kind of inner satisfaction. A little less crazed . . . than when you got here. Maybe a little bit more settled and a little bit more comfortable . . . I've received healings because I've been

An Unreal Estate

here. I've also been so banged up and bloodied working on this place you can't believe it. Bruises and broken bones and cuts and scrapes. For everything that you do for this land, or that the land gives you, let's say, it takes a little in return. There's a balance in there. And this place seems to make sure that balance is maintained. I mean my spiritual growth . . . I don't really like that term per se, but it seems to fit what I'm talking about that's taught me an awful lot; more patience, a little bit better at understanding. Maybe I listen a little bit more than I used to. (Michael, 2006)

Lilith expressed something similar, in more secular terms, with the words, "I think the woods are my therapy." And other interviews and conversations relate this effect specifically to the beauty of the land, as in this comment by Julie:

Being in nature, being able to listen to the animals, being able to watch the moon, the stars at night, and watch as the moon moves and see how clear the star is or how the clouds are moving during the day. I mean just the different elements of nature just help relax—get your mind off of all the stress and the drama—put it back in a lot more simple terms. (Julie, 2006)

Far from being part of capitalist discourse on land in terms of property values, profit maximization, or administration, Faerie is seen by some participants as magical, alive, and powerful, by others as psychologically healing and, from a few participants' perspectives, as having a will or consciousness of its own. But none of these are unquestioning worldviews (if such things exist anywhere). The people I interviewed were familiar and comfortable with scientific and rationalist perspectives on the world. Their view of Faerie is in most cases a choice. This comes across quite strongly in Sarah's words, "It's great that people want to keep magic and things like that alive, because there's not enough of it in the world. There's just commercialism and industry . . ." and in Braze's, "In a way it's real, because I'm perceiving it." Similarly, interviewees frequently spoke self-consciously and self-reflectively about their perceptions of Faerie, able to see more than one vantage point at the same time. For example, Michael's comment, "I mean my spiritual growth . . . I don't really like that term per se, but it seems to fit what I'm talking about," and Bonedaddy's, "I'm not saying I believe in that, but it seems like the universe controls the land," go back and forth between belief and skepticism. Brooks sums up this paradox quite nicely:

They see God in Nature. Whatever God is. (Brooks, 2010)

Faerie and Avalon

Environmentalism at Lothlorien and elsewhere, even Neo-Pagan or Romantic environmentalism, is at least as close to what most people would see as a "scientific" view of human nature as it is to any kind of metaphysics. The more mainstream Euro-American perception of the natural world as separate and even somehow irrelevant to human life can be traced back to strands or interpretations of Judeo-Christian religion where humans dominate nature and are essentially different from it rather than being extensions of it (White 1967). These views are not the only ways to interpret Biblical teachings (and Terry and Michael, two of Lothlorien's four founding members, consider themselves Christians), but they are influential ones. It can also be traced back to illusions of distance created since the Industrial Revolution through lives spent largely among human artifacts.

The relationship between people and the forest at Lothlorien, then, does not involve a retreat to a premodern or nonrational perspective but a deliberate move beyond modernism and into intentional reenchantment, involving an acknowledgment of sensations that are real but not often noticed or honored, like Bonedaddy's experience of the mist, moonlight, and fireflies.

Avalon and the Human Footprint at Lothlorien

My first campfire experience at Lothlorien was with Denise at a Lammas festival in August 2005, and the impressions I received are still vivid. Where the path forked toward a campsite known as Wolf Circle there was a cluster of objects that combined kitsch and mysticism; some squirrels, a daisy with a smiley face, a laughing Buddha. Hanging in the trees further along this short path, was a man's head surrounded by foliage (which may be the Green Man, a Neo-Pagan symbol of rebirth) and a wreath of ribbons. At the end of the path Laura was cooking hot dogs over a fire. There were a few small tents and some iceboxes. Suspended in the trees above us was a broomstick with a gauzy cloth draped across it. Nobody present knew who had put it there, or whether the cloth symbolized anything. A shrine on the ground had a Black Madonna,[2] a construction helmet, a fan, and a dragon, with candles around these. In the low branches of the trees, someone had hung beads and a lantern.

A dozen or so campsites like this, each one surrounded by trees and with its own collection of shrines or altars, tents, and decorations, along with a few larger public buildings, spaces, residences, and shrines, make up the core of Avalon—Lothlorien's festival grounds and residential areas—which cover just under twenty acres. While Faerie is relatively undisturbed, Avalon hosts around a thousand visitors every year, as well as a handful of residents. The

An Unreal Estate

area used to be cornfields. Michael told me that before Elf bought the land it had been left fallow for several years and was full of thistles, Johnson grass, and shrubs. Since the founders did not possess a lawnmower, they had to clear it with weed-whackers and shears.

Lothlorien's festivals are loosely based around what Neo-Pagans call "the Wheel of the Year," celebrating the seasons and the stations of the sun—Solstices, Equinoxes, and "Cross Quarter days" (halfway between Solstices and Equinoxes), which they consider to be the foci of earth-based worship and rural traditions (see chapter 6). The two largest festivals are Elf Fest and Wild Magick, which are based around a late Beltane, or May Day, and the Autumnal Equinox respectively. Festival attendees camp and socialize and attend rituals in Avalon, where humans and nature most often interact at Lothlorien. As with Faerie, many participants at Lothlorien perceive Avalon to be a special and magical place:

> When you lay in the ground here, just with nothing else below you, you can feel her breath here, you can feel her move, and you can feel the rhythm of life here pulsing through her . . . All you have to do is go into Lightning and lay on the ground, and you can feel the amount of power . . . It's the fact that this land for twenty plus years has had magic and energy, put into it . . . Through ritual, through personal transformations, through people just being here. We create our own magic, by our living and breathing and taking care of the land; I feel that that in and of itself is magic. (Lyn, 2006)

As a means to introduce Avalon, I shall list five overlapping aspects of Lothlorien's artisanship and stewardship that distinguish the material culture from that in the mainstream United States, and I will relate these to key features of the site. All of the five represent, to greater or lesser extents, departures from, or critical responses to, prevalent instrumental approaches to land. The features that I have chosen in order to illustrate various points are more or less interchangeable, since any one of them expresses and embodies a number of distinctly "elvin" characteristics.

Lack of Commercial Pressure: The Shower House and Campsites

The first, which is a key to the others, is the lack of commercial pressure at Lothlorien. The land belongs neither to an individual nor to a business. No one is thinking about artifacts, whether these are residential structures, tree art, shrines, composters, or garden features, as selling points for the festivals or in terms of neighborhood housing values, and this is part of why allowing for creative freedom is possible. All work is done by volunteers. Money comes from festivals, which are essential to Lothlorien's maintenance at present, but profits are plowed back, promotion is low key and informative, and the vast majority of planning energy goes into essential services: maintaining the boiler, raking the composting privies, keeping up with paperwork, organizing parking, building, fencing, graveling the roads, mowing lawns, weeding, maintaining fire pits, and clearing trails. People came to festivals before there were any buildings or facilities. Lothlorien is "off-grid," both in the sense of using and generating only solar powered electricity and in the sense of trying to maintain independence from the world around it. It rejects the grid as far as possible and aims to provide an alternative space.

On one hand this means that there is little money to spend on any project. On the other hand, it makes for a great deal of ingenuity in building, gardening, and decoration. Garden beds, trellises, and climbing structures for plants are made from local lumber or sticks from the forest. Bathtubs are made into shrines. On a minimal budget, volunteers have both built the various large structures and added the touches that have created a unique landscape, like the artworks on the walls of Radiance Hall (or the Long Hall), the ornaments hanging in the trees, the shrines, the collages and stone sculptures and painted banners.

Tuna brought up the issue of the shoestring budget in relation to the boilers and shower house. He said, "This is a pure democracy. You get what you pay for. Democracy is free." The shower house, which has hot water at festivals, is heated by an eccentric boiler. The boiler in 2006 had been cobbled together and coaxed into working order mostly by Tuna and Dan, from recycled or salvaged materials. But Tuna said that it had been worked on previously "by twelve different committees at fifteen different times." One of his aims has been to get the water running at reasonable temperatures instead of lurching from too hot to too cold. To me the boiler looks as if it had been invented by an amateur nineteenth-century scientist. A hand-painted wooden board gives some basic instructions in how it is to be run. The shower stalls themselves, and a sauna, also represent collective efforts made over many years. The stalls are wooden, with stone floors. High windows without glass let in both natural light and climbing green plants from the outside. Passive solar power has also been used in the past to heat water, and there are plans to incorporate solar heat into the design in the future.

The campsites are the most public oriented and festival oriented spaces at Lothlorien (although some people stay there for extended periods between festivals as well as during festival times). They are mainly clustered around or

An Unreal Estate

The boiler (with instructions) and shower house, 2007.
Photo by Lucinda Carspecken

within a circle at the western end of the South Road. This is the heart of Avalon, or "the field," as many people call it. Each campsite has a name: Scientists' Circle, Theater Circle, Children's Circle, Healers' Circle, Woodland Tree Circle, Elf Warrior Circle, Faerie Circle, Thunder Grove, Shaman's Circle, Bag End, Upper Boom, and Lower Boom. Some of these names vary or change over time. Also on the field are Merchantsville, where merchants can camp and sell such items as clothes, books, jewelry, and ritual paraphernalia, and Heart Tree Circle, which is a shrine and a place where a lot of handfastings (informal weddings) are held. The furthest campgrounds from the circular road, like Woodland Tree Circle, are on the edge of Faerie.

Camping at Lothlorien is both more primitive and more social than camping at most campsites. Each campsite has its own fire pit. Usually there is free firewood available at festivals. The campsites combine transience with permanence, because there is a tendency for people to go back to the same spots year after year—although there are inevitably also new or different people—so each site tends to take on a fluid character and set of traditions of its own. For example,

Faerie and Avalon

A campsite in Avalon.
Photo by Lucinda Carspecken

Healers' Circle is where a group called the Circle of 42 usually gather. Laura explains why she returns there:

> Those people feel like an even greater, deeper connection to my values. Jef and Vickie are usually down there, and Rodney and Scott and Natalia. These are all people I've become very close to. The whole Circle of 42 thing . . . the science fiction fantasy thing. People who are well educated and study the things that I'm interested in like sociology and mathematics and anthropology and physics. (Laura, 2010)

Bag End attracts sociable people who have no objection to the Trollbar (an informally designated area for sharing alcoholic drinks) being a few feet away

An Unreal Estate

from them. Formerly, Bag End was called the Troll Circle because it was a focal point for the "trolls," who did much of the work for festivals until 1996, and who were also often drummers and musicians. The Wolf Clan, based around a rock group called Dire Wolf, used to camp at Wolf Circle and remnants of it still do. Janie describes the way in which she and a group of friends adopted this area:

> They still call it Wolf Circle. That's because of Dire Wolf. So that band, because they went down there so much, you know, we kind of went as a clan for a long time. Randy and Chaz, they were really good friends and they had established a circle, and so every festival I was assured to go down and I camped—I've camped in the same circle ever since. (Janie, 2007)

Signs indicate most of the campsites. Some signs are carved in wood. A few are missing. The sign for Elf Warrior Circle is embellished with an ancient Greek symbol—the pentagram—hanging from a tree. Its five points represent Earth, Air, Water, Fire, and Spirit, with Spirit at the top. It is also a symbol for Venus, because the shape follows the path that the planet takes in the sky. It is commonly embedded in a circle.

A sign on the south side of the circle says "Merchantsville," indicating the space set aside for vendors, but their stalls and tents may spread all around the circle at Elf Fest and Wild Magick. Vendors are not charged for the right to sell their goods, most of which are inexpensive and some of which are handmade, and they pay the same festival fees as other visitors. The policy of allowing people to vend for free was adopted as part of Lothlorien's ethic of K.E.O.A. (Keeping Each Other Alive.) In between festivals there are no vendors' tents, but the circle as a whole remains one of the centers of social life at Lothlorien. Between March and November there is frequently somebody camping.

Creative Freedom and Inversion: Artifacts, Ornaments and Small Shrines

Closely related to collective ownership, and also related to a policy of respect for individual liberty, is the degree of creative freedom visitors, residents, volunteers, campers, or festival goers have at Lothlorien. It is explicitly written in the Bylaws that sponsors are encouraged to set up any kind of sacred spaces on the land. One can also build any structure (with Council permission) or add any artwork as long as this does not cause environmental damage. Between thirty and fifty people have put substantial work into the many, varied, independently initiated projects I have observed directly from early 2006 to mid 2010: shower stalls, the community garden, a new composting privy, the stage, the Thunder

Faerie and Avalon

Dome, the library, the Ice House, gazebos, a border fence, roads, a pond, parking areas, grounds maintenance, cleaning and trash collection, a patio, fire pits, promotional materials, a website, shrines, bookkeeping, workshops, rituals, a sauna, the greenhouse . . . Project directors, with Council backing and funds, oversee the largest projects, such as a new composting privy or the gravel roads or the garden, but anyone may add to a shrine, or adopt a flower bed or campsite, or add ornaments to the trees, as long as these do not pose a danger to people or wildlife.

Dotted around both Faerie and Avalon, but especially Avalon, altars, art, and artifacts are ubiquitous, in trees or on the ground as well as in the structures. This lends a great deal of combined color and mystery to the place, which is heightened during festivals, when candlelight illuminates the main pathways and there are fires at intervals among the campgrounds. The artifacts, ornaments, and shrines are the most concrete way in which the land is physically and literally "re-enchanted," to use Morris Berman's (1981) term. There are so many examples of "tree art," so many altars, and so many symbolic, decorative, and humorous objects at Lothlorien that the few examples in the descriptions that follow will only represent a small sample of them.

Near the path between the pond and the campgrounds, there is a wooden elemental cross in a circle, surrounded by stars or snowflakes—I am not sure which—hanging in a tree. In Neo-Pagan symbolism the circle represents eternity, and the spokes (like four of the five points of the Pentagram) represent the four elements—earth, water, air, and fire.

At Lothlorien, as in Neo-Paganism as a whole, a variety of themes and traditions are thrown together in unexpected combinations. Symbols of folk traditions involving magic, elves, and fairies, of ancient Greece, of religions—usually European and occasionally Asian—of mundane modern life, of pirates, of humor, of science fiction, and of self-reflection are mixed. The varied items in shrines get put together by different people at different times and for different reasons.

An altar I saw in Healers' Circle was an example of this. The Circle of 42 group, who camp there, took their name from a humorous science fiction novel called *The Hitchhikers' Guide to the Galaxy* (Adams 1979).[3] The altar had the words "Lucky 42" on a mirror, along with a Buddha, painted blue, and a wine bottle—thus combining humor, self-reflection, Buddhism, and hedonism. It drew, then, on imagery from *both* "past cultures and future worlds" (Pike 2001: 78), embodying a mixture of unlimited possibilities and the connection to ancient traditions. The Circle of 42 also used to have a large mysterious sign up,

An Unreal Estate

written in Celtic runes. Anyone with the skills to translate the runes would have been confronted with the following message: "Shit Happens. Things Change." The connection to ancient traditions too, then, is seen ironically.

Another shrine has a Christian Madonna, a Pagan goddess, an American flag, a skull, and a child's truck all in the same space. Like the profane language expressed in a sacred Celtic script, the inclusion of mundane objects along with traditional objects of worship in shrines throws the whole distinction of sacred and profane into question.

Another example of this kind of inversion at Lothlorien was the poetry copied out by Brooks onto the walls of the oldest composting privy. (It is gone now but was in place until 2007.) Much of the poetry dated from Romantic traditions in England and America—words from Blake, Coleridge, Wordsworth, Emerson, Tennyson, and Khalil Gibran—along with some quotes from Taoism and Buddhism. It reinforced my sense of the connection between Lothlorien and a Romantic worldview (see chapter 2). I was also struck by a reversal of the mainstream trend for what is considered "obscene" art to be on bathroom walls and what we usually call "high art" to be out in the public eye. While public sexual activity between visitors is not allowed (and would lead to eviction from the land), there is a tendency in Neo-Pagan circles for art to embrace sexuality openly, to be included in what is sacred and public, rather than hidden away as profane, on bathroom walls. Meanwhile the bathroom walls themselves were elevated to a site of "high art" through the poetry. Shrines and ornamentation, then, tend to support Lucy Kamau's (2002) contention that common distinctions are often lost or diminished in intentional communities as well as in other spaces that she would consider liminal.

There are many other instances of sacred and profane images being mixed, or their usual placement being reversed, at Lothlorien. The way objects are put together or placed is unpredictable. Their juxtaposition is also often, implicitly, a critique, and goes against mainstream expectations in the United States. In contrast both to a rational, modernist approach to material culture and to a fundamentalist, exclusive religious approach to it, where holy objects are on the one hand discounted and on the other regarded as inviolable, the concept of "holiness" itself is opened up and questioned. Gender stratification and class-related concepts of high and low culture are subtly undermined as femininity, sensuality, humor, and mundanity are all included in sacred imagery.

Common words people have used in interviews about their first impressions of Lothlorien are "magical" and "enchantment," largely, I think, because of the combination of these humorous, reverent, sometimes beautiful, and distinctly

Faerie and Avalon

noncommercial creations with a natural setting. There are other associations that can be made, however. When I first showed photos of tree art to my husband, he said that they looked "spooky, like *The Blair Witch Project*."[4] A lot of people not familiar with Neo-Pagan practice might see them as spooky or demonic, since in popular culture many of these symbols are associated with witchcraft, Satanism, and horror stories. Dennis Wheatley, an author of thrillers who wrote some very popular horror novels from the 1930s to the 1970s that claimed to be about witchcraft and who associated witchcraft with Satanism, carries some of the responsibility for this. Large numbers of novels and movies in the horror genre, including *The Blair Witch Project,* have continued to associate Pagan imagery with Satanism. As recently as 2007, MSNBC news commentator Tucker Carlson described a Wiccan lottery winner as "Satanic." This association partly explains why the policemen who first came to a festival run by Elf (see chapter 1) reacted so negatively.

I mentioned above that there can be a range of meanings in each symbol or object for the people who observe it. As a naïve anthropologist in search of meaning I often found this confusing. Scott made a wooden figure in the summer of 2006, just before Lothlorien was rented out for a weekend event for transgendered people. Since the figure appeared male on one side, female on the other, my first thought was that it had been made especially for that event. For several months it leaned against one of the entrances to Radiance Hall.

In the late autumn the ground was cleared for the pond to be dug, and Braze, who had been a prime mover for the pond project, was making a fire at the end of the day and went to get the sculpture to burn. I asked him why he was planning to burn it and he said that the figure was a *golem*. The golem comes from Judaic magical traditions. Sometimes, he explained, magicians put energy into a figure to help with a particular task. He told me that this particular golem was made to help with the clearing of stumps and rocks and trees from the area where the pond was to be dug. Now that the work was finished, the golem should be burned. At this point I thought that I had misunderstood the figure when I had first seen it.

I went to ask Scott about this the next time I saw him. I felt like an archaeologist with a chance to be on the spot and get an insight on some mysterious artifact. I said, "Would you tell me about your golem?" He knew the tradition, but he said, "Actually I was just clearing some wood off Michael and Conney's roof one day and I saw this piece of wood and I thought it would be fun to make a figure out of it." The incident illustrated to me how difficult it is to know why any particular artifact gets made at Lothlorien, and how easy it is for me to

An Unreal Estate

overinterpret or misinterpret what I am seeing, and also how people within the community reinterpret what others are doing. Meanings are very fluid.

To the east of Radiance Hall and to the northwest of the shower house is a limestone patio that was built by Bonedaddy and Heather in 2006 and 2007, with occasional help from others. (Bonedaddy carves bone and ivory and stone—hence his name.) The patio at this end of Radiance Hall and another fire pit with chairs at the west end are the most common warm weather gathering places for people at Lothlorien between festivals. There are some plastic chairs and a table. The two embedded a fire pit into the limestone, a beautiful cross with four equal, slightly curved sides.

When I asked, one day, if the pit was supposed to be a Celtic cross, drawing (proudly) on my newly acquired familiarity with this Neo-Pagan symbol, Bonedaddy said, "I don't know, we just liked the shape." My impression was that he was unwilling for it to be pigeonholed as a religious symbol. A cross with arms of equal length is called an "elemental cross" by Neo-Pagans—the four sides representing the four elements of water, earth, fire, and air, but I do not want to assume that this is what he and Heather had in mind.

Few objects at Lothlorien are easy to define and place straightforwardly. Magliocco (2004: 203) sees Neo-Paganism as "part of the historical movement from late modernity to postmodernity," citing its "holism, community and reflexivity," as well as its stress on "the multivocality of experience." The frequent placement of mirrors in shrines embodies reflexivity in the most concrete way possible. And at Lothlorien, being aware of multivocality is unavoidable as the observer tries to make sense of artifacts with a range of possible interpretations. This can lead to conflict, as, for example, the dividing line between trash left behind and artistic improvements is not always easy to draw.

Besides often meaning more than one thing at a time, or different things to different people, symbols, artworks, rituals, and shapes at Lothlorien may mean *less* than they seem to. A huge tuna hangs in the Thunder Dome. I used to think that it must have some significance. A Lothlorien newsletter had mentioned the "five sacred tuna" shapes at the top of the Dome. I asked Bonedaddy about this one night, and he told me that the tuna was a mascot of the Hell's Tuna Motorcycle Club and had been put there by Tuna. Tuna said later that nobody needs to own a motorcycle in order to join the club. Hearing about it automatically entitles one to membership. The mascot moves around mysteriously, appeared at Lothlorien one day, and may move somewhere else off the land at some point in the future. The club has apparently existed since 1969. In short, the giant tuna does not mean much beyond a joke.

Faerie and Avalon

A third difference—closely related to creative freedom—is the tendency for boundaries between religions or spiritual paths to be extremely porous, as is the boundary between religious and nonreligious objects or rituals.

Officially Lothlorien is ecumenical—a place to welcome all paths. The majority of religious or spiritually significant objects come from Neo-Pagan traditions, including pentagrams, Greek or Egyptian gods and goddesses, fairies, gnomes, mirrors, Green Men, and Celtic crosses. As far as mainstream religious symbolism is concerned, there are quite a lot of Christian images, a few Judaic images, and also some from Buddhist or Hindu traditions. The Christian imagery is most likely to be related to Catholicism, like Madonnas or statues of Saint Francis. Judaic influences or images tend to be from the Cabbala. The Tree of Life, for example, can be seen at various places on the land; a golem is also a Judaic symbol.

Hindu god and goddess figures are rarer, but sometimes appear in the shrines. Forms of Hinduism are easily compatible with Neo-Pagan practice because of their nuanced polytheism and their aim of internalizing divinity through ritual, especially meditation and chanting. Buddhism and Taoism are also open to many and fluid definitions. Buddhism has been disseminated widely and has developed many hybrid and idiosyncratic forms. Taoism is defined so loosely that it can meld easily into an environment where many paths are recognized. There are two or three Buddha statues in Avalon, but there are such a large number of shrines in out-of-the-way places in Avalon and Faerie (a number of which I have not yet seen) that there are likely to be more.

Julie stresses the religious tolerance at Lothlorien as something that offers a model for other places:

> Lothlorien is not really a Pagan-based place; it's where you come no matter what your religion. We have Buddhists here, we have Hindu, and we have all sorts of different religions here, and we all like to get along, which I think is something that the outside world needs to see; that it is doable. (Julie, 2006)

But Neo-Paganism itself includes many traditions, pantheons of divine figures, and degrees and types of faith, including some that are being made up on the spot. It also includes feminine as well as masculine divinities. So although there is a great diversity of religious approaches at Lothlorien, including agnosticism, it is rare to find anyone with a belief system that condemns or invalidates other religions, and this can lead, as I showed above, to unusual combinations and blurred boundaries. I shall use a description of the Thunder Dome to illustrate this point.

The Thunder Dome is an enormous geodesic dome structure beside a sloping path leading down from the northwest corner of the camping circle. It borders Faerie. This structure has a lot of symbolic significance at Lothlorien. Perhaps because of this, it is also a site of ideological conflicts as different people see it and use it in different ways, or even avoid it altogether.

At present the Thunder Dome is a four-story metal frame, open to the elements. In its current form it was constructed in 2005, and is understandably a point of great pride among many at Lothlorien. Braze, who is a welder, came up with the design and tried it out first on a small scale—building Andrea's dome. The larger dome required roughly a thousand hours of welding. River, a long-time elf who is also an architect, checked the dimensions for structural integrity and helped with construction. The surface area is five thousand square feet. It is a shape that combines the most volume inside with the least surface, making it very energy-efficient—or at least it will be when it is covered. All around the inside of the base of the Dome are limestone ledges for seating. In 2005, about thirty or forty Lothlorien regulars got together and put the Dome up in three

The Thunder Dome in summer.
Photo by Lucinda Carspecken

days. All the people involved in the Council and in volunteer work took part (see chapter 4), as well as many others.

The Dome is also called Thunder Shrine. The second name indicates reverence for nature and natural forces. The first name, however, is also associated with the movie *Mad Max Beyond Thunderdome* (1985) in which there is a similar huge geodesic dome, used as a pit for gladiators. In the movie, fighters could attack each other from all angles by swinging from points around the dome. At Lothlorien too, rings were built into the design so that people could swing. This is a popular and unique sport—quite dangerous, since the return swing propels one toward a shrine encased in an upright bathtub with hard edges. (Apparently the secret is to take a long run first and then swing in an oval arc, also to swing in shoes rather than sandals or bare feet.) Like many objects, shrines, or place names at Lothlorien, then, the names for and design of the Thunder Dome juxtapose religious reference (specifically Neo-Pagan reverence for nature) with a less solemn reference to popular and futuristic fiction. Recently I also became aware of other possible references in the name Thunder Dome, as Brooks, who lived at Lothlorien first in the late 1990s, returning in 2009, reminded me of Coleridge's opening words in the poem *Kubla Khan,* which he knew by heart and had posted on the walls of an earlier version of the dome when it was first completed, beginning thus:

In Xanadu did Kubla Khan
A stately pleasure-dome decree.

Samuel Taylor Coleridge (1816)

The Thunder Dome had a previous incarnation. The former dome was covered with wood, so that people could drum until late at night without disturbing the neighbors. However, it rotted and had to be pulled down. Plans to construct a permanent cover for the new Dome wax and wane. As of early 2010 the funds are not in place yet, but early in 2009 some drummers, or "Dome rats" (an informal name for people who spend a lot of time drumming, dancing, or fire tending at the Thunder Dome), covered some of the structure with huge strips of tarp. The idea of covering it is contested, however, as are many issues connected with it.

In the center of the Dome is a fire pit. The fire and the drumming and dancing around it are focal points for festivals. After dark, huge logs, often hollow logs, are brought in, and the fire is often maintained all night. Fire tenders, or "fire trolls," wear red suspenders, and this is a prestigious and skilled task.

There are two major festivals and a number of minor (sometimes unofficial) festivals based roughly around the Neo-Pagan calendar. At Elf Fest or

An Unreal Estate

A bathtub shrine in the Dome. This one is set up to honor
the water element, for Summer Solstice 2010.
Courtesy of Scott Martin

Wild Magick, the two largest festivals, there might be more than two hundred
people in Thunder Shrine on Friday and Saturday nights. At smaller festivals,
like Beltane, Lammas, Summer Solstice, and Witches' Ball, there are usually
between twenty and fifty.

At each of the four directions inside the Dome is an altar, encased in an upright bathtub. These tend to be untidy between festivals and get more care and
attention at festival times. Their contents shift over the months and are varied,
but often include objects that symbolize the elements. The elements—earth,
air, fire, and water—correspond respectively to the compass directions—north,

Faerie and Avalon

east, south, and west. Thus, at the Summer Solstice Reunion in 2007, the southern shrine held several symbols of the sun, the western shrine held a mermaid statue and a shell. In 2010 there were ducks in the western shrine. Mirrors tend to be found in shrines in any direction—symbols of the self as divinity. There may also be flowers or herbs in vases.

Sometimes people who come to festivals set up temporary shrines in the Dome. At Wild Magick in 2006 and Elf Fest in 2007, and on several other occasions between 2006 and 2009, Evangeline, who is half Mexican, and some of her friends, have created a large Santería shrine at the north end of the Dome, which is taken down at the end of the festivals. At Elf Fest in 2007, the shrine held Madonnas and saints with fruits, flowers, and other offerings interspersed among them. A large cloth with peacocks hung in front. There were coconuts, mangos, bananas, edible plants from Lothlorien's garden, candles, fans, and beads. Before the central fire was established the women put flowers and honey from the shrine into the fire pit as offerings.

The Dome itself is a shrine, and thus participation in its activities is often considered religious or "magical." Nights of dancing and drumming usually begin with a collective ritual (see chapter 6), but the traditions involved can be difficult to pinpoint or identify:

> There's a lot of different types and origins of magic that are worked down in the dome . . . There's an energy there, an energy that can swirl about, that can be created out of nothing. And that all comes from multiple people participating to create some sort of energy that can be used for whatever purpose you want to use it for. And 'Vange and Constance, they work their magic with that Santería, and that's their form of working with some of the magic down there; that's their contribution. And, I don't really have any particular form of spirituality that I contribute down there, I just kind of do my thing and I work the magic, and I work with the energy. (Jason, 2008)

While Jason prefers not to label what he experiences at the Dome, and Evangeline and Constance work within Santería traditions, Frank associates the energy with a Christian framework of the Holy Spirit, and argues that drumming and individual religious experiences should be honored:

> The dome is the temple. Are you going to tell people that when they get the dose of the Spirit coming in that they're supposed to relinquish it because you don't like noise? . . . I can't speak for everyone. I can speak only for myself. (Frank, 2009)

An Unreal Estate

The profusion of religious images within the Dome, and ritual styles, also brings up the complex issue, discussed at some length by Magliocco (2004: 205–237) and Pike (2001: 123–154) of cultural appropriation or borrowing—a phenomenon of white people adopting indigenous rituals or practices. Some Native American religious participants in particular—referring to popular Euro-American culture—have expressed resentment at cultural or religious themes being taken out of context or used for commercial purposes. However, I have not seen Native ceremonies conducted at Lothlorien except by Lisa, from the Teehahnahmah nation, who has led several rituals at large festivals.

I asked her, in 2007, if she felt there was a conflict between her Native identity and her involvement in Neo-Pagan gatherings. She answered that she saw the paths as parallel and similar, but with different sets of symbols. The similarity, she said, was that participants in both paths have a sense of unity between humans and the earth. She saw Judeo-Christian religions as believing that humans are superior and different from the natural world with a right or duty to dominate it. Paganism and Native traditions, in her view, see humans and the earth as all part of the same thing.

Lisa thought that attitudes toward sharing rituals or other cultural knowledge varied from one American Indian culture to another. She gave the example of the Lakota as a nation that had become very wary of sharing rituals. The Teehahnahmah, on the other hand, she said, had been intermediaries, traders, and translators between other nations before the Europeans arrived and had developed a long tradition of sharing.[5]

Most Lothlorien participants (like most Neo-Pagans, according to Magliocco) try to strike the difficult balance between religious inclusiveness on the one hand and avoiding cultural appropriation or insensitivity on the other. But religious tolerance is a point of pride, as is the fact that there are symbols from paths *other* than Neo-Paganism on the land. Most of these symbols are from nonexclusive traditions. There is a reluctance to pigeonhole Lothlorien as a purely Neo-Pagan place or to pigeonhole its artifacts or even structures, just as there is a reluctance among individuals to be labeled as Neo-Pagans or as *any* one thing, as reflected in Conney's comment, quoted in chapter 1, "I tend to run from categories. It's safer that way." Religious eclecticism is one way to avoid it. It is also one of the ideals of the community to create a safe space for practitioners of any religion, especially minority religions.

On the other hand, as noted in chapter 2 and by Magliocco, Neo-Paganism is often a way for white people to try to find some aspect of their own history that is not associated with colonialism, capitalism, or patriarchy but that still feels authentically their own:

Faerie and Avalon

I think that fairy tales are probably closer to the seeds of the truth than anything else, at least for me, being, you know, Anglo-descent, White western, that is the mythology of the roots of our people. (Braze, 2006)

Ideally, according to most of my interview participants, the drumming should be steady and unobtrusive enough to create a "trance" state. Michael said that the first phase of the evening's drumming gives drummers a chance to get the more frenetic rhythms out of their systems. Sometimes during this phase at festivals I have heard complaints that the drumming gets fast and expresses virtuosity at the expense of upliftment. After eleven at night some Lothlorien members maintain that drumming needs to be quieter so as not to disturb the neighbors or people whose children are sleeping. Others, particularly drummers, disagree.

There is a rough gender division among dancers and drummers. Women predominate among the dancers and men predominate among the drummers. (There are male dancers and female drummers so this is a tendency rather than a rule.) Children also dance around the fire, especially in the early evening. Once it is dark enough there may be exhibitions of fire dancing on Lower Boom, visible from the Thunder Dome. Jason does this very skillfully, with a whip, through which he creates arcs of fire. Besides the drummers and the dancers, a number of people sit around the circle on the walls, watching or socializing. On some occasions somebody will play a wind instrument or violin or harp.

Janie vividly describes how atmospheric the Thunder Dome can be at times. This memory is from a time when the Dome had a wooden cover:

One of my greatest memories from that wooden dome is sitting on the ledge. I was kind of shy, because there were so many people, they were all so friendly, but at the same time, there were still, you know, little cliques of people where everyone seemed to know everyone and when you didn't know everyone . . . it was still a little intimidating. Just, any crowd of people, you know, no matter how friendly, is still slightly intimidating. But to sit on that wall and just watch everything go by. There was just a scene in my mind that sticks with me and Chris was kind of part of that, tending fire . . . and then sparkly people, you know, with their fairy glitter on and so there were these fairy element people running around . . . very kind of mystical and fun. There was this working group and the drumming was really wonderful and it was full, it was energetic and the fire was so cool—I love to watch the fire tenders build a fire, and that's so neat when they use all the chimney logs and everything. That was a really wonderful, magical night for me. That scene of feeling that energy, community, fun, festive . . . a little bit of back in the day . . . of a day I don't remember, recall in my memory—way back. It just seemed like it was primitive, you know, it was that kind of primitive atmosphere so that was really neat and that sticks with me. (Janie, 2007)

Chris recalls an equally atmospheric but more intense evening:

My first night here, that night when Evangeline and I first came up, the Dome scared me. The energy down there was so intense; they were singing, they were whirling like Dervishes dancing. The pace was huge, the drumming was frenetic, the energy was palpable and I was scared if I went down there and got sucked into that maelstrom I wouldn't come back out. I was afraid of being changed in some way I had no control over. It was majorly attractive at the same time. It scared me so bad I actually—I came back up to the parking field and sat in my car for an hour and a half and decided whether or not I was going to stay. (Chris, 2006)

Many dancers, like Sarah and Andrea, who use dance very expressively and well, consider it a spiritual practice, enabling them to get into a trance state. The continuous regular drumbeat, as opposed to a shift from one dance tune to another, helps:

Some of the same drummers come back frequently, and some people come specifically to drum. A woman called Rowan, who also drums, explained to me that there are styles of drumming that correspond to the elements. "Fire" drumming tends to be fast and is difficult to trance to, although it gives energy. "Earth" drumming is more grounded. Drumming like dancing, according to Scott, is a way of connecting to what he called the "Higher Self." Jason came to me, beaming, at Summer Solstice Reunion in 2009 to try to express what he was experiencing while he drummed. He said, "This is crazy. It's uncommon. It feels so right!"

Andy—whose spina bifida prevents him from dancing—pointed out that just being in the Thunder Dome when there is drumming can be a spiritual experience in itself:

The first time you see Thunder it's amazing down there. Just all the dancing, all the drumming, it's very trance-like. I mean you could go down there, not talk to anybody and just sit and watch the fire and listen to the drumming for hours and hours and just be perfectly happy.

Faerie and Avalon

Doing that it helps center you a lot and you start to really think about what you're doing versus what you should be doing or what you could do. You learn a lot about yourself out here. (Andy, 2006)

Fire tenders, drummers, dancers and other dome rats often stay up all night. Some of these from 2006 until 2010 were Spencer and Evangeline, Conrad, Chelsea, Jason, Andrea, and Scott, as well as Larry in the early years and Frank from 2008 on. At dawn there is a ceremony called Resh to greet the sun. Jason describes it:

Once you start seeing the gold around the trees, you know that the sun has risen, the sun has come up once more, and it's all good. I've been told that one of the reasons that we stay up all night long, especially on longest night, is to make sure that the sun comes back up the next day. And if the sun doesn't come back up, we'll let everybody know. And if the sun does come back up, we'll also let everybody know. Whenever it gets to be in sunrise, we all gather on the east corner of the dome, and we all raise our right hands. And on the count of three, or four, or two, we start . . . and we've all got this memorized:

"Hail to thee who art Ra in thy rising.
Hail to thee who art Ra even in thy strength,
Who traveleth across the heavens in thy bark at the rising of the sun.
Tahuti standeth in his splendor at the prow, and Ra-Hoor abideth at the helm.
Hail to thee from the abodes of night.
Bull!"

   And then everybody screams "Bull!" . . . You just really scream out "Bull!" and just make as much noise as you can. It's kind of an alarm clock for the rest of the land. "All right, we've done our part. We've stayed up all night, we've made sure the sun comes back up. This is your information, this is your infogram that the world will go on, that the sun has risen, and everything's all good," and we continue to drink a little bit more and be silly, and then we stumble off to bed. (Jason, 2008)

Ra was an Egyptian sun-god whose worship peaked in the mid-2000s BCE. Ra-hoor is a combination of Ra and Horus, who is associated with the sunrise. Both of these deities were invoked by Aleister Crowley in his magic oriented organization and ceremonies (which, as noted in chapter 2, influenced Gardner and Wicca). "Bull" has several meanings. The first, and most conventional is

The sky seen through the Dome, just after dawn.
Courtesy of Scott Martin

that Ra was often portrayed as a bull. Then there is the ironic self-deprecation of ending an invocation with the word, "bull," as if it is not to be taken seriously. Finally there are references to "the cult of Azo"—a tradition developed around a battery operated toy bull called Azo by a Discordian named Dennis Murphy. Discordian practices tend to use a lot of word play, and much is made of the double meaning of "bull," which is a symbol of nothingness. Azo is also referred to as a "sacred chao"—"chao" here being a singular form of the word "chaos" as well as sounding like "cow." Around dawn a combination of rum and orange juice known as "Discordia juice" is also passed around.

The fact that the Thunder Dome may be used as a place for socializing as well as reverence is an area of underlying conflict at festivals, since a few regular and long-term sponsors at Lothlorien feel that socializing should happen elsewhere, and are disturbed by the amount of casual conversation that takes

Faerie and Avalon

place in the Dome on festival nights. Chris expresses his frustration with the contrast between what the Dome often is and what it can be or has been in the past:

> If I had to be disappointed in anything it's the way the Dome's turned out. It's become a dance club. There's so much spectation. There is no trancing. People are always talking about trancing but they have no clue what the heck they're saying. When you fall into a trance you stop what you're doing. You fall to the ground. You foam at the mouth. Your eyes roll back. They're zoning, they're getting into almost a light state of self-hypnosis but it's certainly not resembling a trance. We always refer to trance dancing, trance drumming, but that's not what happens. I've dropped into trances a couple of times on the drum and I've woke up with it underneath me and people all around me going, "Oh my God. Oh my God. Are you alright?" They don't even know what a real trance looks like. It's a deep hypnosis. It's deep self-hypnosis. (Chris, 2006)

Eclectic understandings of religion and spirituality at Thunder Shrine, then, as well as very porous boundaries between sacred and secular activity and space, have made for some conflicts at Lothlorien, and issues over drumming—how loud it should be, when it should stop, whether there should be conversation while it is taking place—probably require more negotiation than any others in the community. Some regular participants identify the Dome as a sacred space, and drumming and dancing as sacred activities. Some see it as an extension of their social activities. Other regular participants avoid the Dome altogether, and their commitments and religious expressions at Lothlorien are focused on the land, the plant life, and the opportunities for communicating with nature and for building and gardening in reverent ways. Most see both as sacred. One or two also have concerns about the drumming having a negative effect on their relationship with neighbors and about possible visits from the police. All of these perspectives come up, sporadically, at the monthly Council meetings. Then there are often differences between the perspectives of Council members and casual visitors, with the latter group sometimes having a less reverential attitude toward either the land *or* the Dome.

As mentioned above, also, religion at Lothlorien includes parts of life that are commonly regarded as secular or even profane in the United States and in much mainstream Christian thinking, particularly femininity, animals, sexuality, plants, and the elements. This will be touched on again in the next section, and both religion and ritual will be discussed at greater length in chapter 6.

An Unreal Estate

A fourth difference is that things are often made cumulatively, bit by bit. This is especially noticeable with the shrines, but it is also true even of the boiler for the showers, as in Tuna's comments about this having been made "by twelve different committees at twelve different times." They are added to piecemeal. Each piece might, or might not, be a comment on what was there before. People may also move objects, although this is less common. Removing them from the land altogether would be a kind of theft and would be frowned on. Alterations or additions might be made by someone who lives at Lothlorien or by a visitor who comes only once. It is very haphazard. I noted above, for example, a shrine which combined a Madonna with a flag, a skull, a goddess, and a child's truck. I do not know if these were put in place by one person or by several people at different points in time, but the latter seems more likely. A mundane object shifts the meaning of a traditionally sacred one, and vice versa. An object can also make a humorous or ironic comment on its context, like the recent addition of a miniature statue of the Thinker to the Trollbar, which is an informal gathering place for drinkers at festivals.

Cumulativeness also reflects Lothlorien's nature as an experimental work in progress rather than a finished place. The composting privies, for example have gone through many incarnations, from early semipermanent outhouses to the Old Composter, to the improved Peepee Tipi, to the newest privy. The Old Composter has now been pulled down entirely, but each attempt benefits from the learning drawn from having built, used, and maintained the previous privies. Cumulativeness gives concrete form to the passage of time.

The Old Composter was across the south road from the pond and a little farther to the west. It was demolished in July 2007, since it was unstable. It was not wheelchair accessible—it had a ramp, but it was too steep. The newest, unfinished one will be accessible. There was no running water inside the Old Composter for most of the year, but at festivals a hose used to be connected to a sink at the wall on the far end, so that people could wash their hands. There were three stalls, each containing a cup and a bucket of sawdust to be added by cupfuls to the waste.

In the first few years, before any permanent composting privies were built, human excrement had to be cleared away in barrels and buried:

> We gradually realized that having these little semipermanent outhouses
> was ridiculous; we had to empty them after every festival . . . because we
> started out we were going to move them, and bury it . . . It seemed logi-

The Lower Composter in the snow.
Courtesy of Scott Martin

cal. You move it . . . Pioneers did. You used it for a while then you bury
it. It takes forever to dig in that clay . . . We had all kinds of really gross
icky variations that we went through over the years before we started
building the composters that are permanent. You can clean them out.
(Conney, 2006)

Near the far end of the outer edge of Avalon's circle is a new composter,
within a tipi design. It was built a couple of years ago, and is also known as the
"Peepee Tipi" and the "Excremeditation Chamber." It was mainly the brainchild
of Bonedaddy and Braze, with others helping. Inside the stall walls are made
of steel. A third composter, also in the shape of a tipi, was finished in September
2009. Bonedaddy and Paul, along with other helpers, built this one for $2,000
less than the Peepee Tipi, by reducing the height of the stalls, and Bonedaddy
also used his previous experience to improve the ventilation, with carefully
positioned vents at the bottom and top of the structure. The old and new
composters, then, represent stages in Lothlorien members' experiments with
alternative building—each one an improvement on the one before in some way.

All the creations that appear over the years are more or less anonymous. People might or might not remember who made something. Often they remember

differently from one another. There is an attempt to cultivate individual free-dom of expression at Lothlorien, but since nobody leaves their names on their creations, and since the creations grow and change by being added to, it would be difficult to separate out the individual contributions anyway. This leads to a nonreified form of individualism, which I shall discuss further in chapter 5.

Environmentalism: The Community Garden

Finally, a fifth difference is the commitment to the environment. This is a main focus of the Bylaws at Lothlorien. So, as we noted earlier, permanent structures are made with energy and resource conservation in mind. This last point is often stressed by participants in relation to the material culture, and is central to Lothlorien's mission:

> I was like "I will be much happier in my life if I could literally just walk out on this land, see one tree—just, say, that one right there—*and* know fifty years from now, that tree will not be touched because of what we're doing." That means . . . more than any money, anything like that. (Andy, 2006)

> I'd like to think that we're leaving a legacy. If this place outlives us then we've done a good job. Part of our legacy is trying to keep the ecosystem here intact and not do a whole lot more building. Focus on what we have. Improve where we can. Leave it alone when we should. (Stewy, 2006)

To the right of the driveway in front of the Long Hall is an organic garden based on the principles of permaculture. Braze and Andrea designed it. Braze first tried gardening here in the summer of 2005 in a conventional way, putting flowers in rows. Over that winter he read back issues of *Mother Earth News* and they both read *Gaia's Garden* (Hemenway 2000), which sets out some permac-ulture procedures for small-scale gardening. Andrea grew up in a rural area and her family grew a lot of their own food. Both have a strong commitment to gardening. Andrea says,

> That's my lifelong plan—to be able to provide myself and those around me with healthy food and a healthy simple lifestyle. (Andrea, 2007)

When I began studying Lothlorien I took on the role of an unofficial (and unskilled) apprentice to Andrea and Braze. In March of 2006, we pulled up chickweed for a few weeks, which was added to the compost pile. Then we made a trellis of branches along the north edge of the garden, intertwined around

Faerie and Avalon

four tipi-style tripods for beans and other climbing plants. The trellis doubles as a wind shelter and a barrier to forest animals. Later we built tiered beds. There are designs for these in *Gaia's Garden;* the idea behind them is that the top layer is for plants that need a high ratio of sun to moisture, the lower layer or layers for plants that need more moisture and less sun. Most of the tiered beds are circular, and Andrea and Braze made them from limestone slabs. There are also smaller trellises at intervals, for tomatoes and for peas, the latter planted early in the spring.

Following another suggestion from the book, we made a swale, digging a winding ditch through the garden, which we then filled with mulch—to provide both access to the plants and an even distribution of water. Toward the end of 2006, we replaced the mulch with gravel. (Bob, a volunteer from Tennessee, helped with this also.) Braze has built fences and beds all around the garden out of local timber (dead or dying trees from around the land), and he and Andrea have constructed three entrances. The two of them ordered, collected, and planted a variety of seeds, mostly for edible plants but also some flowering plants. The latter both add to the aesthetics of the garden and attract bees and other insects to help the garden thrive. As in other areas of work and organization at Lothlorien, plans for the garden change frequently—new strains and species of plants are tried out and kept up or abandoned, depending on how they thrive and on the tastes of the gardeners. New approaches to gardening are also tried out sporadically.

Lothlorien is not a self-sufficient community; the garden supplements food for residents and regular visitors rather than being their only source. But a lot of food has been grown in the garden since I arrived, including tomatoes, green beans, lettuce, herbs, potatoes, cucumbers, squash, peppers, kale, garlic, onions, broccoli, and peas. In the winter Andrea and Braze planted carrots, onions, and garlic. They seek out unusual varieties when the community can afford them, and the range of flowering and edible plants that have been added in the spring of 2007 would read too much like a garden catalogue for me to include in its entirety. Altogether there are now hundreds of plant species in the garden, many of them edible, which have taken over from the chickweed that predominated until March of 2006. The flowers are also eye-catching, notably, in 2007, the sunflowers and the bright blue morning glory.

In early 2006 the soil was almost solid clay, but this has been improved through a variety of measures. Braze and Andrea planted first clover, then a mix of clover, alfalfa, and buckwheat as a groundcover between the beds because these fix nitrogen in the soil. There is a compost heap to the east, which has been a good resource. We also added to the soil quality by digging up a small

The garden when it was first tilled in March 2006.
Courtesy of Scott Martin

The garden after cultivation, in summer 2007, with
fencing, painted fairies, and a "dragon" skull.
Photo by Lucinda Carspecken

truckload of decomposed mulch from the bottom of an old wood pile. One of the winter's major projects was the creation of a pond at the west side of the garden. Andrea made a computer design of the pond to help sell the idea to the Council, since it required funds. Braze cut down a few trees to clear a space for it—also giving the garden more sun. Larry and Dan helped him drive diggers and clear stumps for the final groundbreaking and digging. The pond will provide water for the garden and will also attract bats—to eat mosquitoes and to enrich the soil with bat guano. Braze added fish, and shrimp as a source of food for the fish. Dead fish will provide additional enrichment for the garden's soil. In 2007, Braze found a source of horse manure. And in the winter of 2009–2010, Andrea tried covering parts of the garden with cardboard and straw to keep in moisture, cut down weeds, and add fiber to the soil.

There are some colorful artifacts in the community garden that complement the creative approach to gardening itself. At the south east entrance, Andrea painted two statues of fairies. Braze added a dragon's head at the top, with three horns and a light inside for nighttime. There is a goddess statue at the southwest corner of the garden, which Andrea painted blue and silver, and she and Braze put in a plant called Gaelic Magic near the statue, along with sage and rosemary. They added some local stones and crystals. I have never heard the goddess given a name. Soon after this statue and flowerbed were established, they bought a Pan statue, which Andrea painted in brown, gold, and green. Braze had expressed a desire for Pan to have a flowerbed "every bit as good" as the goddess's. At the moment the statue has been placed among some bamboo next to the pond.

Neither Andrea nor Braze define themselves as Neo-Pagans, although they have both been involved in Neo-Paganism at various times in their lives. Andrea has an interest in Buddhism (but is not necessarily a Buddhist either). Braze used to be a Pagan but is now very critical of most organized forms of the movement. He thinks it has gone downhill and lost its edge, and that some Pagans think it is enough to do a ritual once a week rather than getting to know nature, which he feels should be the essence of Neo-Paganism. Braze says that his favorite ritual is cleaning his teeth while looking at the stars. Andrea does not define herself in terms of any religion, as I noted above. But they are drawn to these symbols, the goddess, Pan, the fairies, the dragon. These artifacts add mystery and a haphazard beauty to the garden.

Braze made two stone sculptures for the garden out of local rocks. When I went for a visit to England in the summer of 2006, he asked me to take a rock from Lothlorien, a geode, put it somewhere and bring back a rock from England to put in the garden here, to make a link between the two places. I put the

An Unreal Estate

Lothlorien rock in a secluded spot near the river in Magdalen College Gardens in Oxford and brought back four small rocks from there (I couldn't find a large one, so this seemed to me like a balanced exchange). I showed Braze and Andrea pictures of Magdalen when I came back. Tolkien and C. S. Lewis used to walk together there, so it struck me as an appropriate source for the rocks. I added them to one of Braze's sculptures and to a couple of flower beds.

Building and gardening have been innovative, and these are areas in which Lothlorien's participants have much to teach by example. With a minimum of outlay and without fertilizers or chemicals, Braze and Andrea have improved the clay soil in the community garden and experimented with a number of alternative gardening methods to transform a patch of chickweed into a fertile and abundant source of edible and flowering plants. The trellises, the swale, the companion planting, the pond, and the tiered beds have all played a part in this. Rose of Sharon trees and bamboo have been planted to create part of a natural barrier against deer. Since the addition of the pond and its fish, the garden is drawing closer to being a self-sustaining ecosystem.

The community structures are also innovative and energy efficient in spite of limited funds. The shower house, too, is both aesthetically pleasing—partly open to the elements and surrounded by greenery—and energy efficient. The Long Hall, while it needs insulation and other repairs, shelters hundreds of people throughout the year, uses only solar energy, and works well as a focal point for meetings, shared meals, and, through the library, education. There is also continuing experimentation with unconventional building shapes such as geodesic domes and tipis in the residential structures.

Conclusions

Lothlorien attracts some unusual forms of art and reverence partly because it is a sanctuary of sorts where the commitment to individual, religious, and creative freedom ensures that ideas that might normally be considered strange or shocking can be expressed. This contrasts with mainstream North America in practice if not in theory, since, despite the popular rhetoric of American individualism, there are few avenues in mainstream culture for the airing of individual artistic expression that are accessible to any but a tiny minority of people and that are not filtered and manipulated by large commercial interests. It is unusual because it is "off grid," in the sense that it is neither dependent on nor accountable to an individual or a company. And creations at Lothlorien are made cumulatively and anonymously, sometimes being added to on the basis of experimentation and learning—as in the case of the shower house

Faerie and Avalon

and privies—sometimes developing layers of new meaning or self-reflection as objects are juxtaposed with each other, as in the case of the shrines and altars. Frank's description of building a temporary shrine pulls together several of these points:

> I built my first shrine this year. My shrine—it's my belief. I made this three-tiered kind of thing. On the top level I put a crucifix that was given to me by the best man at my wedding after his wife died . . . If you've noticed there aren't any crucifixes down there . . . And I bought this metal Buddha, and I put Buddha on the second tier. Buddha was a teacher and he taught the same things Jesus did . . . The next morning I woke up and there was a fertility goddess that somebody had put up there. There was a totem. Over the course of the festival, I went from having the crucifix and the candles up there to the crucifix and the Buddha and the fertility goddess and the totem and the My Little Pony™. And by the time I left I think there was a little truck. People had just come in but they respected my top tier . . . What was nice was that they respected my belief enough to leave the top tier alone yet they had the freedom to put what they wanted up there and show their belief . . . It's not my shrine. It's there for everyone. They don't have to agree. They have to be tolerant of my belief—as tolerant as I am of them. (Frank 2009)

Lothlorien's artifacts are often difficult to define, as I often found in my early attempts to understand and pigeonhole what I saw. This relates to another kind of creative freedom—the freedom to define things in a variety of ways, as well as to make them. The choice of the name Lothlorien—"dream flower" in Tolkien's invented Elvin language—suggests a place conceived and experienced within the mind as opposed to in an objective realm. Because there is no strong pressure, either from economic necessity or from group norms, to look at the world in any single way, the definition of each landmark or object is very subjective. Transience adds to this. For example, when I talked about "Andy and Julie's campsite," I was aware that by 2007, the same area was being used as a base for children at festivals. The campsite now known as Bag End used to be called the Troll Circle, and perhaps will be again. This kind of perceptive or ideological fluidity and shift can lead to conflicts, as when, for example, some see the Thunder Dome as essentially a place for religious experience, while others see it as a place for socializing.

At the same time that it expresses an ethic of freedom and fluidity, there is a distinctive aesthetic identity infused in the material culture at Lothlorien. There are visual references to the distant past and imagined future, to litera-

An Unreal Estate

ture—both Romantic and traditional—to folk stories and to various religious or spiritual belief systems.

As noted above, boundaries between the sacred and the profane, the sublime and the humorous, are often blurred on the land. Both of the background traditions that I described in chapter 2 and into which Lothlorien loosely fits—intentional communities and Neo-Paganism—tend to juxtapose seemingly incompatible categories. From Kamau's perspective, intentional communities are liminal spaces, where normal distinctions do not apply. Neo-Paganism also has a tendency to question boundaries. Magliocco says "For most American Neo-Pagans, who grew up in mainstream culture, intentional marginalization is essential to their ability to critique the dominant paradigm and come up with creative alternatives" (Magliocco 2004: 203). As examples she offers the Pagan songs and imagery that embrace "oppositional culture" such as symbols of witchcraft or horns worn on the head. She quotes Starhawk's advocacy of "power from within" as an alternative to "power over" or domination of nature or of other human beings.

There is also a strong environmentalist ethic at work at Lothlorien as members attempt to create an example of respectful stewardship of the natural environment. The trees, plants, and animals, along with the rocks and creek and elements (earth, air, fire, water), are respected as essential parts, even members, of the community, and provide its rationale. On a subtle level, whether because of people's attempts to heal a perceived rift with the natural world or for some other reason, a few participants experience an almost physical relief when they come onto the site. Janet is empathetic and sensitive to atmosphere and she notices a shift as soon as she arrives at Lothlorien:

> Over time I started to really love this place . . . If you are a person working with natural energies and such, you feel a difference in atmosphere around your body as soon as you step out of your car. I can feel it as the car is pulling into the front gate. (Janet, 2009)

On a more practical level the environmentalist ethic means that the forest has recovered well from its history as cornfields, and the land has been a gathering place for idealistic and talented artisans, who have created some potentially valuable examples of ecologically sensitive building and gardening. This is a feature of life there which I hope attracts attention at some point in time, because of the benefits it could offer to others who are looking for efficient, low impact, and inexpensive ways to deal with waste, pollution, and energy.

Lothlorien's material culture has grown piecemeal, through trial and error, with the help of a variety of people at a variety of times. All these factors make

Faerie and Avalon

for a chaotic, unpredictable, recognizable, if odd, whole. But not everyone is comfortable with the nature of the human footprint there, at least not for the long term. I have heard several people express the wish that there was one clear owner or a small group of owners in charge, or that there wasn't so much "tacky," tasteless stuff in the shrines. The haphazardness is one of the reasons that some people move on. It is also what makes Lothlorien unique. Once I asked Andy, Julie, Ethan, and some others what they thought an archaeologist would make of the artifacts on the land five hundred years from now. Ethan said, "You wouldn't want to know." Andy added, "Even we don't know what it means."

An Unreal Estate

Radience Hall set up for a Council meeting in 2007.
Photo by Lucinda Carspecken

4

"A Loose-Knit Anarchy"

Reimagining Organization

> To me it's always been kind of a loose-knit anarchy—we have formal
> organizational processes and all that, but we're also very individually
> responsible for what we do. So in that regard I think it's a lot different.
> We're usually not so in each other's faces all the time.
>
> *Stewy, 2006*

> There's something about human nature. If you could have a community
> and just not have any humans involved it would be all right.
>
> *Tuna, 2006*

At any given time over the year and a half I was researching Lothlorien Nature
Sanctuary, a core of about ten to fifteen people—not always the exact same
group, but with a fair degree of consistency and drawing on a slightly larger
group—worked cooperatively on maintaining the grounds, running the festivals, and making decisions. In practice this usually involved each person
individually and independently taking on particular projects or tasks and then
the group coming together as a whole at intervals to share plans or feedback.
Most current members distrust authority or the control of one individual over
another. Yet there was a remarkably balanced sense of responsibility and sharing
of work. The loose collective stewardship also enables a great deal of freedom
in creating or adding to the structures, shrines, gardens, and ornamentation.
This system presents a contrast with typical approaches to land and property
in the industrialized world, where private or corporate ownership and management are the norm, aided sometimes by paid employees who carry out the
physical tasks involved in maintenance. Collective grassroots management and
ownership of the land—the predominant Lothlorien pattern at present—also

differs from mainstream patterns and affects the relationship between people and the physical environment.

The land is owned by all the members of its legally incorporated nonprofit, ElvinHOME. (As noted in chapter 1, HOME is an acronym for Holy Order Mother Earth.) Membership (and hence legal part ownership) involves paying a $25 yearly fee, which also gives one the right to reduced rates for festivals and for camping. There were around nine hundred members in 2007, but the number fluctuates frequently as memberships go out of date and new members are added. Living permanently on the land or having a vote on the Council involve the further commitment of putting twenty-eight hours of work a month into the community. This work is not closely monitored, but the governing Council retains the right to vote on a member's continued residence every six months.

While I was doing my fieldwork, in 2006, a group named IFRI (International Forestry Resources and Institutions), based at Indiana University, came to continue a long-term study of Lothlorien's land use policies and their impact on the forest. They had visited in 1997 and 2001 to study sample areas of the property and examine tree and plant species and changes over the years. They found the forest maturing and recovering from the time before ELF had originally bought the land, with larger trees slowly taking over from less competitive, smaller species. Tree trunk diameters had increased while the stem count had decreased—both signs of a healthy forest ecosystem (Bauer et al. 2006).

Elinor Ostrom, one of the senior IFRI researchers, has written extensively on the relationship between land and human organization (Bauer et al. 2006, Ostrom 2006). In her recent articles based on comparative studies of forest density around the world—in India, Africa, Nepal, South America, the United States, and elsewhere—she refutes the popular perception of forest preservation and ecosystem protection being best handled by state-run parks or other top-down legal institutions. Locally managed forest ecosystems preserved *more* dense growth over time than public parks overall. She and her colleagues have found that local involvement and ideological investment in environmental aims are more reliable predictors of continued forest health than are state regulations and penalties:

> When the users themselves have a role in making local rules, or at least consider the rules to be legitimate, they are frequently willing to engage themselves in monitoring and sanctioning of uses considered illegal, even of public property. When users are genuinely engaged in decisions regarding rules that affect their use, the likelihood of users following the rules and monitoring others is much greater than when an authority simply imposes rules on users. (Ostrom and Nagendra 2006)

Construction on the Upper Composter
Courtesy of Scott Martin

This kind of engagement has been increasingly characteristic of Lothlorien's organization, particularly since late 2005. Those who work for the community in kitchen duties, lawn mowing, composter maintenance, tax filing, newsletter writing, and promotion—which is to say all mundane and white-collar tasks alike—and those who make the decisions are officially the same group. And the work is done entirely on a volunteer basis. Apart from the system of voting, it is not, then, an arrangement typical in industrial societies, where administration, work, and decision making are usually separate, and are motivated by wages and guided by principles of efficiency. Yet the organization manages to hold two large festivals and several smaller ones a year, drawing hundreds of people at a time; it manages to maintain the grounds for campers from March to November, to keep up with a mailing list of almost a thousand people and a regular stream of email, to cover road surfaces, to remove the trash and recycled items, and to build, invent, or improve innovative, environmentally friendly structures and gardens.

"A Loose-Knit Anarchy"

Sometimes this seems amazing to me. I remember Jef saying at a Council meeting before Elf Fest in 2007—the largest festival of the year—"It always works out," with characteristic optimism. It does, somehow. But from the point of view of formal economics or most business or organizational theory, the way Lothlorien runs could seem baffling. Formal economic theory assumes that individuals and groups in all societies and communities tend to maximize their profits and minimize their efforts. This is clearly not what is happening at Lothlorien. Nor does the organization's volunteer-based, egalitarian structure fit with common conceptions of human beings as innately, inevitably hierarchical and in need of material motivation of either the "push" or "pull" variety.[1]

Anthropology has been valuable in exploring reasons why the rules of classical economists do not apply in all communities, demonstrating a point that is more obvious to the layperson, often, than the academic—that people may have other motivations than the desire to maximize profit. Stephen Gudeman's edited volume *Economic Anthropology* (1999)—a collection of essays showing up the conflicts and common ground between economists and anthropologists over the last century—points out many cases and places where anthropology has helped make sense of what would seem to be instrumentally irrational behavior but which provides intangible benefits, like prestige, creativity, self-validation, pleasure, role expectations, religious conformity, altruism, camaraderie, or social harmony, and also points out that these vary depending on cultural context. Intangible and hard-to-measure benefits like these—which are sometimes referred to as the "soft" elements of economics and organization—are keys to understanding Lothlorien and ElvinHOME. Recently, organization theorists have paid more attention to such elements, for example Losada and Heaphy (2004) and Sutcliffe and Vogus (2003), and their views will also be discussed briefly in the course of this chapter.

Lothlorien's combination of unusual features, then—collective ownership, a link between volunteer work and voting rights, creative freedom, environmentalism, lack of hierarchy or supervision—means that it embodies from various angles both a potential critique and an example of new possibilities through its organization. *What* it is critiquing, implicitly, may loosely be described as instrumental rationality, a mainstay of formal economics.

Some of the most trenchant insights on instrumental rationality still come from Max Weber's writings—although these date back more than a hundred years. His genius was in noticing the clusters of norms that played a large part in people's identities and ideals and expectations of everyday life, and the way that some groups of norms became self-perpetuating. Like Franz Boas, Weber was cautious about reducing one cultural, economic, material, or social

An Unreal Estate

phenomenon to another, and was always aware of the particular contexts of the norms he described. In *The Protestant Work Ethic and the Spirit of Capitalism* (1904), he descibed the mutually sustaining themes within European Protestant working life—noting the particular influence of Calvinism. Calvin preached that only an elect few were chosen by God for an afterlife in Heaven and that there was nothing the rest of the population could do to ensure such a future, but that work and wealth accumulation were ways to honor God's creation here on earth. God himself, however, was wholly transcendent and separate from the material world.

Calvin's philosophy popularized the idea of a "calling" and ideals of work and prosperity as ends in themselves, signs and reassurances of elect status. Profit calculations were associated with the quest for prosperity, but material and sensual enjoyment of goods were not, since human sensuality and emotion were sites of "the corruption of everything pertaining to the flesh." A focus on profit lent itself to a preoccupation with efficiency, rules, and numbers, features that could be measured and planned for. Competition and inequality were also key factors of this worldview, because elect status was proven through individual accumulation rather than shared wealth or generosity. Since, until the twentieth century, well-paid professions and rights to private property were largely out of reach for women and nonwhite people, due to both legal exclusions and practical reasons (responsibility for small children and lack of access to education, for example), those who were regarded as elect would also typically be male and white.

This emphasis on individual accumulation became a core element of capitalism, lingering long after Calvinism itself had lost much of its appeal. Bureaucracy also, in law, politics, and industry, perpetuated (and was partly created by) a rule-based administrative approach to rationality. And the spread of rationalization was associated with the "disenchantment of the world"—where the importance attached to capital accounting and administration took precedence over the importance attached to relationships, desire, nature, aesthetics, emotional satisfaction, and other aspects of life that were impossible to measure. It is this *kind* of rationality, rather than "Reason" as a whole that informs much of classical economics and organizational theory. In chapter 2 I noted that the Enlightenment, like Romanticism, had more than one trajectory. The Protestant work ethic and bureaucracy use forms of rationality, but these are infused with values and beliefs. The values and beliefs underlying Lothlorien's organization and economic system are different, so that its rejection of instrumental rationality in its organization does not necessarily constitute a critique of rationality itself, nor of science, but of the particular set of goals for which these are used.

"A Loose-Knit Anarchy"

In this chapter I will describe the organization, internal and external policing, conflict resolution, decision-making process, and economics at Lothlorien
with attention to the way its own varied cluster of worldviews plays into all of
these aspects of life.

Organizational Structure

When I first began visiting Lothlorien, in early 2006, it had been through
some major organizational changes, and democracy was a new development.
In the past—up until 2005—Lothlorien's organization was more of an oli-
garchy than a democracy. Terry and Nora, who were the other couple, with
Conney and Michael, to found what was then called the Elflore Family, had a
lot of influence over its running. Terry, in particular was said to have played a
charismatic leadership role. (His is the predominant voice in earlier writings
about Lothlorien, such as early newsletters.) Nora, meanwhile, played a key
role in handling finances and registration, which were later taken in hand by
Vic and Lyn. Terry and Nora also owned a small piece of the land, where their
house, Biostar, was built, using ecological construction principles. (Biostar
has since succumbed to black mold.) In 2004 and 2005, some philosophical
differences between this couple and the rest of the community came to a head,
and they left.

During the earlier phase only Eldars had decision making power on the
Council. Agreements were made by consensus rather than a majority vote. To
become an Eldar, one had to first apprentice with an existing Eldar for a year
(which made it necessary to get the permission of that Eldar), as well as com-
mitting to the twenty-eight hours of work a month.

In 2005, after about three years of research, attempted applications, and
fleshing out of the Bylaws, Lyn managed to get 501(c)(3) status for ElvinHOME
(the legal name for the organization associated with Lothlorien) establishing it
as a not-for-profit religious nongovernmental organization. It was at this point,
also, that a new organizational structure was formed, which had a broader voting base and involved more accountability than the previous structure. This
was a shift that had been desired, although not always articulated, for several
years, according to Stew:

> I think that our current system for voting came from the Council's desire to
> be more inclusive with the elendil [members] and people who are more closely
> involved with our organization. In previous times, there were those on the
> Council who used their position as one of power, no matter how imaginary or
> not that it was, and often got away with ruling under a heavy thumb . . . Anyway,

An Unreal Estate

when we changed to this more democratic system . . . my opinion is that it was because we wanted more of us to share in the responsibility of this organization and I think that we now collectively are more apt to seeing ourselves as having positions of service. (Stew, email communication, 2008)

Stewy said that for him, the shift from consensus to a majority vote was at least as important as the inclusion of Stewards along with Eldar Stewards. His comments also clarify some of the incentives involved in this aspect of the change:

Back when it was only the Elders [sic] who had a vote, a measure could only pass by a unanimous vote (with abstentions, if applicable). One "no" vote would veto the measure and there was a lot of internal bullying to make sure that a measure would pass. The way that we do it now is more democratic, to me, but strong arguments can be made for either way. (Stew, email communication, 2008)

Braze describes the current organization as an "anarchic democracy." In Amartya Sen's *Democracy as a Universal Value* (1999), he lists the following essential elements of a democracy. First, it involves voting and respect for the election results. Second, it involves the protection of liberties, specifically a respect for legal entitlements and the right to free speech and freedom in the media. Thirdly, parties or representatives should get opportunities to present their agendas, among an electorate which is in turn free to obtain news and information about them. Besides these points raised by Sen, checks and balances are essential aspects of democracy—with one section of government in place to keep an eye on others, and vice versa. From 2005 until 2010, Lothlorien has been democratic along all these lines.

Council meetings at Lothlorien happen once a month. Anyone who is contracted to work twenty-eight hours a month—thus qualifying as a Steward—gets to vote, and contracts are renewed every six months. To be a Staff member, as I was for a year, one contracts for fourteen hours a month and has a say on the Council but no vote. To be an Eldar Steward, the most senior position, one must get a unanimous vote of acceptance from the other Eldars and a majority, advisory vote from the Stewards once a year. Finally, since 2009, members have had the option of taking seasonal Staff contracts, which give them the right to live full time or camp sporadically on the land for a three month stretch of the summer season in exchange for work.

Voting, other than to approve a contract, is usually related to projects or to allocations of money for projects. There is an understanding that proposing a project means being willing to see it through rather than delegate the practical work to others:

You can't get anything passed without voting and if the vote doesn't go your way you have to live with it. And if it does go your way then you have to do something about it . . . If a person really wanted it to happen it would get done. And if they just wanted to put it out there because they wanted to see it done, and have someone else do it, it won't happen. (Frank, 2009)

There is usually very little mutual surveillance of one another's hours, but the general consensus on whether a member has pulled his or her weight in terms of work is reflected in whether the Council members vote for a contract to be renewed. As yet, in 2010, I have never seen a contract voted against by the majority or even a close vote, although I have seen several people grilled about their contracts or about a project before a vote was taken. Usually the Council expresses appreciation rather than a close attention to hours.

Volunteer hours contributed by non–Council members are recorded and the records are kept in a "black bag." Whoever is in charge of the bag is also in charge of making sure festival participants and campers pay their dues. This was Andy and Julie's role for most of 2006, Lilith's for parts of 2007 and 2008, and in 2010 it is Bonedaddy's responsibility. General volunteers, unlike Stewards or Staff, are required to find a Steward or project director to work with.

Besides the monthly Council meeting, Vic and Jef have been holding weekly "office hours" on Wednesday evenings since 2006, where people can come to their home, get reimbursed for petty cash expenses and talk over community issues.

Regular volunteers often help one another out and consult one another. For example in 2006, when I worked in the garden with Braze and Andrea, they each built and adopted certain beds, with help from one another, ordered and planted particular plants, and coordinated this at intervals through garden meetings. For a hard task the three of us would combine our efforts, as with digging wood mulch and filling the swale with gravel. From 2008 until 2010, the fence around Lothlorien's borders has been a collective project, with core participation by Owen, Chris, Jacob, Bonedaddy, David, and others, and with supplies from Uncle Dan. In 2009 and 2010 the sauna and shower house were built up and maintained by Tuna, Shay, Rod, Korey, and others. And Frank built a new stage for musical performances in 2010 with help primarily from Uncle Dan but also from Jason, Katina, Michelle, Chuck, Conrad, Keith and Richard McAdams, Torcyr, and many others

As for other cooperatively handled tasks, the raising of the Thunder Dome was the largest project involving concerted group effort that I am aware of. The

An Unreal Estate

The new stage near completion in 2010. Frank is at the top of the ladder finishing the roof. Uncle Dan is on the right. The mural at the back was painted by Dawn and Andrea.

Courtesy of Keith McAdams

Dome was raised in the summer of 2005, over about three days, with thirty to fifty people involved. Raising the structure required a lot of coordination, and Glacier for one considered this a high point in the life of the community because of the camaraderie and the mutual sense of achievement.

A great deal of the work done by Council members, however, is self-directed. Among this collection of highly self motivated people, surveillance or a strict accounting of hours by one person over others would make no sense even from a purely economic or "efficiency" point of view. There are three privileges associated with being a Steward or Eldar Steward. One is the right to attend festivals free of charge. The second is the right to vote on Lothlorien's management. The third—and the one with the greatest material value, at least according to the way this is usually measured by economists—is the right to establish a semipermanent residence on the land, with the stipulation that any permanent structure would be the property of the organization as a whole if the resident were to give up his or her contract.

Most volunteers do not live on the land. The Freese Posthumas are the only family to have lived at Lothlorien from the time of its purchase. Braze lived there for nine years, and Larry from 2006 to 2008 (and sporadically in previous years also). Andrea moved in during late 2005, and stayed until August of 2007. Julie, Andy, Josh, Scott, and Sarah were also on the land for

"A Loose-Knit Anarchy"

a large part of 2006, and Stewy has a permanent campsite (although he also lives in Bloomington). Bonedaddy has lived there on and off since 1993, and was building and improving a complex of three tipis for permanent living from 2008 to 2010. Also in the summer months there are often a few long-term campers.

There is limited access to water through one or sometimes two faucets for most residents or campers. Electricity is available at Radiance Hall and the Lightning Shrine through solar power rather than through an electricity company. Food, warmth, and shelter and any additional energy use have to be provided by the individual resident. So, apart from water, the presence of a resident or frequent visitor does not represent a material cost for the organization, and rarely one that would outweigh the value of their volunteer work. (This is an issue I will discuss further in the section on economics.) Occasionally, however, a resident may be seen to be taking advantage of his or her presence by neglecting work or leaving trash on the land.

So long as they build or bring their own structures and put in their twenty-eight hours, residents can live rent free, if not luxuriously. The Freese-Posthumas live relatively comfortably in that they have running water and electricity through local companies. They live in a structure they built themselves over the years, around a trailer by Lothlorien's entrance, and they are on the "front line" as far as dealing with the outside world and the festival goers is concerned. Braze and Bonedaddy have also lived fairly comfortably, mainly because they have put a lot of work and practical skill into their tipis. Summer and winter in Southern Indiana are a challenge since both the heat and the cold can be intense. Braze built his own woodstove, and used an inner tent with the woodstove inside it for the coldest part of winter. Bonedaddy has innovative methods of ventilation in his current tri-tipi complex. He built a composting privy in one of the tipis, and even uses a marble bathtub that he found in a secondhand store.

Braze built a small white dome as well, which he sold to Andrea and her friend Sarah in 2005. He designed it partly as a practice run for the Thunder Dome. This also had a woodstove, surrounded with big pieces of stone, to absorb and radiate heat. In the winter, spring, and early summer of 2005–2006, Andrea shared the dome with her friends Sarah and Scott. After they moved out she stayed on there alone until August 2007. On one side of the dome was a shower arrangement, which required first heating water on top of the stove. When I visited in the winter, the inside of the dome was comfortably warm. There were clothes on coat hangers, furniture painted purple and green, patches of

An Unreal Estate

The white dome.
Photo by Lucinda Carspecken

carpet covering most of the floor and a few cats. One of her oil paintings added splashes of yellow and red to the dome's color scheme. The place reminded me of a hobbit house, if there is such a thing as an artistic hobbit, especially after dark in candlelight or lamplight. But it had mold problems, which gave her serious allergies, and she was also plagued by raccoons.

Andy gave me an idea of some "pros and cons" of residence in a tent at Lothlorien—both the increased complications of life in the campsite he shared with Julie and Josh and the relief he felt from household expenses and of having time to spare:

> In your apartment you go to the faucet and there's water there. Not here. You wake up in the morning, you need water; you don't have it up there. Then you have to get the big old container and haul it all the way down to here, fill it up, go back and then you can do whatever it is that you're going to do, but you find different ways of doing things. I mean there's times out here when we won't even go into town to do laundry, we'll do it old fashion by hand—two wash bins do it that way—just— and you really don't have to worry about doing it that way because you

"A Loose-Knit Anarchy"

have so much time. You have the time to sit there. When you would normally just be sitting there doing nothing but looking up at the sky, take
an hour to do laundry. And it's not going to affect your day one way or
the other. You don't feel like you have to do it . . . The stress level is the
major thing, that's the main reason; that and when we were living in
Louisville—doesn't matter how much you work, doesn't matter—things
just have a way of ends not meeting. (Andy, 2006)

In the summer months of 2009, a seasonal Steward called Aaron worked on
building a shelter out of cattail mats. It was much more time-consuming than
he had imagined and he ended up making walls from debris (largely weeds)
and only the roof from cattail mats. While the mats were surprisingly effective
at keeping off the worst of the rain, he left before winter.

Several people, over the years, have lived in a white bus on the north road,
including a family of mice who lived in the transmission box for a while. Scott
shared it with some wasps through the heat of one summer. Brooks's experience of living there over a couple of winters was grueling, although he took
it in stride:

It was very cold. It was like a three-year vision quest. . . It was not insulated and [it had] a very small woodstove. It would burn out in two
hours. If you didn't wake up every three hours you'd have to restart
the entire fire . . . It was very Ranger-like. A peaceful Ranger. A green
Ranger. A druid Ranger. But I like that. I have to have some inurement
to the elements. (Brooks, 2010)

Joe describes a few weeks in a makeshift, rickety tower he helped build in the
1990s, which let in the rain in most places:

We spent two weeks out there building this thing that was four stories
tall—a shack that was four stories tall. It was so dangerous and so completely not right. . . . (Joe, 2010)

Joe and his wife Pam did manage to find one corner of the building that kept
them dry for the length of a rainy Elf Fest. But long-term residence at Lothlorien, while a valuable opportunity for those with well-honed construction skills,
is not an easy option.

Living on the land, away from water lines and electricity, then, is not always
comfortable, convenient, or in some cases even safe. With rare exceptions volunteers bring in more material value than they take from Lothlorien, and strict
surveillance among Council members would make little sense at present. It also

An Unreal Estate

presupposes a hierarchy—a distinct group to carry it out—that does not exist there. The difference between Eldars and Stewards is slight in practical terms. Eldars have the final say on purchases over $500 and must be unanimous in voting in a new Eldar. In terms of prestige the difference is also insignificant. My sense is that the position of Eldar can either add some additional authority to individuals who are already respected on an informal level, or can provide the appearance of official leadership when dealing with outside institutions like banks and grant-giving institutions or with festival participants who are relatively new to the organization.

Eldar and Steward status in the first years of my time at Lothlorien tended to correlate with a long-term and stable commitment to work at Lothlorien. All of the Eldars and all but one of the current eleven voting members of the Council in 2008 had been involved in some capacity on the land for more than ten years. Beginning in early 2009, however, some relatively new Stewards joined the Council. The first of these, Frank, was married to Dawn, who had come to Lothlorien frequently as a teenager (and is Janie's sister). Joy also joined, and volunteered regularly, in 2009. Michelle and Korey joined the Council in early 2010. They had spent almost every weekend at Lothlorien, volunteering and sharing food, the previous summer. Keith, Torcyr, Chuck (also known as "Land Chuck"), and Don joined in mid 2010. All of these volunteers had worked on the land before and were familiar to, and trusted by, Council members. Currently, then, there is a good-sized pool of both long-term and more recently involved volunteers and organizers for festivals and land maintenance. There are also some new sources of conflict as long-standing guidelines and assumptions get clarified and sometimes questioned by newer Stewards.

Leadership and organization have "soft" and "hard" aspects, translating roughly into informal and formal aspects respectively. Steward and Staff contracts represent commitments and are useful in that sense, but they are not formally measured, rewarded, or penalized. The word or advice of a respected, familiar, and hard-working volunteer, whether or not that volunteer has a contract and is part of the Council, will carry weight as well as the word or advice of an Eldar. The respect given to Council members is also often given to Staff members with no vote and to active volunteers with no formal contracts. I noticed that this applied, for example, to Michael, who is looked up to as both a founding member of the organization and a dedicated participant; to Tuna, who puts a lot of time into plumbing and electricity; to Janie, who was an excellent facilitator; to Chris, who has worked on construction and fence building. This group avoids Council meetings, seeing them as more frustrating than constructive. It is telling that the newly established "Elf of the Year" award was given to

"A Loose-Knit Anarchy"

a non–Council member in 2007—Tuna—and in 2008 was given to another non–Council member—Michael.

There are also three titular positions for legal purposes—President, Secretary, and Treasurer. I have seen Uncle Dan, Andrea, Lily, Vic, and Frank elected President, with the clear understanding that the position conferred no real power. In effect it adds a level of checks and balances to the other Council positions. For example, Lyn and Vic were the people working on finances from 2006 to 2008, but the figurehead Treasurer, who was not directly engaged with bookkeeping, *also* had legal accountability. Should a problem arise, three sets of eyes would be overlooking the finances and three people would be accountable.

In order to propose a contract at the Steward or Staff level, participants have to come to a Council meeting and describe what they plan to do, usually in line with their skills or experience, for the next three months. The Stewards and Eldar Stewards then vote on whether to accept the project or not. As I have noted above, keeping track of work hours at the Council level is done on an honor basis. At the Eldar level the process is similar, but renewal of a contract happens yearly.

The five Eldars in 2006 and early 2007 were Jef, who did promotion, organized events, designed and led rituals, produced a newsletter, coordinated volunteers at festivals, and also helped with the physical work on the land; Vic, his wife, who handled all the petty cash, registration, and mail, helped coordinate volunteers, and also led rituals; Lyn, who dealt with legal and larger-scale financial matters, who oversaw the shift to nonprofit organizational status, and who continued, until 2008, to work on related matters, including grant applications; Conney, who wrote regular online announcements to the public, newsletters, and the latest *Greenbook* (which contains guidelines and other introductory information about Lothlorien), organized the kitchen, and helped clear the campsites and trails; and Stew, who handled the online communication with the public as well as maintaining fire pits and flowerbeds.

At the April Council meeting in 2007, Glacier, who is Lyn's husband, proposed a new Eldar contract. Traditionally, anyone proposing a contract at the Steward or Staff level takes on an elvin identity as part of their commitment. This has been part of the official process at the Eldar level. Such names may not always be used in day-to-day interaction but may be kept for the website and online communication—like Fimbrethel, Glorfindel, Ratman, and Briar (names for Lyn, Stewy, Jef and Conney respectively.) Making a statement of spiritual intent is also part of the official process of becoming an Eldar, along with a statement of practical intent:

ELDAR STEWARDS shall be of the age of maturity in the State of Indiana. Only committed persons that are ELDAR STEWARDS and have met the following criteria, have a consensus vote on the following items. Other qualifications for ELDAR STEWARDS elected to The Governing Council of this corporation shall be as follows:

Members of ELVIN H.O.M.E. Inc. who have spent at least one year as a STEWARD and have fulfilled the following (Time period may be waived by the ELDAR STEWARDS):

I. Submit a written statement (commitment) to The Governing Council outlining the petitioner's Elvin Persona and/or a statement of spiritual intent, and Elvin Name, their skills and talents which may be applied to ELVIN H.O.M.E. Inc.'s benefit and working, this to include their area of specific knowledge as it pertains to Section 501(c)(3) of the Internal Revenue Code, their means of personal livelihood (how they will provide for themselves with food, shelter and/or cash flow), and exactly what they will do for ELVIN H.O.M.E. Have the above mentioned petition accepted by the consensus vote of the ELDAR STEWARDS.

II. Have signed a commitment with ELVIN H.O.M.E., to fulfill the above—also stating that their sponsorship as an ELDAR STEWARD is null and void if the commitment is violated.

III. ELDAR STEWARD sponsorship to be reviewed on a yearly basis. (www.elvin HOME.org/bylaws)

Glacier decided to take the name Treebeard, which comes from a leader among the talking, slowly moving male trees or Ents in *The Lord of the Rings*. (Fimbrethel, Lyn's Eldar name, is also the name of a talking, slowly moving tree—in this case a female one, or Entwife.) His proposal was written out and delivered formally. It encompasses the main area of responsibility he wants to take on, as well as his symbolic role and elvin identity. I include parts of it:

I, Treebeard, have walked the forests of Lothlorien for many years. I have heard the calling of the trees and to hear them is to know that they are more than just trees; they are my long time friends. Lothlorien talks to me as a whole and as individuals. I have helped but just a few, and yet I hear the call of many more . . . I would prefer to be called by the ancient name, "Ent," or "Shepherd of the Forest." I belong here within the forests of Lothlorien as surely as Fimbrethel is my mate. And may the bright blessings of the Hobbits be with us all.

I swear to uphold the By-Laws of Elvin HOME, Inc. and be mindful of the duty of care that comes with being one of its Eldar Stewards. It is I, Treebeard, Lothlorien's faithful caretaker of the orchard, of the trees that bear nuts and the vines that bear fruit, and perhaps in time, several other wild fruit places contained upon this sacred land, that comes here now on this most humble of quests. (Glacier, Eldar contract, 2007)

After he read out this statement, the Council members asked him questions. Braze and Bonedaddy asked him why he wanted to become an Eldar and whether he thought it would change him. Glacier's answer was that he felt having an official leadership position would help in dealing with surveyors and nature preserve experts. Vic commented, "It's too bad they read more into titles than we do." Braze said that he hated hierarchy but saw that it could be helpful when dealing with "the Beast." Vic added that she thought there really shouldn't be a delineation between Eldars and Stewards. "I never say 'Hi, I'm an Eldar,'" she said. Lyn pointed out that it was sometimes important to have an official position in order to put a signature on a piece of paper, at the bank, for example. After this conversation there was a vote, and both Stewards and Eldars unanimously supported Glacier's Eldar contract.

Lyn and Glacier resigned their Eldar positions in 2008 due to a combination of other time commitments, travel challenges (they were living in Chicago) and disagreements with the Council over approaches to leadership. Bonedaddy took up an Eldar position the same year, this time without a prepared statement of application but with the expressed intention of continuing his work on building a new Composter and helping with other aspects of land maintenance. He also received unanimous support at both levels of the Council vote.

The Shift to "Anarchic Democracy"

When I first started to come to Lothlorien in March of 2006, several people—including Andrea and Braze—told me that they thought the place was experiencing a revival because of its new, more democratic organization. In by far the majority of cases, participants expressed the recent changes as positive developments in spite of all the paperwork involved in adjusting the system. Vic, for example, says,

> We're under this new guise now, and we have to make sure we do certain things differently and we're doing it but it's still a changing thing . . . So we're getting certain policies in place . . . and it's going to be good and I'm enjoying it, and I see big things coming and I'm still willing to give blood, sweat, and tears, and time. (Vic, 2006)

According to Bonedaddy,

> Most intentional communities when they lose their figurehead don't survive. Lothlorien has thrived. (Bonedaddy, 2006)

Scott expresses his perception of a change in the atmosphere of Council meetings, which he said he used to avoid "like the Plague," before the more democratic structure was established:

An Unreal Estate

Certain members bowed out of Council. There was still . . . a little bad blood and infighting. You know, you'll always have that, but I think Council recently has come to the idea that if you just get rid of that, because it's a business meeting now, as opposed to going ahead and entertaining it, you can get a lot more done. (Scott, 2006)

Conney makes it clear that the process of change had its problems:

It was supposed to be a whole new breath of fresh air . . . Because it happened at the end of the year we had to figure out all this stuff in a hurry and we didn't really have time to have all these new systems in place, so a lot of it was just like this whole birthing pains thing . . . There's all this stuff that's underlying structure and habit and tradition and trying to figure out what's good out of that to keep . . . Figuring out how it all fits together is kind of complicated. (Conney, 2006)

Larry was the only Council member I interviewed who expressed regrets over the change, and his comments reflect more mainstream views on economics and leadership than those held by most participants:

Part of the problem is because it is a not-for-profit volunteer group. If everybody did have an investment in the land to where they actually had—'That piece of land was mine,' there would be a stronger purpose. It's one of the things that has gone away. The people that did have the physical investment in the land for the longest time were the ones that were here every weekend . . . Believe it or not, Terry was one of the strongest elements on this land. (Larry, 2006)

In keeping with the "anarchic democracy" description, while there are a variety of approaches to organization on the land, a significant number of active participants have egalitarian, anarchistic ideals. These fit well with one of Lothlorien's two mottos, Every Child Is a Star, which Conney, in the *Greenbook*, described as "an important underlying philosophy at Lothlorien." They are reflected in Vic's comments above. Stew also expresses this:

We . . . need to consistently promote self-governance to lessen the need for the Council to get in the middle of folks' private dealings, whether it's visitors, Elendil, Staff, Stewards, or Eldar Stewards. (Stew, 2007)

Likewise Braze:

Some of them—it takes them a while to realize that they don't have to use the same defense mechanisms that they use to protect themselves

"A Loose-Knit Anarchy"

in the outside world as they do here. So that they could like maybe benefit by dropping all that weird, territorial, hierarchical . . . shit and just work on getting along . . . And doing stuff as a team, as a whole, as opposed to a leader and his followers or her followers. That's a real hard thing. A lot of new people come here and say "Okay, who's in charge?" (Braze, 2006)

Bonedaddy:

I prefer people lead themselves, but some people don't know how. If people want to call me a leader, I would rather do it by doing what I do and them watching. I'm wary of people who want to be leaders. "What is it you want to control? Why are you acting this way?" It's often people who are not in control of their lives. (Bonedaddy, 2006)

And Chris:

Anything that makes us more egalitarian is a step in the right direction. I'm not into that *Animal Farm,* "first-among-equals" kind of thing. (Chris, 2006)

Frank explains participants' wariness of leaders in terms of bad experiences with authority in the outside world:

The people who are there don't feel as if we fit into mainstream society. You do what you're told [outside]. That's the only way it can be done, and if you don't do it that way you're going to get into trouble . . . We're all the people who have gotten into trouble. (Frank, 2009)

A couple of interviewees expressed a need for more leadership at Lothlorien. Larry was already quoted above as missing Terry's input. And in 2010 I have noticed more expressions in Council meetings of a desire that Stewards and newer volunteers show respect to the Eldars and those who have been involved since the early years. These remain minority positions, however.

Lothlorien's current egalitarian leadership structure is fairly typical among intentional communities since the last quarter of the twentieth century. There has been a shift since the nineteenth century and early twentieth century in organizational styles in North American communes. Many successful eighteenth-century, nineteenth-century, and early twentieth-century communes had charismatic leaders—John Henry Noyes, George Rapp, Father Divine, Ann Lee (although she died after ten years of Shaker community, her influence and the structure she had established lived on). Exceptions to this are the socialist

An Unreal Estate

experiments in the early twentieth century. But some of the most successful, or at least long-lived, late twentieth-century communes and experiments have been egalitarian, like Twin Oaks, East Wind, and the Rainbow Family. While the Farm started out through the influence of a charismatic spiritual leader, Stephen Gaskin, this influence has waned and leadership there is now more dispersed.

Hilke Kuhlmann studied a handful of communes inspired by the work of B. F. Skinner, the author of the behaviorist utopian novel *Walden II* (1948) and found that they ran up against an intractable problem Skinner had not foreseen. In the novel, a contented community is run smoothly, almost invisibly, by a behavioral scientist named Frazier. But in the real life intentional communities that sprang up in the 1970s, sparked by the novel or by behaviorist philosophy, very few people wanted to be planned for, however brilliantly. Almost everybody wanted to be the behavioral planner, the Frazier character. In the long term, the *Walden II*–based communes that had overly powerful leaders either changed their structures or ceased to continue as communes. Kat Kinkade, from Twin Oaks, who had been an advocate of behaviorist leadership, was an early casualty of this tendency. People wanted to be *involved* in decision making—they didn't just want the decisions to be wise. In 1970, she was denied, through veto, a renewed turn as a Planner, "simply because I had 'too much power' and they were tired of it."

> The big shock was discovering just how much I minded when it happened . . . Now I found myself deeply depressed because I had been effectively deposed. My 'sharp self-awareness' went through the painful process of becoming even sharper.
>
> I had a choice. I could either despise myself or I could change my theory. I chose the latter. (Kinkade 1994: 26)

Contemporary secular intentional communities tend to be very conscious of gender and racial equality as well as hierarchy. At Twin Oaks, for example, the word "co" is used in place of "she" or "he." In its early years, all the car mechanics were women, to buck stereotypes of "women's work" and "men's work." Twin Oaks also gives labor credits for housework and the work of caring, which tend to be invisible in mainstream industrial societies and are not remunerated. In line with this tendency, ElvinHOME's leadership has been well balanced between women and men.

Workplace organizations in the wider society normally operate through chains of authority. Those who have stepped away from the mainstream in North America (at least in secular or ecumenical communities) seem unwilling

"A Loose-Knit Anarchy"

to tolerate this. Lothlorien fits the egalitarian pattern common to contemporary intentional communities, and it is difficult for me to envision many of the people there—all creative in their own ways, in charge of their own projects, and wary of authority—going back to a more top-down system. The group's previous organizational history surprises me even now, because the current loose, collective leadership style struck me as coming so naturally to most of the participants. Many of them are temperamentally or philosophically anarchic, and a significant number, though not all, seem wary of any kind of hierarchy. However, even in this very egalitarian organization, some informal policing is required.

Informal Policing

In part, the move to found Lothlorien Nature Sanctuary was motivated by a desire for independence from, or removal from, mainstream law enforcement in Southern Indiana, which has tended to be deeply suspicious of Neo-Paganism, as noted in chapter 1. Buying the land enabled a degree of separation from local policing, local politics, local energy and land usage, even local cultures of private property and fundamentalist Christianity, but has not completely resolved problems of vandalism or hostility.

In the early 1990s, a group of members took on the task of organizing parking at festivals. They referred to themselves as "parking trolls" or "trolls." A few trolls also took it upon themselves to patrol the borders of the property at festivals to keep an eye out for intruders, and to be arbitrators in case of disputes within the festival site. Chris says he was one of these security trolls and still takes the responsibility seriously:

> I'm not a My Little Pony™ hippie, so if there's some drunken guy that's getting loud and getting ready to raise his hand to his wife—and it's happened to me twice—I've had to step in between. I stopped one guy from taking his belt off and whacking his fourteen-year-old son, right there at that fire pit behind us in broad daylight, by having to stand in between them. (Chris, 2006)

Recently the system has become less formalized, with all Stewards and Staff members and active volunteers taking responsibility as necessary. In a loose sense this constitutes Lothlorien's system of policing.

Some Council members have made an effort to stay on good terms with the official police, too, and over the years tolerance has developed. It is standard practice now for volunteers to call and let the Lawrence County police know on which dates festivals are to happen and on which nights there will be drum-

An Unreal Estate

ming. Also some long-term residents of the festival site take it on themselves to try to ensure that the festivals do not disturb the locals.

Michael has often been in the position of the mediator and diplomat with the community surrounding Lothlorien. He notes an improved relationship between ElvinH.O.M.E. and the police. For example, in the past the police used to come around if there were complaints from neighbors about noise levels. Recently they have taken to telephoning, relying on the community to take care of the problem itself. Michael also helped improve relationships with the neighbors by visiting a number of them in person and letting them know that festival participants would not drum on Sunday mornings out of respect for their church services at that time. He said that his experiences in theological school had helped him in this task, since he was thoroughly familiar with all the branches of Christianity represented in the neighborhood.

As for informal policing within Lothlorien, the fluid boundaries between Council members and festival attendees mean that those responsible for maintaining the Bylaws are very deeply embedded in the community, so that the community could to some extent be said to be policing itself rather than one group policing another distinct group. And since any participation at Lothlorien—either as a festival attendee or an organizer—is voluntary, there is no question of the informal policing involving much power over any other participant. Leadership has to be accountable, and Stewards can rarely afford to lose volunteer labor or festival attendance through top-down or heavy-handed approaches (although this has happened sporadically).

At Lothlorien, the Bylaws have recently been drawn up, due to the community's change in legal status, and are being amended and fleshed out as time progresses. As they stand on the website (which is often updated), they are quite general. They do make it clear that "needless" violence, killing, or pollution of people or the land is prohibited, but do not say how needless and needful versions of these might be distinguished. They also prohibit violence toward or theft of personal property, and rule out private ownership of the land. The toleration of all faiths and creeds is expressly mandated. At a recent meeting, a recognition that an individual was to be considered innocent until proven guilty of any infraction was spelled out and added. Beyond these points, rules are minimal.

Warnings or banning a member from the land, either temporarily or permanently, are the only responses I am aware of to infractions, with majority approval from the Council. Someone's contract may also be refused, which would prevent him or her from living on the land or voting on Council, but, as noted above, I have never yet seen this happen. (I have, however, seen new participants encouraged to take the recently established seasonal Staff contracts instead of Steward contracts. These enable them to camp on the land for a few months but not to vote.)

Community oriented monitoring on a small scale like this, and among people who are perceived as equals, is challenging. For one thing it is uncomfortable and disruptive to point out perceived wrongdoing in someone who is part of a close-knit community. As Frank puts it, "No one wants to be the asshole there. Which is why people get away with gate crashing and noise and everything else. No one wants to be the hard ass there." For another, because authority is informal and somewhat invisible (many festival attendees do not know who is on the Council or the nature of some of the rules), there is a lot of individual discretion, which leads to differences in dealing with disturbances that might be defined in different ways at different times.

As to serious infractions, anything amounting to a threat to personal safety or property is actually quite rare. I have been comfortable, as I noted in chapter 2, in leaving my money and belongings in one area of the land while I wander off to another, and have never failed to find them on return. Donation boxes are left at various spots on the campground, and festival vendors usually have a high level of trust at Lothlorien. At Elf Fest in 2010, for example, a vendor named Karen went "missing" for four or five hours, worrying her friends. She had simply been in Bloomington and showed up eventually in one piece, surprised about their concern. What was interesting to me about this incident was that she had been quite at ease about leaving her stall unattended for a large part of the day.

However, Eldars or Stewards have occasionally had to remove festival attendees who were behaving in unacceptable ways, like the infamous "shower peeper" who was removed from a festival a few years ago. Other infractions leading to removal or bans have included physical assault or threats of assault, misappropriation of community funds, drug sales, taking photographs when permission has been refused, and indecent conduct in public. Bans are usually in place for limited stretches of time and can be appealed if a perpetrator agrees to come and state his or her case before the Council and if necessary make amends. A list of banned people is kept at the entrance booth, but this list currently consists of only about seven people after twenty-five years of festivals.

Dilip Das and Arvind Verma (2005), Herman Goldstein (1990), and Wilson and Kelling (1982), among other scholars, have stressed the importance of police and citizens working together on small day-to-day issues. They compare a crime control approach to policing with a service orientation. Police participation in community projects and a service oriented, community policing approach are important assets in keeping a flow of communication between citizens and the police. This flow of communication in turn is an important component in preventing or resolving crime. According to their research, maintaining a relationship of trust with communities is not only desirable for its own sake, it is more desirable for its efficiency in upholding the rule of law than is the crime control approach. Moreover, according to Das and Verma's research, this is true across a range of cultures. This research implies that an emphasis, where possible, on relationships alongside rules would be desirable not only for "soft" reasons, like mutual goodwill, but also for "hard" reasons, like rule compliance. Using this framework, ElvinHOME's Staff mainly fit the model of a service oriented and problem oriented style of policing or monitoring. Bylaws and due process get clarified and amended as a particular problem arises.

Finances and Volunteer Labor:
"You need to be able to give more than you take"

With a group of volunteers, and with a lot of outdoor work that depends partly on weather conditions, the work that gets done depends more on individual initiative than on planning or scheduling. However, planning and scheduling happen. Around March, meetings get longer than those in January and February as more people come, and more ideas are proposed. Here is a section of the meeting minutes from March of 2007, with plans for the Earth Steward weekends to come:

- **March 23rd to 25th.** General clean-up; getting rid of the rusty freezer in the kitchen.
- **March 31st to April 1st.** Painting new composter. It needs paint, Penetrol and about 5 gallons of latex for the inside. Bonedaddy is in charge of this project.
- **March 31st to April 1st.** The Trollbooth's roof and awnings need fixing. We have the materials for this and will also need to replace the table, which is disintegrating.
- **April 6th–8th and April 13th–15th.** Painting the rusty bits on the Thunder Dome which will require a couple of gallons of paint, an air compressor and about 250 human hours.
- **April 20th–22nd.** Thunder Road needs 8 or 10 inches of gravel spread on it to make it safer to walk on.
- **May 4th–6th.** Painting, tiling and upgrading the Long Hall kitchen. This requires gloss paint, about 6 boxes of tile, possibly a simple pan rack and some plywood and glue for the drawers. Jef may begin earlier if he has free days.

"A Loose-Knit Anarchy"

- **May 12th (date is tentative).** Adding a handicap/wheelchair accessible shower. This requires railroad ties, gravel, limestone slabs or concrete for raising the ground, caulking, screws, a wrap around curtain rod, a curtain, handbars and three panels. Dan Henline, Scott and Jef will be in charge.

    Also . . . Conney will call the Fire Department or David to find out how many fire extinguishers we need, where they need to be, etc. (Meeting minutes, March 2007)

Most of this work got done, along with several other ongoing tasks, such as the clearing of dead trees, a good deal of landscaping of Avalon, and garden work. The reality was more haphazard than the plan, however, depending on weather and other unpredictable elements. At festival times, the work is more intense and the list of tasks grows.[2]

ElvinHOME's income comes mainly from festivals and camping. Prices are low. The largest festival, ElfFest, which lasts for six days, costs $120 per adult. Camping overnight at non-festival times costs $5 and is available only to sponsors, between mid-March and late October. There are also day passes for non-sponsors costing $3 a day. Sponsorship, which makes one a part-owner of the land, costs $25 a year.

Since 2006, Lothlorien has been running at a profit.[3] It has no remaining mortgage, but it pays land taxes every year. Economic organization has changed along with leadership organization, and a previous use of contract labor, usually involving Lothlorien hiring its own members, has been discontinued. This has made an appreciable difference to the budget. ElvinHOME ran at a loss in 2005 and in many previous years.

As I have already noted, Lothlorien is managed entirely by a group of volunteers. Many of the participants first came to Lothlorien at festivals, and were drawn in through the festival experience. The festivals, then, both bring in the funds for Lothlorien's maintenance and act as a form of recruitment for those who may become volunteers later. Regular volunteers and visitors at Lothlorien bring in a variety of skills. Some are experienced and knowledgeable in construction, others in computers or accounting, crafts or gardening, cooking or handling large machinery, writing or designing. They also share a willingness in most cases, to put in raw labor, either clerical (like addressing envelopes), domestic (like dishwashing) or physical (like moving lumber). According to classical economic criteria, they bring in, and have brought in over the years, an enormous amount of value. Volunteer work and organization at Lothlorien seem to go beyond "give and take" in the usual senses that are given to these

An Unreal Estate

words outside the community. The chance to work itself is a gift. An exchange I had with Chris expresses this well:

> LUCY: It does amaze me how much gets done . . .
> CHRIS: Yeah, that's because we want to do it.

In spite of all the volunteer work at Lothlorien, labor is still barely sufficient. But considering how much work needs to be done for the larger festivals, things run remarkably smoothly, with only the occasional glitch. This is partly because of the long-term commitments many of the Eldars, Stewards, Staff, and volunteers have made to Lothlorien, so that problems get solved through experience. And experience itself is another valuable economic asset at Lothlorien. Financing smaller projects, for example, has become relatively easy, easier than it had been in past years:

> Getting the money to do necessary things at this point in time really just requires that you go up and say, "Hey, this needs to be done. If you haven't seen it, come on down and look at it. I'll show you what I'm talking about, then write me the check [for materials], 'cause I know how to fix it." And we want to fix it and we've got the time to fix it. Our volunteer base is popping back in . . . So there isn't really any supervision, but now we sort of, like—it's almost an old boy network, talk among ourselves, "Have you ever seen him do this? Do you know if they can do that? Why don't we watch them first and then write him a check next week"—so that our money isn't wasted—it's not our money, it's somebody else's donated money. (Chris, 2006)

Andrea describes a change from when she began, as a new resident, working on the garden:

> At the beginning of the year [2006] I put all the money into anything that we got except for some donations, and they paid for some of the seed, but I put a lot of money into it. [That changed when] I didn't have the money to put into it anymore and they started giving us money when they saw the changes and that, you know, something was actually happening, so, I think that people like the progress. (Andrea, 2007)

Her comments illustrate the way her time on the land and proven track record with garden work gave her more access to ElvinHOME funds for further supplies. Financing projects that cost large sums of money can be more contentious, due to different ideas about what constitutes a priority at Lothlorien.

"A Loose-Knit Anarchy"

So far, I have noted some of the economic gifts that participants bring to Lothlorien, as well as the benefits that go along with Stewardship, such as the opportunity to live on the land. What they get back is less tangible in classical economic terms but nonetheless real. According to interview participants, these included the chance to experience the physical beauty of the land, the opportunity to be of service, the opportunity to be creative—sometimes on a large scale—the chance to live out environmental ideals, and the chance to feel grounded through hands-on work. There is also the experience of teamwork.

Janie described the way her work for the community evolved from the care of a specific shrine in the camping circle she loved, highlighting one of the routes that can lead from festival attendance to regular volunteer work:

> I took on the shrine there after a few years, you know, of just attending and hanging out and partying, having a good time . . . I'd start to notice it kind of looking bad or I'd start working on it . . . and then it just became my little pet project over the years . . . [It] was certainly probably one of the projects that I took as a pet and then from there, it's like, "What else can I do?" (Janie, 2007)

She also expresses the sense of empowerment she gets from the basic, hands-on level of work:

> You have so many pressures of what's expected based on today's world . . . I mean what's happening in New York has to be the thing to be happening all over. I just never really believed that was true, and you can go down [to Lothlorien] and see that that's not the way you really have to live, it doesn't always have to be that, you don't always have to have everything and be everything, you know . . . You can go down there . . . ground a little bit and gain a little in yourself and say, "You know, I could take care of myself, things are okay here." I think I just enjoy the simplicity of life; I think it keeps me in touch with, just the real basic way of doing things. You don't have to have all the high-tech equipment. (Janie, 2007)

Comments by Janie and Stew express the satisfaction they get from working with and for a community, which was something that came up frequently in interviews:

> I think part of it, too just makes me feel good, it's my opportunity to really get out there and be physical and feel like I'm doing something good. It is that community effort. It's because I know I'm going to camp

down there next time and I know I'd like it to be nice like this and I know other people would like that. (Janie, 2007)

The way things are now I get plenty of time for solitude and just experiencing the woods, and other times, like it's nice to not only be working in the gardens and the various things that I do, but to see younger people doing the same thing; getting their hands dirty; or being upstairs in the library and working on that; seeing all the different projects and doing my work and really happy about doing it. (Stewy, 2006)

Similarly, Joe described the way help with festival parking and other essential tasks emerged from a friendship group in the 1990s, and became part of the group's identity. They are still remembered for their work as well as for their drumming circles:

We were the parking trolls . . . At some point we established the troll circle. There were a lot of the guys from Bloomington who were involved in the music scene that were going down to drum. I was a flute player and a sax player. I went down, it was really for camping and for partying and for music . . . The Council . . . really appreciated the trolls because we would help a lot. (Joe, 2010)

The environmental ideals that were a draw in the early phases of people's involvement also factor into keeping them involved:

Really, we can't go on being the use once and throw away kind of culture, because we're going to throw away everything that we had and we won't have anything left. That's why I think it can be done where it's just the same amount of convenience, it's just more preparation and doing it right the first time so that you aren't doing it wrong constantly and it's falling apart on you so you have to redo it . . . Building a house that is super energy efficient run on solar . . . I think doing that and growing your own food is doing it the right way the first time. (Andrea, 2006)

Another reason that some people visit and help out frequently between festivals is their attachment to the physical environment, as reflected in this comment by Chris, who was explaining why he stayed on at a point when many of his friends had left following a conflict:

I had formed an emotional attachment to the place, almost more than the people . . . because the people make the place, but the place is a physical geographical location and it has the natural beauty that's here. You know, I have a favorite rock back there in Faerie that I sit on and just watch the woods from. (Chris, 2006)

But the most commonly expressed reason of all for engaging in volunteer work was a desire to contribute something, to be of service:

Part of how I define my sense of self-worth and self-esteem is—this is going to sound really, really sappy, but I like to help other people, I like to pitch in, I like to work. And there's always plenty to do around here, so I started working, doing stuff. (Chris, 2006)

[At Lothlorien] I fix plumbing and electrical systems. I do stuff to make things better. That's what I do with my life. (Tuna, 2006)

Brooks's service orientation was, in part, an expression of his appreciation for Lothlorien and his life there:

I had to do 28 hours a month. I did 40 hours a week . . . I was a Ranger. It was such a special, magical place, I wanted to make sure I gave my best. "This is definitely the best highlight of my life. I want to make this work." (Brooks, 2010)

Scott expresses his desire both to do service and to act as an example:

A lot of my drive in being out here and doing stuff is to show people that my being of service and helping other people—they can do that too . . . I believe my purpose this time around is to be of service to as many people and bring as much happiness as possible. (Scott, 2006)

Heather's comments highlight service again, combined with an expectation of the work being appreciated and the creation being enjoyed:

The patio, for example; whether I was part of Council or not, that's going to be there for years to come and it's just the joy of watching it and knowing that people appreciate it. And it's useful. So that's what compels me to do that. (Heather, 2006)

The desire for service and the opportunity to express oneself creatively—noted in chapter 3—often combine. Lothlorien is a place where alternative or experimental building designs can be tried out. Bonedaddy and Braze were both drawn by this possibility:

I was good at design and I liked to mess with things. I like to do really hard, impossible things. So I worked that position as a volunteer, com-

An Unreal Estate

muting from Indie basically every weekend, and then at some point realized that the task was so large that I had no option other than to re-center my efforts on the land. The staging was killing me, and the expense every week with gas . . . So I moved down here in the spring of 2002; 2001 was my first volunteer year, and I moved down here in spring and like March of 2002. Then I built a scale model geodesic dome just to make sure that the math I was working under was right. And get some practical experience with the scale structure. (Braze, 2006)

Bonedaddy says that his involvement meant

being somewhere where I could be artistic without anybody messing with me . . . Lothlorien has given me a chance to do the stuff I've thought about for years. (Bonedaddy, 2006)

And Scott appreciates the way Lothlorien gave him a chance both to develop his carpentry skills and to be involved in progressive, environmentally conscious building:

This place really provided a missing part for me, because, you know you couldn't talk about alternative building practices with anybody in Columbus, they just sort of don't care. It's all here already, it's forever old. (Scott, 2006)

Finally, work in the unpressured atmosphere of Lothlorien can be experienced as healing and transformative. Paul F., who has been volunteering since 1993, explains this eloquently:

My direct involvement with the land has always been a great source of meditation and healing. Because just wanting to give is a big step for spiritual growth . . . I was in a space when I worked alone, or usually alone, gardening, and it was very "chop wood and carry water." I was so involved in what I was doing that my cares melted away and I was able to stand outside myself at some point and look at it as some other time and space, some other expression of me, and look at the things I wanted to examine about myself. I think it was a result of that, and because of the permissive environment between people—just working directly with the process, the natural process.

[The process] enabled the very work itself, for instance, and my approach to that work. By being just allowed to be and do. That, I think, allowed me to let down my defenses enough and become vulnerable, in what they call a state of learning. And you can really lay down your guard to be open and present. And again another tentative Zen philosophy: you become the machination of whatever work you do to such a degree that that occupies your entire consciousness and that can be your expression, and it can also be your practice on how to retain a really firm grasp on the now . . . so that's exactly how I was healing through my work out here . . .

I am rewarded by giving because I get so much and I can't really quantify that—just being allowed to be here and people put up with me is enough I suppose. (Paul F., 2009)

"Hard" benefits, of the kind that are usually considered in economic analyses were discussed above, including the right to live on the land. The chance to attend festivals free of charge is cancelled out, in effect, by the fact that almost all of this group work through festivals as a matter of course, and often put in more hours (and more valuable hours, due to their experience) than visitors who volunteer. In the main, then, participants work because they get gifts of intrinsic or social value from it rather than money, cheap lodging, or other means to ends. Based on the perspectives of most of those I interviewed, it seems that strict surveillance or hierarchy would detract from the motivation to work rather than add to it

Heather sums up the ethics involved in volunteer work:

There's a lot of people that give more than they take. And I think that's what you need in life. You need to be able to give more than you take. (Heather, 2006)

Conflicts

Coming and living in an intentional community is like the diamond in the rough being placed by the jewelsmith into the tumbler. The inner potential of every individual is there, but there are rough corners. And there are places that need polishing. And when you're in that tumbler with bunches of other people, those beautiful stones get created by the friction and abrasion and sometimes your corner hits another somebody's corner and there's negative, crazy, intense drama that results and you take it seriously and you think it's all about them, but Grandfather Maple,[4] his reply to me after saying all that negative bullshit was, "So what part of that have you contributed?" (Braze, 2006)

To reiterate Conney's words from chapter 2, Lothlorien is always changing. Because of this, and because Lothlorien is such an ideologically tolerant place,

An Unreal Estate

there are inevitably disagreements or differences in ideals over the way the land is used, the way festivals are run, the way meetings are organized, and many other issues. Areas of minor conflict or tension often revolve around the allocation of funds to various projects. Then there is ongoing but low-level disagreement about the Dome—some thinking it should be covered, others thinking it should remain open, some thinking it should be funded through general funds, others thinking it should be funded separately with help from drummers or other Dome aficionados. The Trollbar has also been a bone of contention. On one occasion, the Trollbar was physically destroyed, only to be resuscitated a few years later. It has also been removed. And another sporadic source of conflict is gate jumping, or failure to pay festival and camping fees.

Recurrent problems like these tend to highlight Council members' diverse approaches to enforcing and defining the rules and bylaws. Fee collection is an example. At the two larger festivals—Elf Fest and Wild Magick—the Trollbooth (where fees are collected) is staffed from 8:00 in the morning until 12:00 at night. But some visitors are aware of Trollbooth hours and arrive after midnight to avoid paying. At the smaller festivals and Earth Steward weekends there is nobody at the Trollbooth, and whoever is in charge of the black bag is required to check up on campers and visitors and ask for payment. People on the Council (or others with real but less formal authority) take a range of positions on how or whether the rules are to be enforced. Overnight camping, for example, is defined as staying after midnight. But how do you deal with someone who leaves at 12:30 AM? Or 12:15 AM? Some find *laissez-faire* approaches frustrating and worry that Lothlorien gets taken advantage of, while others are wary of heavy-handed or top-down styles of dealing with infractions. I have seen conflicts arise fairly frequently over the difference between these styles. The challenge of defining rules adds to the scope for potential conflict.

A definition problem that has come up frequently in the years of my research is the difficulty of deciding what level of drumming volume constitutes a potential disturbance to neighbors after 11:00 PM. Some worry about inviting problems with the local police, others consider the Dome a distraction from the real work of caring for the forest, and yet others resent the intrusion of complaints about noise during what they feel to be the spiritual experience of drumming. In this dispute, as in many others, the style of attempted enforcement of the rules has been as much an issue as the rules themselves.

One of the most intense specific incidents of conflict about drumming took place in 1996. It involved a birthday party, for a woman named PJ, among trolls on the South Road. They were drumming and had achieved a trancelike state. Council members who objected to the noise came into the circle and expressed

"A Loose-Knit Anarchy"

intense anger toward them. At this point, many of the trolls left Lothlorien, and it would be years before some of them returned. Brooks experienced this incident as traumatic, and as a deep disruption to the community:

> Brigadoon went away . . . The trolls took off . . . They were ones who did all the work parties . . . They were the ones who did the work and attracted the people. They were the heart and soul of this place. (Brooks, 2010)

Another conflict took place in the early 2000s between Terry and other Council members, and this was partly centered around definitions of the land and its purpose. For Terry, Lothlorien had been a "seed sanctuary" to inspire others, a site for a variety of individually run fundraising festivals (most related to music), and an educational project. He bitterly regrets the direction the land has taken since the early 2000s, when he ceased to be actively involved. In particular he laments the legal labeling of Lothlorien as an ecumenical religious center, and the lack of focus on training and education:

> What's this got to do with fixing this planet or greening this globe? . . . That's the work. We're supposed to be training people. This sanctuary was supposed to be the seed sanctuary that started a series of sanctuaries. You've stolen it for yourself and turned it into a religious place and it's completely taken it off from the track that it's supposed to be doing in this world . . .
>
> It's good that it still exists. It's good that the forest has not been cut down and developed. It's nice that people have a place to party . . . It's good that people get a taste of working with each other. But I can't help but see the total lack—I used to bring out Harmony School kids out there and teach them classes. I had them building solar panels. It's all gone. The education thing—the actual thing of bringing people in and teaching them is gone. The workshops are gone from the festivals. (Terry, 2010)

People who are active at Lothlorien are extremely idealistic, and yet because the land can represent different things, primarily, to each person—a center for ritual, a forest preservation project, a place for experimental ecological building design, an opportunity for collective land stewardship and egalitarian organization, a festival site, an education and training center—their ideals may run up against one another. Conflicts, then, often reflect deeper differences of opinion about Lothlorien's purpose, and different worldviews.

As an example of one set of views and resultant criticisms of the way the land is run, several Council members or active volunteers value work and the

An Unreal Estate

aesthetics of Lothlorien's land over the wilder elements of festivals. This can be seen in the words of Heather, an artistic, hard-working, and gentle person:

> I'd like to see a lot more people work harder . . . More of an art atmosphere. Functionable art, like the garden . . . and there's a lot of function and beauty. And the tipi composter and the patio, things like that. (Heather, 2006)

Stewy expresses the importance, for him, of the nature sanctuary and its educational potential over festivals:

> I think that if we continue in the direction that we seem to be headed now, we should be pretty well thriving years from now . . . The library has books now. It's becoming a lot more organized. Not necessarily because of any formality. I think the people that are here now are here now more for the nature sanctuary as opposed to in the past, a lot of folks were involved specifically for the festivals. It was almost kind of a down time in between. (Stewy, 2006)

And Andrea expresses her desire for a stable, environmentally conscious community over a festival site:

> What I would like out of Lothlorien for the long term is probably is not what the general membership wants out of it for long term, because they do kind of view Lothlorien as a summer life and a place to just come to pay to hang out in the woods and be hedonistic and free, which is fine. But, and most people aren't willing to put the extra effort into making it more of a community that produces sustainable food and other things. That's more of what I wanted. (Andrea, 2007)

These comments do not necessarily point to overt conflicts over priorities. They do highlight one set of values that might contrast with those who come for festivals, some of whom, in Tuna's words, regard Lothlorien as "party central." When I write about any project or structure or event, I am conscious that there may be people who do not consider it to be in Lothlorien's best interests because "Lothlorien's best interests" can be interpreted in so many different ways. Several of the Council members whom I respect and like the most are at odds with each other on a number of issues.

Tuna said to me at one point, "If you ask one hundred people to define Lothlorien you'll get two hundred definitions." The community attracts diverse people with diverse goals. But while the conflicts, major and minor ones, have

"A Loose-Knit Anarchy"

sometimes run deep, as in the two examples described above, the very diversity of the organization makes for resilience. When any given set of emphases fades, another tends to comes to the fore.

Finally, as an epilogue to one of the conflicts described above, in 2009 and 2010 some of the former trolls who had left in 1996 returned, including PJ. They have held two beautiful rituals at the Summer Solstices. Brooks, who remembered them, and who had been especially inspired by PJ in the past, returned to the land, with the Troll Circle sign in tow. He was delighted:

> It was . . . *wonderful.* PJ made the stars come out inside the dome back when the dome was covered. She could do incredible things . . . It's back! It's back! . . . The beautiful vibe out there in '96 is back. It's enchanted. It's Brigadoon. It's safe. I danced for six hours. (Brooks, 2010)

Meetings, Conflict Resolution, and Accountability

Most decisions, festival plans, and policing issues are handled at the monthly Council meetings. They were facilitated by Janie for a few years until late 2007, then by Bonedaddy, and beginning in July 2010 Braze will take a turn.

Meetings have a lot to cover. A (fairly) typical meeting in June 2007, for example, had an agenda of thirteen items, including new contracts and contract renewals, the pet policy for festivals, finances, plans for the Fourth of July, alternative banking possibilities, notes from the Grand Council meeting at the recent Elf Fest, website design issues, and the removal of the old white bus. A contentious or sensitive item will add to the time required. Council meetings have been known to last up to as seven hours, and members, understandably, often complain that they are too long. Jason explains his initial reluctance to take a Council position for this reason:

> I didn't want to get onto the Council. . . . I didn't want to get involved in the politics. Some of these Council meetings can go on and on forever, and one of the downsides of being such a communal type of community: we listen to everybody, take everybody's thoughts. . . . And some of these people can just speak on and on and on, and keep on going and you're just, like, "Okay, we've heard that now from about four other people and now you're saying the same thing twice. Let's get on with this, we don't want this meeting to last eight hours." It has been better lately, it has been better. But people just didn't want to get involved in those kind of politics. (Jason, 2008)

An Unreal Estate

Besides meetings, the Council members, including Staff members, have an ongoing listserve where suggestions get made, items are announced for the agenda, and occasional crises on the land are dealt with, discussed, or argued over. Several members, however, do not have email access. Council and general members alike may also go to Vic and Jef's office hours, which is a valuable forum for unofficial discussion.

There is an inherent tension involved in using ElvinHOME's monthly meetings for the large number of functions they have to handle. Everyone is a volunteer, and almost everyone has a job in the outside world as well as their work in the community. Besides this many people have children. Grassroots democracy has historically often been correlated with lengthy deliberations. In many Native American communities this has been allowed for and supported (Bonvillain 2001; Samson 2003). But at Lothlorien, participants are often trying to balance their work in an alternative community with demanding lives in a less forgiving wider world. Because of these factors, people can get impatient when "personal issues" rather than "essential issues" of running Lothlorien get brought up in meetings. And as a result, at times incidents that are brought up at meetings do not get talked through fully or calmly and some conflicts and miscommunications go unresolved.

Like styles of enforcement, styles of interaction vary. The active volunteers at Lothlorien tend to be strong-minded, independent people who do not "herd" easily. But speakers during the meetings I attended between 2006 and 2010 were more often positive and respectful than not, enabling at times the kind of interaction, exchange, and subsequent mutual learning that Sen (1999) sees as a benefit of democracy. At one meeting, for example, Jef said, "I talk to everyone. And I trust everyone."

Based on my interviews there are at least two representative schools of thought among Stewards about the value of expressiveness versus the value of positive, calm speech at meetings. Two Council members I interviewed emphasized the need for calmness and rationality in discussion. Two others, however, talked about the need for full expression of issues, including the need to occasionally "explode" in dealing with anger or hurt or outrage. Occasionally in meetings and on the listserve there is a harshly critical tone. While I can see that this may provide a valuable expressive outlet for the speaker, I associate it, on an informal level, with a "crime control" approach rather than a service approach to conflicts, since it tends to shut down rather than open up communication, whatever its intention. It can be intimidating and discourage other people's full expression or resolution of contested issues. At the April meeting in 2010, Vic made an effort to set the tone of the meeting at the beginning by remind-

"A Loose-Knit Anarchy"

ing participants not to use inflammatory phrases when disagreeing with each other over issues. It is difficult to strike a balance between the two styles—one keeping communication safe and open, and the other giving vent to emotions.

Andrea sees a need for more timely communication at Lothlorien and outlines her own thoughts on how to achieve this balance:

> I think that if something is taken care of quickly enough and everybody involved is told both sides of it, that keeps people from talking and speculating things that might not be true, and it gives people a chance—I mean if you are communicating face to face about something and you don't have those assumptions I think that it's going to be more friendly and clear and the compromise will be come to . . . because even when people talk and they converse after the fact that they may have some assumptions, it doesn't always provide an opportunity in the conversation to bring out all of those assumptions to address them and so if they're left unaddressed they're still being assumed, and I think that's what happens in a lot of the interactions down there. I don't think that there's a way, you know, to completely eliminate it, but I think honesty is the best policy and as long as it's put in a tactful way and it's not personally insulting . . . When it comes to business, there shouldn't be any personal attacks. (Andrea, 2006)

Robert's Rules of Order are the official guidelines for meetings at present, and these are included in the Bylaws. Here there are some quite detailed specifics about conduct at meetings and they have potential value in helping resolve conflicts without damage to interpersonal relationships. For example, criticisms are supposed to be aimed at actions or measures only, with no comments about personalities or motives. If followed scrupulously, this could give people a means to express their indignation without burning bridges with each other or leaving residues of wounded feelings or resentment, thus resolving some of the dilemmas mentioned above. I do not know how familiar most members are with the details of Robert's Rules.

Often enough the atmosphere at monthly meetings has been affirming and peaceful. At one meeting I attended in early 2008, Jef began with a ritual to give positive energy for the group, Stew aired some concerns with the culture of the Council, which he had written out, and people clapped. Braze and Glacier both said that they could be too gruff at times, and expressed their desires to overcome this and their appreciation for other Council members. Jason made everybody hot chocolate. All the money requested for various projects was allocated by unanimous votes. Eldar contracts were unanimously renewed. Four-

An Unreal Estate

year-old Haven sat on my knee, and there was a blazing fire in the Long Hall. A bonus, in many minds, was that Bonedaddy facilitated well and the meeting was finished within three hours (which made it substantially shorter than usual).

As another positive example, Braze described a past incident where he and an Eldar had helped resolve a conflict involving two computer technicians who were having some disagreements while setting up the community's website. The four of them sat together; each of the troubled parties got a chance to express their views fully and listen to each other. The two Council members had made a few encouraging comments and the issues were resolved with no hard feelings. This kind of small-scale process might be a good complement to meetings and allow for less rushed, more focused interpersonal resolutions. In more sensitive cases, like accusations of sexual harassment, it could also be valuable to have spaces for accuser and accused to make statements separately, in nonintimidating contexts, before coming to Council meetings for a resolution.[5]

The right to be heard and the right to have access to information are other important aspects of Sen's definition of democracy, as is a safe and consistent way of dealing with infractions or differences. With any luck, conflict resolution at Lothlorien, still in a formative phase, will be fine-tuned and fleshed out to a point where disagreements, perceived infractions, and personal or sensitive issues can be talked through in safe contexts outside of meeting time as well as being discussed and voted on later, when necessary, at meetings.

At Lothlorien, effectively, each person on the Council oversees all the others. Checks and balances, important elements of democracy, are certainly in place with fifteen or so strong-minded people around the table. Membership is open to anyone willing to work, so there is a steady stream of outsiders coming in and previous members dropping out, which prevents the Council from becoming too insulated from the rest of the world. The Bylaws are available online or in booklets that are handed out at festivals. Also, because Lothlorien has legal nonprofit status, meeting minutes and financial records have to be available for public inspection. Various researchers from Indiana University besides myself have paid close attention to these—for example, the International Forestry Research Institute group (IFRI) who visit at five-year intervals. Democracy is a messy business, but accountability at Lothlorien is strong at present.

Organizational Culture and Democracy at Lothlorien

Peters and Waterman (1982) did a large-scale study of successful organizations and found that they shared some common themes. A high degree of autonomy among low- or middle-ranking employees along with clear and consistent guiding values were important elements of companies that thrived. Other factors were staying close to the customer and putting a high value on employees.

Some recent research on organizations has looked at positive reinforcement and connectivity between employees or from management to employees, and related this to success. Losada and Heaphy published their findings in 2004 from a study of sixty companies; they found that a ratio of positive to negative comments correlated to effective business performance. Sutcliffe and Vogus (2003) came to similar conclusions, their study factoring in a sense of organizational altruism as well. On a much smaller scale, Gottman (1994) has found that a high ratio of positive to negative comments within a marriage (or live-in relationship) predicts its longevity and strength.

Lothlorien both allows for a lot of autonomy and shares a core of common values—like environmentalism, religious tolerance, and a distrust of commercialism, which makes it a good example of the kind of organization Peters and Waterman found to be successful (except for the fact that it is not stratified along the lines of the organizations they were studying). On the whole, also, social interactions are accepting and positive. And the kind of altruism or sense of doing something valuable that Sutcliffe, Vogus, and others have found efficacious is embedded in work at Lothlorien, which is all volunteer and generally related to a wider vision of conserving nature and energy and creating a sanctuary for nonmainstream religious expressions and lifestyles.

These organizational researchers have focused on the industrialized world, which has cultural norms that may or may not translate into other contexts. However, looking cross-culturally, Elinor Ostrom and Harini Nagendra found in their (2006) study of forest management that grassroots, participatory organizations or communities could be as efficient by any standards as bureaucratic organizations, and in most cases were more so. Based on their findings, from a range of different, mostly nonindustrial, parts of the world, people seemed to work more effectively when they were involved in decision making than when they were being told what to do. Grassroots involvement is certainly in place at Lothlorien. All of these organizational qualities might help explain why this festival site has proved so resilient in comparison with many other alternative communities.

The sometimes competing needs, on the one hand for expression and on the other for a safe, positive atmosphere in which to express, mean that it will probably continue to be challenging to resolve conflicts. An attention to Robert's Rules guidelines for interactions at meetings and online, and due process for resolving conflicts, as noted above, could improve on organizational culture further. In his new role as meeting facilitator, Braze plans to ensure a closer

An Unreal Estate

adherence to Robert's Rules beginning in July 2010, and it will be interesting to see how effective this proves.

ElvinHOME is an extremely democratic organization, with all the confusions, changes of course, and conflicts that tend to go with this. And as in any democracy, the time spent in group decision making is often a source of frustration. But as Ostrom and Nagendra pointed out in relation to forest management, as Das and Verma noted regarding policing, and as Losada and Heaphy, Sutcliffe and Vogus, Culbert, and Peters and Waterman observed about organizations, it is not only ethically desirable but effective and practical to try to adhere to elements of democracy and community engagement—the assumption of innocence until guilt is proven, platforms and tolerance for varied points of view, respect, accountability, positive feedback, autonomy, voting, and a community oriented rather than crime control approach to enforcing rules. For example, the danger of letting a real culprit go unnoticed in a festival crowd by being too quick to remove the wrong person would be more substantial than the danger of taking time to establish the real facts of a case.

Also because Lothlorien relies entirely on volunteer labor and festival attendance, the danger of any one individual having too much power over others, so that other groups or individuals become alienated or disenfranchised and stay away, is more substantial than the danger represented by the messy negotiations involved in voting and group leadership, or by an occasional shortfall of hours. Similarly, the danger of breaking the trust between Council members and the campers, neighbors, other Stewards, or festival community through a punitive or high-handed organizational style may be more long term, but is none the less real, than the danger of delays, disagreements, and uncertainties involved in a more community oriented style. Based both on this consideration and on the organizational research findings cited above, the attempt to establish "anarchic democracy" at Lothlorien is not only an expression of idealism, in line with its ethic Every Child Is a Star, but of hard-headed realism.

The protection of liberties is, if anything, greater at Lothlorien than in the society around it, partly because ElvinHOME supports a wider range of religious freedom. In practice, religious freedom for Neo-Pagans in North America has been curtailed by social norms and prejudices, including by the police, and it can be uncomfortable to hold public ceremonies that fall outside of the Judeo-Christian religions. Creative freedom is also unusually strong, with neither the constraints of private property nor commercial interests to consider in adding to the land, as long as the Bylaws are observed. Some manifestations of this are the constructions for practical use or artistic expression—geodesic domes, tipis, shrines, sculptures, flowerbeds, organic gardens, and decorative objects of all

A Council meeting in July 2010.

LEFT TO RIGHT: Rowan, Jason, Jef, Scott, Keith, Andrea, Richard, Leslie (holding picture of Stewy), Jacob, Joy, Frank (AT BACK), Braze (AT FRONT), Conney, Vic, Chuck, Michelle, Torcyr, and Uncle Dan. The sketch in the insert is a portrait of Bonedaddy (who was also present) by Jef.

Photo by Lucinda Carspecken and sketch courtesy of Jef Stelzner

kinds among the campsites and in the trees. These unusual areas of freedom spring partly from collective ownership, partly from an ethos of individual expression. Lothlorien meets Sen's criteria of democracy well, and in some ways goes beyond them because it is operating outside the frameworks of mainstream economics or religion.

Conclusions

Lothlorien's maintenance depends on service, mutual respect, and group negotiations rather than rewards or leadership. It imposes some behavioral limits—for example on violence, verbal threats, sexual harassment, tree cutting, use of pollutants, drug dealing, or public sexual activity—but its ideological boundaries are very broad. No obligation binds one to staying. No conditions or

An Unreal Estate

behaviors, other than those that directly threaten other humans or the natural world, exclude one.

From interviews, and from the level of dedication I've observed over the years of involvement among volunteers at Lothlorien, I have been impressed by the strong investment people have in the mission there. Part of this is commitment to the natural world and to environmentally conscious building, and part is a commitment to other people and to festival experiences. The level of freedom people have in guiding their own work and creating their own structures, newsletters, gardens, or festival workshops is an essential aspect of this investment.

Stew, in the statement with which I opened this chapter, distinguishes the informal work culture of ElvinHOME from the more formal process of meetings. Based on current research, positive reinforcement is much more effective than criticism, and self-direction rather than top-down direction is a feature of successful organizations. Based on the values of ElvinHOME too, and of most of the Council participants, meetings and governance should be egalitarian and respectful. This is often the case, but due on the one hand to the tension between time pressure and a great deal of ground to cover and on the other to different styles of communication, and different interpretations of rules, meetings can also be contentious. Grassroots democracy is time-consuming and can be especially frustrating if one is living in two worlds at once. But ElvinHOME seems willing and able to adapt.

There has been a move away from hierarchy since the group's early years, and this move seems to fit well with what I see as a mix of independent, self-motivated people and, arguably, with the strand of "alternative" culture that secular intentional communities have drawn on, especially since the late twentieth century. As at Twin Oaks, it is hard for me to envision the present participants at Lothlorien putting up with much top-down leadership. Also, for the reasons cited above, there would be much more to lose through such methods than to gain. People work and contribute partly because they enjoy the creative freedom, the camaraderie, and their engagement in decision making.

New or unusual social formations are often rejected, resisted, or despaired of before they are tried, because what is common tends to be perceived as what is "natural"—in accordance with current perceptions of human psychology. Lothlorien provides an excellent example of the "soft" aspects of both economics and organization taking precedence over the "hard" aspects that form the core of classical economic theory and much organizational theory. Impressive amounts of work are done with minimal monetary outlay and minimal top-down supervision. Along with other contemporary experimental communities and communes, it throws modernist tenets about human nature into question, such as the belief in innate tendencies to establish hierarchies or pursue profits. Once such tenets can be questioned, there is new ground from which to explore social stratification and bureaucratic approaches to organization.

The economic and political organization of ElvinHOME reflects a cluster of underlying ideals about individuals, communities, and the natural world and the way these interrelate. These are unusual in many respects. Individual freedom is often seen as something at odds with *communitas,* yet both ideals seem to be strongly held at Lothlorien. It is this juxtaposition that I will turn to in the next chapter.

An Unreal Estate

5

"The Land of Misfit Toys"

Reimagining Community and Freedom

These eccentric, beautiful, talented, wonderfully creative people who
are also stark raving mad by most standards—get attracted here.

Braze, 2006

This is the land of misfit toys . . . it does attract the less social
individual—the person who's more likely to hide in their room . . .
There are trains with square wheels, there are squirt guns that
shoot jelly, dolls that cry milk, all those things are here.

Larry, 2006

In 2009, a friendship group from Indianapolis began spending most of their
summer weekends at Lothlorien. Besides working to beautify the Heart Tree
Circle and shrine, and helping with other volunteer tasks, they regularly served
food to anyone who was around. Paul N. acted as gourmet cook to twenty or so
people at a time. Others—including Linda and Joe, Michelle, Korey, Beka, and
Paul's partner Dan T.—helped and were welcoming to anyone wandering by.
The campsite, sometimes known as Wayne's World, sometimes as Lower Boom,
became a center for coffee, food, bad jokes, and gossip; a heart of social life at
Lothlorien for that stretch of time. This small circle of friends, who had met
through a meditation group, combined gay and straight people and a range of
ages, from twentyish to sixtyish, and they became gradually absorbed into the
community of Council members and other regular volunteers. Michelle and
Korey joined the Council as Stewards in early 2010, and they have been active
in many land projects.

Between festivals, centers like this one form and shift in Avalon, changing
places and composition over the months and years. Each end of the Long Hall,

for example, has chairs and tables and draws people who might have been working on the sauna or the Composter, the garden or the fence, at the end of their day. I was nervous about joining these circles in my first few months, in 2006. I wasn't sure whether I would be an outsider among people who knew one another very well, or whether I would find anything to say. When I finally took a chair it surprised me how little time it took to feel comfortable, and to be absorbed and accepted into the various configurations of people, who seemed to shuffle and reshuffle themselves like a pack of cards. The groups were rarely divided up by age, interests, or other predictable delineations and tended, I soon realized, to include newcomers as well as people who had been involved for a long time. People who volunteer are appreciated, and I did not feel pressure to think or talk or live in any particular way. It was easy, then, to feel that I belonged, and the feeling of belonging grew over time. In 2008 I interviewed Braze over breakfast in Bedford, at a diner where he often went and where he was on good terms with the wait staff. "This is my anthropologist," he said, by way of introduction. The truth was, though, that I had already "gone native."

While the people who attend ElvinHOME's festivals are quite diverse in terms of occupation, religion, sexual orientation, and age, many participants expressed a great deal of emotional connection with others there and had been involved for a decade or more. In chapter 1, I noted that a sense of community was one of Lothlorien's strongest draws, and this is expressed in a comment by Scott:

> I was just blown away again by the community, everybody was so cool, supportive, people working together—there was something special about it. People could drop away their exterior armor and be like relaxed monkeys around here. (Scott, 2006)

Dropping away external armor is characteristic of what Victor Turner would call *communitas* (1969). It refers roughly to the bonding, mutual loyalty and sense of belonging in a group. In his view communitas is directly opposed to structure, or the usual laws and stratifications that pervade a society. It often emerges, he argues, in situation where normal social categories are in crisis, as people shift from one stage of life to another, as in a puberty ritual. Distinctions between the members of the group going through such a ritual are lost and an intense camaraderie develops. Kamau (2002) considers communitas to be an integral experience for the participants in intentional communities like Lothlorien, because she sees these as liminal spaces, neither clearly a part of, nor clearly separate from, society. While communitas can often be an almost accidental by-product of liminality, Lothlorien takes this a stage further because

An Unreal Estate

the community and organization consciously strive to overcome distinctions of religion, gender, sexual orientation, color, class, age, lifestyle, personality type or even species—distinctions which are prevalent in the mainstream world outside the festival site. There are times and places where it does not succeed, but it is an ideal and is one of the senses in which Lothlorien regards itself as a sanctuary.

Turner (1969) describes three different stages in communitas. The first is a spontaneous stage, where it emerges in unplanned ways and often in liminal situations, and provides a revelation of shared humanness. The second is "normative," where people plan occasions to experience communitas deliberately. The third is "ideological," where particular conditions for, and types of, communitas are advocated as general principles, and attempts are made to regulate and structure them. But the third stage will inevitably fail, he argues, since communitas and structure are mutually exclusive. While Turner's point about regulation and spontaneity being two very different things is well taken, this final claim seems to me to be overstated, as laws to prevent discrimination, for example, create more opportunities for spontaneous experiences of shared humanity as people's paths are increasingly likely to cross.

Communitas at all three levels aims to be broader at Lothlorien than in many ritual contexts because it ideally includes all groups of humans. (Among Turner's first research participants, the Ndembu, for example, the neophytes were all young males.) It also encompasses nonhuman species and plants. All three stages are expressed at Lothlorien to greater and lesser extents at different times. Festivals are normative expressions of communitas. They are gatherings where community spirit is deliberately cultivated. The Bylaws and organizational self-definition express some ideological communitas in that they try to mandate religious and lifestyle tolerance. There are also spontaneous experiences of connection and empathy at festivals or in between them.

Turner used the case of the hippies as an example of the shift between different stages of communitas. They were often inspired at first, he argued, by shared minority perspectives and lifestyles, by drug- or otherwise-induced experiences of connection (the spontaneous stage), after which they started to seek out events, communities, or music that would recreate it (the normative stage), and eventually they tried to establish guidelines that were universalizable, whereby communitas could be established on a wide scale (the ideological stage.) At this point the hippies became part of the establishment they had begun by rejecting, as they influenced (or owned) music, media, and clothing companies, developed new ideological contexts for laws, and created new norms for family life.

"The Land of Misfit Toys"

This description of the process whereby Turner sees communitas developing into structure looks fatalistic at first glance. The visceral, immediate sense of fellowship gives way to a new established order. But at second glance, communitas moves structure into new places, and the new structures open up possibilities for expanded levels or layers of communitas. Using examples further back in time, the camaraderie that gave birth to the Declaration of Independence was antistructural in that it opposed colonialism and monarchy. Once it was established, further levels of structure became more visible and contestable—for example, the legal, economic, and political exclusion first of the landless, and then of nonwhite peoples and women. Communitas tends to expand, which means that its shifts into new structures are not failures. It is associated, especially in its first two phases, with liminality and fluidity and the possibility of rethinking and recategorizing what has previously been taken for granted, bringing new strategies for change into view.

Here I see a parallel with the research done by Carl Rogers (1980) in psychological counseling. Rogers, who began writing in the 1940s, found that in therapeutic relationships, a stance of what he called "unconditional positive regard" led to much more autonomy and emotional adjustment in his clients than had his previous attempts to assert his insights along traditional psychoanalytic lines. In other words, love, communitas, unconditionality, *agape*, or acceptance (all these seem to me to be closely connected and I shall be discussing agape more below) create possibilities for change and reinforce change; changes in structure on a social level, changes in personality on an individual level.

One interesting difference between these two perspectives is that Rogers argues that the unconditional positive regard, a kind of communitas for two, helps create the necessary condition for change; whereas in Turner's scenario the causality is reversed and the state of liminality, a part of the process of change, creates conditions for communitas. Turner's second and third types of communitas, however, are more amenable to will or choice. At Lothlorien there is a culture of acceptance, and there are some deliberate policies that reinforce it. It would be difficult to establish with certainty whether communitas there is a product of the community's liminal and marginal position within a larger society or whether it is the result of conscious ethical choices, which then create conditions for further changes.

Two overlapping aspects of Lothlorien's social ideals came up frequently in interviews, in conversations, in organizational policy, and in my observations of interactions. Together these make up the core of what I perceive as communitas on the land. The first was the accepting or affirming nature of the community and the correlation of this quality to participants' sense of freedom—a kind

An Unreal Estate

of small-scale liberalism. This was reflected in the Bylaws, also, in their official stances of religious tolerance, creative freedom, and respect for nature. The second is its role as sanctuary for people who feel out of alignment with mainstream values. Lothlorien gives people with unusual viewpoints and lifestyles a place to step beyond the world into what Chris described in an interview as "a little slice out of time," and which Turner and Kamau would describe as a liminal site.

Lothlorien upturns some popular conceptions about the relationship between community and freedom. Land and structures are owned collectively, which is unusual in a North American context, so "freedom" is not defined around property rights. Its maintenance also depends entirely on volunteer labor, which in turn relies on a desire for service either to other people or to the land and its living organisms, or both. These two features make the site look like a communitarian's dream from one perspective.

Yet it involves a culture that also allows for a great deal of individual agency. There is little supervision by one person over another, everyone is free to leave at any time, and most lifestyles are officially, and usually unofficially, honored. Normative restrictions on an individual are thus minimal. As an example, the Council was discussing a group who espoused bondage, domination, sadism, and masochism (BDSM) one day and someone asked whether that could really be considered a spiritual path. Jef said, "It is if they say it is." He went on to say that he was hardly in a position to judge anyone's spiritual or religious beliefs, since he was in the habit of "blessing" cars before road trips.

Lothlorien has two guiding mottos, which are included in the *Greenbook* under "Traditions and Symbols," and which endorse both communitarian values and an affirmation of equally valued individuals. One, already noted in chapter 3, is Keeping Each Other Alive, or KEOA for short (with a sly reference to KOA camps). This entails mutual support of many kinds. It translates, in practical terms, into vendors being allowed to set up for free and a guiding ethic of helping one another out with jobs, repairs, counsel, childcare, or any other necessity. The other is Every Child Is a Star, and I will let the *Greenbook* speak for itself here: "We are all equal. We are all stars. We are a circle and we all get our chance to shine and to help others to shine" (*Greenbook* 2010: 5–6). Individualism and collectivity exist side by side at Lothlorien and, ideally, reinforce one another, although, as I noted in the last chapter, there is also frequent conflict.

Before going further into a discussion of individual liberty, emotional ties, and communitas, including a look at some of the smaller identity groups within the community, I will offer a rough overview of the demographics of the general membership and of the regular volunteers who were involved at Lothlorien

"The Land of Misfit Toys"

in 2006 and 2007. This will be an incomplete description, based mainly on face-to-face interactions and meeting attendance during this time, along with mailing list data. There is a fairly high level of consistency and long-term commitment among the core group, but people come and go month by month, so any portrait is more a snapshot than a definition.

Demographics

Depending on who you talk to, Lothlorien draws "misfit toys" (Larry), "flakes, nuts, and fruits" (Jef, in humorous mode), kind people, brilliant people, sociable people, talented people, socially awkward people, creative people, earth-loving people, accepting people, or cliqueish people (two participants wrote this on survey forms). Bloomington residents I have talked to with little direct experience of the place associate it with nudists and drug users. "Do you walk around naked there?" was a question I was asked several times in Bloomington. (I never have, although there are usually several nudists at large festivals.) In a kitchen conversation in 2008, Paul F., who has been volunteering at Lothlorien since the early 1990s, described people who chose to spend time there as both intelligent and "marginalized." Jason disagreed, saying, "I'm not marginalized." Conney added further confusion with the comment, "You're not marginalized, you're butterized." As I noted in chapter 1, people are often reluctant to be defined by others, and people at Lothlorien define themselves in wildly disparate ways.

ElvinHOME's mailing list from March 2007 consisted of 958 people, which did not include children. The genders were evenly balanced, with a slight preponderance of men—442 men and 434 women. However, there were a significant number of names that could have been either male or female (like Kelly), or initials, or adopted names like Phoenix. Reluctant to guess, I left these out of the count.

Just over half of those who included addresses, 478, came from Indiana. Just under half, 472, came from other states. Quite large numbers—157 and 80 respectively—came from Illinois and Ohio; 46 came from Kentucky, and 45 came from Michigan or Wisconsin. Other than these concentrations, participants came from all over the United States, and one came from Canada. Broadly speaking, then, Lothlorien's festivals draw people mainly from the surrounding Midwest or Kentucky, in particular from Indiana itself.

All except a handful of people at most festivals are white. It has been typical, over the last five years at Elf Fest, to see only three or four African Americans, two or three Asians, one or two Hispanics, and one or two Native Americans out of the three or four hundred visitors.

An Unreal Estate

Promotion for Lothlorien's festivals is often done at Pagan Pride processions and gatherings in Indianapolis, or on Neo-Pagan websites like *Witchvox*. There are pockets of Pagans in most cities, and while ElvinHOME is officially an ecumenical organization, with people describing their religious affiliations in a variety of different ways, most festival attendees are in touch with Neo-Pagan networks. A loose web of communities feeds into Lothlorien's festivals. Bloomington, fifteen miles to the north, is home to the majority of current regular volunteers, and also to many of their friends, boyfriends, girlfriends, schoolfriends, workmates, family members, and friendship groups, some of whom come to the large festivals.

I can provide more details only about the participants who volunteered regularly at Lothlorien in 2006 and to a lesser extent in early 2007 based on my participation during that time. Anything I say about this group, however, will provide a partial portrait at best, since the volunteer staff changes, ebbs, and flows even over one year, with summer campers coming and going. I include thirty people, including all the Eldars and most of the Stewards and Staff—unless their contract lasted an unusually short time—two Eldars Emeriti who frequently visited the land, several volunteers who were not officially Staff but had been working on the land on a regular basis, and six younger people of school or (traditional) college age from the second generation, ranging from Haven, who was three (in 2007), to the high-schoolers Jacob, Lilith, and Lily, to Owen and Josh, who were nineteen during most of my research time at Lothlorien.

All of this group were white, except for Leslie, who is half Chinese. There were 18 men (or boys) and 12 women (or girls), which put men in the majority of active volunteers overall. Of the 24 adults, 14 were men and 10 were women. Just over half—13 people— were over forty years old; 3 or 4 of these were in their late fifties or were around sixty. Of those under forty, 6 were in their thirties and 5 in their late twenties.

Of the 30 people, 25 were of working age. (I am excluding Josh here, since he moved off the land when he was nineteen.) Of these, 4 (16%) had white collar jobs, two of which probably paid decently—Jason's in computer network repairs and Lyn's as a software trainer in a law firm. Glacier was an archeologist for the Indiana railroad, and Conney worked as a secretary and administrator at Indiana University. (She has recently been promoted to a dean's office.) Four people, all women (16%), Heather, Vic, Sarah, and Janie, had service jobs, although very different ones—Heather in a retirement home, Vic in a call center, Sarah at Hobby Lobby, and Janie in the ticket office for the Indianapolis Orchestra.

"The Land of Misfit Toys"

Just over half of the adults of working age, by far the largest grouping, had artisan jobs or were self-employed at jobs requiring some combination of artisanship and physical labor. Leslie, Larry, and Stewy did landscaping, Jef painted houses, Braze was a metal worker and also worked on various construction jobs, Scott was a carpenter, Dan fixed heating systems, Michael worked in crawl spaces, Tuna did solar and conventional heating systems as well as plumbing and wiring, Chris drove a forklift truck and also worked in warehouses, Owen was driving a delivery truck, Bonedaddy worked on and off in construction and had a background in crafts—although he was caring for Haven for substantial periods of time—and Andrea did T-shirt designs for a shop specializing in sorority and fraternity T-shirts. This represents 14 people (56%).

Hedwig and David were on the borders of this category. Both sold crafts at festivals, some of which they made themselves. If I include them as artisans rather than salespeople, this brings the percentage of the artisan group to about 64 percent of the working-age adults.

At the time of most of my data collection, in 2006, Andy and Julie had decided to give up their work in Louisville, get by on Andy's disability payments and put their energy into collecting fees at and calculating barter hours at Lothlorien. Previously, Julie had handled welfare claims—a service job. Also occasionally one or more of the artisan or service group may be unemployed or underemployed depending on the local demand. So this adds another category (around 10%), sometimes more, sometimes less, who are not (or were not) working at outside jobs.

Almost all the people I have met at Lothlorien between festivals like to read as well as being skilled in arts or crafts, and their erudition often puts me, the university researcher, to shame. The beauty and insight expressed in people's words in interviews was striking and made it difficult to choose among quotes to illustrate points. Conney, I hope, will write her own book about Lothlorien some day, and if 2010's *Greenbook* and her online postings are anything to go by it will be spectacular. I could give many more examples involving people on the land. As a small sample, Michael has two degrees, as does Larry; Andrea is a talented artist, as is evident in her work on the cover of this book and on Elvin-HOME's website; Vic and Jef are avid readers; Bonedaddy has a lot of skill, both on the design and practical level, in eco-building and crafts; Jason is skilled in web design and electrical work. Braze gave an excellent, hour-long lecture to one of my university classes on the ecosystem of the community garden and is knowledgeable and eloquent on many aspects of horticulture and building. Stewy and Janie are good writers, and Tuna, besides his degree in agriculture and expertise in electricity and plumbing, also has an unusual gift with words.

An Unreal Estate

(I like his name for Purdue University, "Undue Perversity," as well as some of his other phrases quoted in this volume.) I remember a construction worker—a friend of Andy's visiting for the day—talking about the early life of Leonardo Da Vinci, Scott coming up with phrases in Welsh, Japanese, and Latin, the walls of the Old Composter covered entirely in poetry (thanks to Brooks, and to Conney's poetry books), Chris talking about the epic of Gilgamesh and its influence on the Bible, and many other instances of erudition.

In interviews, community, commitment to environmental ideals, and creativity were stressed and valued more than material goals, as expressed in this statement by Michael:

> To me it's not all about money. I mean if it was all about money I sure as hell wouldn't be living like this. I'd be living in town and I would have made my own business . . . I don't need all of that . . . This is better for me. (Michael, 2006)

Some participants prefer the freedom and flexibility involved in self-employment to more prestigious career tracks. Braze's comments express this idea:

> I was making fifty to sixty grand a year in the other profession, and I went and took a job, nightshift, for $8.35. It was a big change seeing a two-hundred-and-fifty dollar paycheck at the end of a forty-hour week. But that was a time when I said, "Okay, I don't really know what substance I want out of life. I don't know what it means and I don't know what it wants. But I do know I need to set myself up in a very versatile trade—where my skills are mine and I'm valued because of my skills, not because I'm this person that's existed inside of this company that can do a preordained job very well, specific to that company." (Braze, 2006)

Whatever the reasons, based on my research and during my time at Lothlorien, the core of volunteers, residents, and regulars were predominantly artisans or skilled laborers with a few people working in service jobs or white-collar professions. They were not a good fit with the dismissive common image of those involved in intentional communities as "hippies" or "Trustafarians." They were widely read, creative, hard-working people of average or below average income, ranging in age from their twenties to their early sixties. And there was a larger proportion of men than women. This rough description still holds true in 2010.

As for the membership as a whole, the overall culture seems very different from Kat Kinkade's description of the long-standing intentional community she helped found at Twin Oaks (see chapter 2.) Kinkade notes that although Twin Oaks strives to be a diverse place, it has a culture she sees as both middle class

"The Land of Misfit Toys"

and "New Age," a culture of tofu, left-wing journals, and natural fiber clothing (with stains.) This is not always comfortable for her—she likes polyester and air conditioning—and she expresses the worries she contended with over returning to this social environment after an absence of nine years: "Would I be content gently fending off suggestions that I try aerobics and brewers' yeast? Could I stand overhearing earnest conversations on topics I privately considered nonsense?" (Kinkade, 1994: 202).

Piercings and tattoos are more common at Lothlorien than natural fibers. And there is certainly not much of a New Age ethos. The spring seasons in 2009 and 2010 were kicked off with pig roasts, generously hosted by Phelan, Aurora, Torcyr, and the McAdams brothers, with kegs of beer and bottles of soda. I told Chris one day that I was planning to share a "tofu turkey" with my family for Thanksgiving, and he responded with a sympathetic shake of the head and the comment, "Oh, I'm sorry." Cigarette smoking is pervasive, as is swearing. Overall, the community is more diverse in terms of Kinkade's definitions of class-related behavior than is Twin Oaks, and it is more subcultural.

Overlapping Communities

The community at Lothlorien spills over into Bloomington and other places, and the connections between people go beyond their involvement in festivals or site maintenance, crisscrossing in complex ways. Sometimes bonds like family, work, school, romantic relationships, or combinations of these, precede the bonds at Lothlorien; sometimes they happen as a result of time at Lothlorien. Either way, relationships outside the site often reinforce (and occasionally damage) relationships inside.

Often more than one generation of a family will be involved at Lothlorien. Anyone from these generations may bring friends in, and sometimes these friends will bring their own children or parents or siblings or grandparents. As a small sample, Robin, whom I met on my first Earth Steward weekend, is the mother of two young adults (one is Lunis) who have now made their own friends on the land and come without her. Tuna's son, Jonathan, has become friends with Owen, and Lily and is part of the FLC (Feral Land Children) group. So is Alicia, who is twenty and is David's daughter. At Elf Fest of 2006 I met a three-generational family of festival attendees, which included Peacock, her mother, and her teenage daughter. Uncle Dan's son Zeke used to be the main computer consultant for Lothlorien. Chris's daughter Caitlin is a part of the FLC. And Vic and Jef's teenage daughter, Lilith, helps out and attends festivals.

An Unreal Estate

Romantic relationships spring up fairly frequently, especially among the younger generation, and create more crisscrossing ties. For example, Conney and Michael's son Owen is dating Vickie and Jef's daughter, Lilith. Chris Caehall used to date Tuna's daughter. People are often introduced to Lothlorien through a romantic relationship also, brought to the land by a spouse or partner, as Frank was brought by his wife, Dawn, who is also Janie's sister.

School and work also play into relationships. Quite a few of the children and teenagers who come to Lothlorien have attended the same alternative school in Bloomington, called Harmony. This includes all of the Freese Posthuma children; Songbear, who is Leslie's son; Vic and Jef's daughter Lilith; Emmy, who is Laura's daughter; and a few other regular visitors who originally came because of their friendships with children who have ties to the site. It is probable that this kind of link also occurs at schools other than Harmony—in Indianapolis, Louisville, Bloomington, Cleveland, or Chicago, for instance. Since I was connected to Harmony through the attendance of one of my own sons, this is the school community I am most aware of.

Work contacts and working relationships off the land are common. Braze and Bonedaddy, for example, have worked on construction projects together in Bloomington. They helped work on a store called Sahara Mart. Michael Posthuma and Tuna got to know each other through a construction-related work project, and Tuna then became a regular volunteer. Uncle Dan has frequently found work for Frank. Shay worked on Rod's house in Illinois. People who work in construction-related projects especially tend to help out, employ, and include each other, creating supportive networks. KEOA, or Keeping Each Other Alive, applies, or can apply, to members giving each other work if they have a choice.

In Bloomington and other nearby cities or rural area, Lothlorien members sometimes share housing or choose to live close to each other. To offer a few examples that I am aware of, Jef and Vic have a house next door to Chris. The Freese-Posthumas' oldest daughter, Eva, used to be roommates with Tuna's son Jon. Jason and Spencer have been roommates, as have Larry and Evangeline, with Aurora and Julian—Evangeline's children. Also, Alicia used to live with Jason, and Larry used to live with Leslie, so there is a certain amount of shuffling and reshuffling as relationships change.

Community members at Lothlorien, then, are often linked to each other in a variety of ways rather than simply through the land. After a few years of time there, the person in the next tent but one is likely to be not only a camping associate but the sister of an ex-boyfriend or the daughter of a work colleague.

"The Land of Misfit Toys"

Agape, Eros, and Philia:
Love, Agency, and "Chosen Family"

While there has been much excellent interpretive work on historical communes,[1] research on existing intentional communities in North America has, until recently, been mainly the preserve of sociologists,[2] and has been oriented toward a search for predictive social laws. The study of contemporary communes has hence often prioritized what can be measured and has left out what cannot be measured. Looking for recurring patterns has been a common approach in surveys and comparative studies (for example, Kanter 1972; Wallace 1956; Zablocki 1980). These provide valuable information and food for thought, but certain experiential aspects of community life—relationships, emotions, and intentions, for example—have been missing. Community, from the perspective of social laws, appears as something that largely *happens* to its individual members rather than being created, interpreted, or experienced by them and affect is rarely fore-grounded (Hillery 1992). And even in more interpretive descriptions of social relationships in general—in anthropology, for example—power, rather than emotion or experience, has been the main focus in the last few decades.

George Hillery is one of the exceptions among the sociologists of Euro-American communal life. His ethnographic study of contemporary monasteries, *The Monastery: A Study in Freedom, Love and Community* (1992), focuses on the affective aspects of relationships there, looking at love in different forms as an essential and binding factor of community in monasteries.[3] I will follow his example and use some of his terms in looking at the affective features of community life at Lothlorien.

The Greeks had at least three distinct words for love: *eros*—romantic or sexual love; *philia*—affection and loyalty toward friends and family; and *agape*—universal or indiscriminate love.[4] Philia is what Ferdinand Tonnies (1887) had in mind as the binding factor in small communities. Eros is a strong organizing factor in Euro-American culture, because it is the basis of the nuclear family, and because the latter has become increasingly mobile and cut off from extended family and long term friendships. Hillery sees agape, universal love, as the most crucial form within his field site, replacing, and compensating for, the lack of familial love—philia—*or* eros. These distinctions between different kinds of love provide a useful framework with which to analyze the affective elements of communitas.

Only recently have researchers on intentional communities (Andelsen 2002; Pitzer 1997; Smith 1999) begun to question Rosabeth Moss Kanter's (1972) conclusions that eros and family love are inversely related to group communitas.

An Unreal Estate

Kanter's *Commitment and Community* was long the standard work on communes. Her thesis was that the greater the number of "commitment mechanisms" in place—sacrifices required in order to be a part of the community—the more long-lived the commune was likely to be, and that nuclear family relationships tended to be a distraction from the necessary focus on the wider group. However, in a wide ranging comparative study, Smith found that many successful intentional communities do include strong nuclear families. The Farm in Tennessee, for example, is thriving after thirty-one years and has a strong ethic of valuing families. Many long-lived communes also require few sacrifices or commitments of the participants. Lothlorien and Twin Oaks are two that throw Kanter's conclusions into question—demanding very little from their members and certainly no fixed ideological commitment or sacrifice of the family.

Hillery is inconclusive on this issue, not surprisingly, since eros is excluded from monasteries. On the one hand, he concludes, regarding philia, that, "Different forms of love support each other: the data suggest that the more we love in one form of love, the more we can love in other forms" (1992: 216.) On the other hand, he seems to see eros as an exception to this, requiring the compensation that helps cultivate agape.

All three kinds of love are in evidence at Lothlorien. Although people did not often use the word "love" in interviews (the word has become confusingly identified with romantic love in the English language), agape in particular seems woven into the ethic of acceptance in the community. It did have limits, however. As is clear from the last chapter, differences in ideals and styles of interaction bring up conflict on a regular basis.

In Hillery's view, agape is the one form of love that is amenable to will or agency. He says, "One chooses to love, and one should be able to love the unlovely" (1992: 204). It would not make sense to order someone to love another person erotically.[5] It would not make sense to order someone to make friends or to develop affection for another person. But agape can be chosen. It is the word used in early Greek translations of the Bible for Jesus' and others' commandments about love; "Love your neighbor," "Love your enemies." It is unconditional because it does not require a particular kind of behavior, appearance, or belief system on the part of the person loved, nor even any return of love. It is also nonpossessive. It fits Turner's description of normative communitas because it is chosen rather than arising spontaneously. The idea of community-building as choice is reflected in this comment by Scott:

> A lot of times it just has to do with trying to bridge gaps between people. [You get] two people who can't stand each other out here and if

"The Land of Misfit Toys"

there's some kind of common ground they can get . . . you can forgive just about anything. It's within human capacity. It is a matter of choice. (Scott, 2006)

Hillery's description of agape and Carl Rogers' writings on psychotherapy have much in common. Rogers (1980) prescribed both "unconditional positive regard" and empathy on the part of the therapist as essential for a successful psychotherapeutic relationship, along with a third factor, congruence, or genuineness. Again this points to a possibility of choice in the affective relationship. It makes sense to tell someone to cultivate a stance of unconditional positive regard (although in some cases this might be easier than in others). Lothlorien has attempted to create a culture of positive regard.

Frank told me about his first festival experience and his impressions of the campers. He had been stressed at work, and his wife, Dawn, who had grown up going to Lothlorien festivals, decided that he needed a break:

> She brought me down on a rainy Friday night and said, "Here, you go to Elf Fest" . . . and she said, "Have a good time," and she left . . . The next morning I cocked my head out of my tent to see a bunch of people— I had no idea who they were—sitting around the campfire. And I sat down around the campfire with them and we talked and had a great time . . . and I was accepted immediately and unconditionally with people not knowing who I was . . . That's unique. Not only do they pass the time but they do it with gusto . . .
>
> We think differently than the rest of the world. It all comes back to that old 1960s hippie thing, where everyone is friendly, and you take people for what they are, and even though you don't know who they are you make sure that they are alive and are acknowledged in some way, which is not like the rest of the world. How many people are going to cook waffles for fifty people at a campground? Lothlorien is set up so that you have to interact with other people . . . You're going to be tolerant of what other people believe whether you believe in it or not. (Frank, 2010)

Related to the sense of easy acceptance is the building of friendships and interpersonal safety in a way that is more usual in families. This brings up another aspect of Lothlorien's culture; the way people bond in small groups or identify with the community as a whole.

Jef told me that he loved a group of friends he had made at Lothlorien festivals, the "Circle of 42," more than a family. He said that he and Vic had known them for many years and that they had become his chosen family. "Chosen family" is a powerful phrase—combining the element of choice with the strength of affection and willingness to help usually associated with biological ties. Denise, a former active member at Lothlorien, also talked about the friends she made there as being her chosen family, as does Braze:

> There's a group of people here who are part of my clan, my inner circle, that I dearly love as if they were family—I'm closer with them than my own family—that I will always know. And we're spread out across five states. And this is the central place for us. And Healers' circle at festival time is a place we go to commune. And that will always happen. And those people I would never lose touch with . . . They're like cousins. (Braze, 2006)

Lilith also describes her early years in Indiana, when she was spending almost every weekend at Lothlorien, as a process of "becoming family":

> It was friendship and then becoming family. Everybody just seemed like a second family . . . I see you guys actually more than I see my own (extended) family. Everybody working together . . . It's a great community. It's a loving family. I know that sounds cheesy, but it's true. (Lilith, 2009)

Jason expressed a slightly less rosy view of family at a Council meeting, following some disagreements. He said, "Siblings fight. We're still siblings though."

"Chosen family" does not usually replace consanguineal or affinal family, but complements it. I do not know of any regular Lothlorien participants who are completely estranged from their kinship groups (although this may have happened, given the large numbers of people who have been involved over the years). Only one of my interviewees, Julie, described strained communication with her family resulting from religious differences and from her romantic relationship with Andy. However, those with Pagan associations may feel guarded around their relatives, and nuclear or extended family members may choose to stay away from festivals and from Pagan ceremonies like handfastings.

In North American culture, especially among the middle class, the nuclear family tends to be the focus of social life and eros is emphasized over philia. The United States and Canada are particularly mobile societies, where people move for jobs and education and often end up separated from extended family and from friends. Lothlorien fulfils the desire for a broad-based but still close-knit community:

> This place always held a very special place in my heart, because it was really the first community experience . . . In suburbia you kind of

"The Land of Misfit Toys"

know your neighbors on the left and on the right. There's one couple like six houses down my parents are friends with because the kids play together. There's all that. But you really don't have much more than a once a year block party kind of thing. It feels disconnected, it feels very consumer-based, kind of, the nuclear family are here to consume and we're here to make our lives easier by consuming. But the waste we're generating . . . I think there's a better way. (Scott, 2006)

Laura also values the way Lothlorien creates a sense of connection beyond the nuclear family. She refers to the community there as a "tribe":

Braze and I have been talking a lot about that a lot lately. How when we go down there we feel like we're part of a tribe. I think that that's some-thing, anthropologically, that's been lost, in this whole American idea of individualism . . . We've got little nuclear families stacked in little houses in little neighborhoods, and nobody's really connected any more . . . (Laura, 2010)

Friendship, community and fictive kinship all depend on Lothlorien as a physical, geographical gathering place, as is clear from this comment by Vic:

That's been really great connecting with people from all over. That I re-ally like, because some of these folks you might only see twice a year and you make really good friends, some people might come back every five years or whatever, but . . . people come back. You might never see them again or you'll see them all the time, it just depends. I really like the idea of just being able to always know you can come back here. No mat-ter what goes on in the rest of your life you can always come back to this community and there is a place for you and to share what you know . . . Every time we'd come we would meet more people over here and make closer friends. (Vic, 2006)

Even when friendship groups exist independently of Lothlorien, experiences on the campsite can help to consolidate them:

We spend time up here (in Indianapolis) together, but it was nice to . . . go down there and you really camped in the same circle. It was definitely that community feeling and hermetic community feeling where you really have to depend upon each other—who's going to go get the water, who's going to start the fire? (Janie, 2007)

The level of safety and ease at Lothlorien, more common in large blood-related kinship groups, has its roots in the community ethic of accepting

An Unreal Estate

people unconditionally in most instances, and it is most evident in the culture at festivals (which is why friendships are made easily there). The dividing line between friendship and agape is not always clear, but there is a willingness to give people the benefit of the doubt at Lothlorien, over an unusually wide range of issues, that encompasses agape. Lothlorien, then, combines philia and agape and sometimes eros too, as people bring spouses, lovers, girlfriends or boyfriends—or in some cases meet romantic partners on the land.

"Growing From Within": Sanctuary, Acceptance and Freedom

In "Life Not Death In Venice," Schmiel, an elderly Jew in Los Angeles, describes his small town in Poland to Barbara Myerhoff in words that powerfully express the value of a safe space in the unsafe world he remembers: "In that little town there were no walls. But we were curled up together inside it, like small cubs, keeping each other warm, growing from within" (Myerhoff 1986: 284). Like Schmiel, many Lothlorien participants expressed the idea that safety and growth were linked. This was a very common theme in interviews. Visitors and volunteers had often found a greater degree of safety in friendships and acquaintanceships on the land than in the outside world. This discovery of a safe place, a sanctuary, contributed to an enhanced sense of freedom and an ability to explore and make changes in themselves.

Communitas within Lothlorien sometimes contrasts with previous experiences of alienation in the larger society. The two comments at the opening of this chapter eloquently describe a misalignment between people who spend time at Lothlorien and the world in general. Larry's comment places the responsibility for the misalignment onto the community participants. He adds,

> Something didn't work right and they weren't the hip kid in school and they didn't figure out how to ask the girl out. Or whatever makes them the misfit. (Larry, 2006)

Braze's comments shift the responsibility for the lack of fit, by implication, from the individual to mainstream social norms. For him, those who come to Lothlorien are exceptional, "eccentric, beautiful, talented, wonderfully creative people," and mainstream society comes up short, finding them "stark raving mad." Either way there is a mismatch, and people find an alignment in the community that had often been missing outside. Frank, like Braze, puts the responsibility for the misalignment on society's shortcomings rather than on shortcomings in participants at Lothlorien:

"The Land of Misfit Toys"

I think a lot of people who go there have been disillusioned in one way or the other by the way the world is or the way religion is . . . I think people go there to escape the world as it is. (Frank, 2009)

Paul F. also sees a mismatch, and describes it in terms of the marginalization of various groups in the United States, including intellectuals. He makes it clear that marginalization and outsider status are increasingly becoming normal rather than exceptional, as middle class aspirations move out of the reach of many people:

You are expected to work hard and get a good education and get a good job and have a family—all of these very typical things . . . But you can't really even get a good job any more regardless of your degree. There's so much competition over so little. And the political bill of sale in this country that we are expected to believe is widely divergent from reality. And that's a lot of what I think this society does, is inculcate us into this form of capitalism. And it's just blind. You are asked to enjoy their consumerism and not really ask for anything more. People know better. Especially groups of people who've been kicked out of all the groups that say, "Hey, we're cool and you're not."

Just because one person has more money and can have a lot of toys . . . [they can have] nice objects and they can hang out with other people who have nice objects. But a person with equal intellectual capacity, or maybe superior intellectual capacity and talent, who doesn't garner as great an income and therefore doesn't have the same types of objects, can, for that reason alone, be ostracized from that group. There's a varying array of reasons why you get kicked out of groups or are not acceptable to groups, and just find yourself marginalized by default. And in the United States the most glaring thing, I think, is how intellectuals are marginalized . . . they don't want people to question the paradigm . . . There is a veil of illusion we're asked to accept in some form. And people are finding the veil very thin—it's just wrong. They're looking for ways to survive when it's obviously going to come crashing down because it can't go on like this any longer. And how do you become more self reliant? [There is a] huge, wide array of ways [here] that we teach each other and help each other. (Paul F., 2009)

In contrast to a sense of misalignment that some people described in the outside world, feeling unconditionally accepted or valued at Lothlorien—which

An Unreal Estate

I associate both with communitas and with the egalitarianism implied in Every Child Is a Star—was a theme that came up from several different angles. The need to be accepted as a Neo-Pagan practitioner will be discussed in the next chapter. But most often the emphasis in interviews and conversations was on acceptance in more general terms, as an individual. These comments came from people with a range of different personality types, rather than one particular kind of personality. The following insightful statement, for example, was made by a young man called Lunis, who sometimes camps at Lothlorien for stretches of summers and who has earned the nickname Dishman through his dishwashing at festivals:

> [I was] fourteen when I first came here. I was shy and I wasn't really capable of talking to people. The society and reality I had lived in before, I was bullied on, a lot of people picked on me and my values, and what I was wasn't really appreciated. But when I came here I learned that I was allowed to express part of myself that seemed inexpressible outside and that allowed me to open up a lot of myself . . .
>
> When I first came here I had quite a lot of problems. I would have a really hard time talking to people because I would think I would have to create a whole conversation before I even started one. I would have this problem where I'd create this whole scenario before I even got into something. It's like I'd write this mini dialog and jump into something and it always got me into trouble, because nothing turns out how you expect it, especially when you're trying to live out life in sort of a scripted manner. So I think over time that's degraded and I've come to the point to where I can say what's on my mind and not really be afraid. (Lunis, 2006)

Lunis's growth in confidence and expressiveness involves different personality traits than those described in this comment by Chris:

> When I first got here everybody accepted me for the idiot that I am. I could act completely and naturally, which is half the time relatively foolishly because I'm a clown. And I found I was able to make friends easily, which is not something I normally do. I'm relatively withdrawn actually. But there were so many goofy people who were totally comfortable behaving the way they were behaving—who accepted me unconditionally. (Chris, 2006)

Or this by Jef:

"The Land of Misfit Toys"

I'm kind of an outgoing guy and I don't mind just like walking into a group of people. Either they like you or they don't. And they always did, so that was what I thought was really cool about Lothlorien—I could be this motor-head, urban Elf kinda guy and there's still a place for you there. So there's a place for almost everybody. There really is . . . Everybody wants to fit in somewhere. I mean everybody wants to fit in. I mean if you try at all you can fit in at Lothlorien. (Jef, 2006)

Lothlorien provides a safe place not only for a range of personalities but for a range of lifestyles. Neo-Paganism is only one of these among others, since acceptance is valued in itself:

I think that Pagan culture, the Wiccan earth-based religion culture . . . because they're more an accepting group, I think there's a lot of those people down there. But I think you also get just a variety of people that just simply want to be free or be accepted for whatever ethnicity or eccentricities that they have, you know. You really just want to be accepted, and I think that culture has been more accepting than most others. (Janie, 2007)

We encourage people who practice all kinds of alternatives: whether it's their sexual preference, their marital status, their religion; whatever it is, we are there to give you a place to feel comfortable doing something that most everyone else in society would look at you weird for. (Chris, 2006)

This is especially true at festivals, where the large group is composed of many small circles of friends, acquaintances, or like-minded people—drummers, covens, or those of similar sexual orientation, for example. People also feel freer to wear clothes that might be thought strange in the outside world, like sarongs, capes, or kilts.

Because of this atmosphere of tolerance, participants often expressed a greater than usual sense of freedom on the land. Vic says she can

share a meal, do a ritual, just hug for the hell of it. These are people that you can do that with. You can dress anyway you want, do anything you want to do, and there's not going to be open ridicule. (Vic, 2006)

Conney expresses an appreciation for fixed ways of life, but comes out more strongly on the side of freedom:

I really have a lot of respect for people like Amish who, like, "This is what you do and this is how you live your life" . . . but at the same time I

An Unreal Estate

have this whole, "Why should someone tell me what to wear and how to dress and, and what to eat because that's my religion?" This real internal thing where I see both of those things and they don't really mesh together very well. (Conney, 2006)

A comment by Andy points to his sense of freedom from feeling judged on superficial or material grounds at Lothlorien:

Society's standards don't apply. You're not judged on what money you make like anywhere else, [it's] just a lot more laid back. From the very first day you start to learn that there is a lot more than what you think of on a daily basis when you're in society, because they're more worried about their cell phones and their cars and their—than the earth itself, and you start to see that from day one out here, so it makes a big difference . . . Even amongst [my] family it's a big show on who has what and does what. So I never did follow in his [my father's] expectations and things like that. But I mean—I had gone from that to coming out here where there's hundreds of people that were just their own people; just not going to judge you, not going to be uppity like so many other people, and you just feel like home from the minute you set foot on the property, and that's the way they work on making it, is everybody is welcome—it is home, whether you live here or not, you come out here it's just an extension of your yard. (Andy, 2006)

And the following comment by Julie expresses her relief in coming from the relatively materialistic values of the outside world to a more supportive place:

Everybody is here to help each other out . . . Outside . . . I wouldn't feel comfortable going and asking anybody, "Do you have some sugar?" or if you've got a loaf of bread, because they'll look at you like you're crazy; "This is my stuff. What in the world?" Well, it's not like that here. It's nowhere like that here, it's a lot more relaxed. (Julie, 2006)

Janet talks about some of the ways her behavior changes at Lothlorien as a result of a sense of safety in being herself. Her comment is reminiscent of Scott's comment, above, about dropping armor. She says,

I am a little bit more verbal, a little bit more receptive to whatever is going on because you don't have to hide things here. Because most people who come here, like 95 percent of people that come here, are pretty chill and pretty cool and pretty understanding. It's the whole environ-

"The Land of Misfit Toys"

ment. It's . . . receiving information data from the whole environment. Everything is in a different playing field. It's pretty cool . . . It's like you are allowed to be your true self here. A lot of places you have to put on a mask. Here you don't. (Janet, 2009)

Frank appreciates the freedoms at Lothlorien but seems to take a more pessimistic or cautious view of the way people change there. Rather than a "true self" emerging, he notes the danger of people adopting personas on the land:

You can go down there as an alter ego. How you are in the outside world can be very different from who you are inside Lothlorien . . . You can go there and be as flaky as you like and people will flock to you because of your flakiness. (Frank, 2009)

Teal, in a way, combines these two perspectives. In her view, feeling free to be oneself has led, for some people, to the possibility of making personal changes or experimenting with different sides of the self:

I think it's actually two things, which may even sort of contradict in a way. I mean on the one hand you felt like you could completely be yourself. You didn't have to put on a different face. You didn't have to pretend that you were someone else or something else. And if you had ideas about things that were not quite what everyone else thought, you know . . . So it was okay to be different. But on the other hand it was the freedom of actually being with people that supported both that difference and the similarities, because then you had a lot of people that actually felt kind of like you so you weren't as different when you're in this context.

And also I think that on the opposite side of that, you also had the freedom to experiment with who you were—just start to learn things about yourself that maybe you didn't even have the context for in your regular mundane life. Like people play around with new names and they play around with—and not play as in like it's a game but in trying to understand themselves better—then they try it here in a safe place, and then a lot of people may extend it to their mundane life; but here in a safe environment you can run around without your clothes on and I don't know, just all kinds of things. I've had some of the best conversations with people here about things, and healthy debates, not crazy arguments, you know, but healthy debates where we try to challenge each other to think in different ways, or at least consider a different perspective. (Teal, 2007)

An Unreal Estate

Laura describes Lothlorien as a place where she has felt safe enough to mature, without the negative connotations associated with maturity and age in the culture at large. Like Teal, she relates safety to the ability to change:

> It puts me in an environment where I feel safe to grow . . . Being out in the normal world and figuring my own stuff out was a lot of, you know, being deviant about it. And here it's just accepted and encouraged. And so it is fertile soil, as it were, as an analogy, for people to come and plant themselves and grow in their own way and still be influenced by other people, but it's people you kind of want to be influenced by. . . . Through my interactions with various people down there I really feel that I've been encouraged to find my own path and mature in a way that doesn't scare me. . . . For a long time I fought really hard against that whole adult paradigm. But down there I feel like I can do that and I'm not getting old and crotchety. It's a positive experience. (Laura, 2010)

Lunis also expresses very clearly this freedom both to explore and to make changes:

> When I came here I learned that I was allowed to express part of myself that seemed inexpressible outside, and that allowed me to open up a lot of myself. So when I came here I guess I could say the transition was from being afraid and unaware to accepting and slightly more aware. And that's been a slow progression over time. And each time that I've come here, even though it's only a week at a time, I feel like I do three or four months of work in a week, and it just seems like I make so much progress. (Lunis, 2006)

Lothlorien's culture of acceptance and affirmation, then, was often described by interview participants as a factor that enabled them to risk expressing new sides of themselves. It opened up options—for Teal, to try out different points of view; for Lunis, to interact with others more; for Janet, to be both receptive and communicative; for Laura to shift more easily into her identity as an adult; for Chris, Andy, Jef, and others, simply to be more comfortable in being who they were. Frank noted too that some people shift into more "flaky" identities. But overall the people interviewed saw Lothlorien's community ethos as a factor that helped keep their identities, their senses of themselves, fluid. So whether or not this aspect of the culture keeps people at Lothlorien for the long term, it enables changes that they themselves (in most cases) interpret as valuable and positive.

"The Land of Misfit Toys"

There are always, of course, limits to acceptance. Violent behavior, theft, sexual harassment, and a few other misdemeanors will result in expulsion from the land, as I noted in chapter 4. Also, while there seems to be tolerance for a broad range of personalities, destructive or rude behavior is not appreciated, as Jef says:

> If someone is obnoxious and rude you don't get accepted. But I mean if you just a little bit show like you really cared and you want to learn and want to just be part of the Lothlorien scene, if you want to call it that, people would just accept you. (Jef, 2006)

Negotiating difference: Sexuality, Race, Gender, and Age

Since both agape and normative communitas *are* by definition unconditional, the conditions, stratifications, or distinctions which often mark off one set of people from another in the mainstream world—race, age, gender, sexual orientation, religion, political affiliation, ability, appearance—should be ignored to the extent where these principles are espoused or reflected in alternative communities. Hillery finds this to be true in the monastery. On the whole I also find this to be true at Lothlorien.

As noted above, only a handful of African Americans come to festivals, along with a smaller handful of Hispanic or Asian people, and only two of my interview participants, Janet and Ethan, were African Americans. Anthony, who has been coming to Lothlorien since the land was first bought, said that he was "terrified" when his friends from Indianapolis first drove him down to the place in 1987 and dropped him off alone. Everyone in the community at that time was white except for himself. In his words, "When I first came here, the only dark things were me and the night." But he added that the visit had turned out well and that he had been coming to festivals ever since.

Ethan also shared his experiences of time at Lothlorien as an African American. He too said that he had originally been nervous about coming to Southern Indiana, because of its lack of diversity (as noted earlier, the area has a population which is close to 99 percent white.) His past experiences of racism in big cities had made him wary, but it ended up being a positive experience:

> They've worked on whatever racism they have within themselves, you know? I think a lot of people at Lothlorien have . . . actively worked on that kind of stuff. So if that was, or is an issue, I think it would have been brought to the forefront rather than kept inside or whatever. I think it would have been talked about—you know I would have been

An Unreal Estate

talked to about it. It wouldn't have been something that I would feel so strongly that a negative kind of aura from that person or people. So it was really comfortable for me. (Ethan, 2007)

He speculates about why so few nonwhite people come to the land:

The thing that really kind of struck me is that there really aren't other brown-skinned people as members of this community, you know, the Lothlorien community, and I wonder why that is. . . . I've been thinking about this a lot and part of it I think is the Pagan aspect of this community and a lot of us, a lot of American brown-skinned people have been raised in certain Western religious traditions . . . It's almost like it's part of your DNA or something so it's hard to break out of that . . .

All my life I've wondered why, about the things that I was taught in terms of Christianity, and not really believing the things that I was told but taking it in nonetheless. So most of my life I've done research, because that's what I do . . . Because I like to find out, I want to know, because I'm not going to just blindly believe in something. I think that's not a healthy thing. I don't think that's a healthy thing at all. So, and what I found was that most of the quote unquote "Christian" traditions come from Paganism, so that made it easier for me to be involved in the Pagan community and embrace it, you know . . . Pagans have always been talked about as Devil worshipers and baby killers all that . . . and unless you do the research, that stays in your head, you know. And so I think that's part of the reason. I think another part of the reason is that it's really hard sometimes to break into predominantly Caucasian spaces. (Ethan, 2007)

While I have not seen conscious racial discrimination at Lothlorien, the symbolism that pervades its material culture draws largely on European historical or mythical themes. Coupled with this as background, for a nonwhite person the predominantly white population of festival goers and volunteers might be daunting or alienating, given experiences of racism in other contexts.

Women and men have usually been equally represented among the Eldars over the time of my research. There are more men among the Stewards and Staff, largely because there are more male volunteers overall. Leadership, then, is unusually balanced, and as far as the informal culture goes I have experienced Lothlorien as an inclusive and safe place to be a woman. Teal, who has been coming for many years, reinforces this impression:

"The Land of Misfit Toys"

I've always felt, for the most part, that there was somebody watching my back, you know, and I feel safe here. So I definitely feel safe to be naked, you know, and I feel safe to get to know people and I feel safe enough to drink. (Teal, 2007)

I see clothing styles at Lothlorien as subtly indicative of a positive attitude to women and to femaleness. In *The Snake Charmer Queen*, Stoeltje notes the way "appearance and dress specifically serve to define gender" at a Texas beauty pageant. In that context, feminine formal clothes draw attention to women's bodies, while a beard competition for men, including a prize for the ugliest, creates a deliberate contrast and a backdrop of masculinity. At Lothlorien, men and women dress similarly. At festivals or when they are not engaged in physical work, both genders tend to wear clothes that are usually considered "feminine"—sarongs or loose skirts. This is unusual in mainstream contexts. Women have been dressing in masculine clothing in Europe and North America for as long as they have been able to get away with it—taking on, or trying to take on, the higher status associated with masculine identity. Similarly they have moved into parts of the workforce previously considered masculine domains. But the reverse is not true in most mainstream contexts. Because of the higher value given to masculinity in most of North America, it is rare and can be shameful for men, especially straight men, to associate themselves with clothing or activities usually associated with femininity. Scott describes the shift he made when, on his first visit to Lothlorien, someone gave him a skirt:

I'd never worn a skirt before. But I . . . knew that skirts were one of those things that were originally created for men, like earrings were. Earrings were originally so Christian sailors could have Christian burials. So I put one on and it was a weird adjustment. I kind of felt like "Well, I'm cross-dressing, this is a weird taboo kind of thing," and you get over that pretty quick. It's a funny thing. (Scott, 2006)

I have also noticed a tendency in the Lothlorien community for men to spend time with, and take great care of, their girlfriends' or former girlfriends' children in cases where there was no biological relationship. I observed this with Bonedaddy and Haven, Andy and Josh, Braze and Phoenix, Stew and Songbear, and in several other families. Again this is a case of men showing willingness to take on work usually done by women—work that is often accorded a lower status than traditionally "male" occupations.

Divinity is female as well as male in Neo-Pagan spiritual philosophies, and the shrines are full of female as well as male figures. As an illustration of the

An Unreal Estate

rationale behind this, Scott expresses the problems he had, growing up in a strict Christian environment, with the idea of God as exclusively male:

> I wanted to know [how come], if we're created in God's image, half the population, in fact more than half the population, according to *Entertainment Tonight,* is female. That means that God is more female than male. (Scott, 2006)

The visual environment, then, expressed through clothing and artifacts, reinforces a worldview in which women and items or imagery associated with women are valued to an unusual degree. This is not to say that one will never hear a sexist remark, as people come in and go out with varying levels of identification with the culture of the world outside, but it is less common than in mainstream contexts.

Lothlorien is predominantly a straight community, but it has a policy of accepting all sexual orientations, and this has been an important aspect of the land as a sanctuary. It can be valuable for people of minority sexual orientations to feel that they have allies or a safe place in the world, since so many have experienced rejection from family members, acquaintances, or friends. Even those who are "out" as gay or lesbian in their day-to-day lives can express themselves more fully at Lothlorien:

> We have one of our members of our campsite, he's got a pink skirt on and he can feel free enough to do that. I'm not sure that even though he's out as gay, that he would go home and wear this pink skirt. And here we're like, "Oh you're wonderful, we love you." (Teal, 2007)

Ethan's minority status as an African American, his life with cerebral palsy, and his experiences first as a lesbian and then as a transgendered man have made him a pioneer in many situations. For this reason, acceptance in a community is very important to him, and Lothlorien has been a reinforcing experience. Here he talks about being a transsexual:

> I think that there's an atmosphere of kindness and openness and honesty that I don't often find in the outside . . . Here you can just be whoever you are and it's okay. Especially for me as a transsexual—people don't get it out there. Here it's like I don't have to explain anything, it doesn't matter. I'm Ethan, and that's it, you know, and people get it or they don't, but it doesn't matter whether they don't get it or not because they know who I am and that's just who I am. Whereas when people find out in the outside world, it's like there's all these questions and

"The Land of Misfit Toys"

just different expectations, and people treat me differently once they find out, and things like that, and that doesn't happen here. So I feel much more comfortable being myself here, but it's also translated into me being able to be much more comfortable out there, because I know that it doesn't matter what those people think, because I'm comfortable with who I am. They see what they want to see and that's their business; that's not my problem. That's part of what makes it good for me—coming here sort of renews my spirit so that I can go out there and do what I need to do out there. (Ethan, 2006)

The accepting attitude toward alternative sexualities and gender identities partly reflects attitudes in the Pagan community, especially in large urban areas:

I think that Lothlorien sort of fits into . . . what I would call a larger Pagan community . . . In general it was the larger Pagan communities in Indianapolis and Cincinnati that seemed to be more accepting of both homosexuality and polyamory, and it was the sort of the smaller communities that were less . . . Most of the people that I actually talked to who were bisexual or gay or lesbian seemed to feel that for the most part they felt really accepted in the Pagan community and definitely more accepted in the Pagan community than by society as a whole. (Teal, 2007)

Teal goes on to discuss a more controversial aspect of her sexuality—polyamory. This is certainly not the norm at Lothlorien, but it is a recognized and accepted choice there:

I felt that a lot of things about myself were, I don't know, maybe a little bit unacceptable. For example, like I'm polyamorous . . . and now I'm out as a lesbian, but I was out as a bisexual for many, many years. And here it's like "Whatever," you know and . . . these aren't things you can always talk about to just anybody. (Teal, 2007)

Polyamory is a composite of two words—the Greek word "poly" meaning "many" and the Latin word "amor" meaning "love." The term was coined by Morning Glory Zell in the Neo-Pagan journal *Green Egg* in 1990. Zell (now Zell-Ravenheart) was a High Priestess in the Church of All Worlds (see chapter 2) in the 1970s. It refers to a philosophical position as well as a lifestyle choice, which advocates (or allows for) having intimate long-term relationships with more than one person at a time.[6] The difference between polyamory and "affairs" is that the consent of all people involved is required. Ideally secondary or satellite

An Unreal Estate

partners would be friends with both members of a primary couple as well as the lover of one of them. Or there may be a primary threesome or foursome. The relationships are not merely sexual: "It is expected that the people in such relationships have a loving emotional bond, are involved in each other's lives multi-dimensionally, and care for each other" ("Ravenhearts' FAQ," quoted in www.Wikpedia.com). Zell considers that polyamorous arrangements revive some of the advantages of an extended family, but that "they are better because the ties are voluntary and are, by necessity, rooted in honesty, fairness, friendship, and mutual interests" (Zell 1990). Polyamory has become something of a movement in the last couple of decades, with its own symbols and flag.[7] It is more wide-ranging than what has been known as "open marriage," since it does not necessarily involve marriage, and the term involves more self-definition and solidarity with others living by similar principles.

While polygyny is practiced in many parts of the world and polyandry in a few, Paganism is one of the few Western spiritual traditions that acknowledge polyamory as an ethical option. As Zell notes, there has been a history in religious groups that endorse monogamy to enforce the rules more rigorously for women than for men: "In a patriarchy, men's deviation from that norm is ignored and women's is punished, often by death" (Zell 1990). Polyamory is a good fit with both Neo-Paganism's view of sexuality as sacred and its endorsement of gender equality. Yet some people within wider Neo-Pagan circles are wary of this lifestyle because it is so far from being accepted in mainstream culture that they fear that the movement will be tainted by association.

> I think there's more of a taboo about polyamory than homosexuality or bisexuality . . . Because I have met some Pagans who were somewhat hostile . . . this is not the case with most Pagans, but the few that I have who had issues with polyamory, their biggest thing is, is exactly what my friend did, that they're like, "We're pissed off about it because we don't want everybody to assume that all Pagans are poly." (Teal, 2007)

At Lothlorien, polyamory is a possibility that can be considered in an atmosphere of tolerance:

> There are people that, some good friends of mine that are looking, exploring polyamory, you know. And they can come here and they can talk about it and they can actually explore it, like have another person with them and they know that they're safe to do that, that the people here, not just their friends at their campsite, but the other people here are not going to be condemning about it. (Teal, 2007)

"The Land of Misfit Toys"

There seemed to be less diversity of sexual orientation among Council members, residents, and volunteers, however, than in the festival population. This led one young lesbian woman to tell me that her friends were reluctant to come with her to the land, not because of overt discrimination but because of the prospect of being in a mainly heterosexual environment. There was also one survey response that referred to "subtle homophobia" as a problem at Lothlorien; so there must be exceptions to the accepting social environments that Teal and Ethan described.

The children, teenagers, and young adults who have spent a lot of time on the land as they were growing up are often described as the Land Kids, or the FLC or Feral Land Children (see chapter 1). The core of this group consists of Conney and Michael's children, Eva, Owen, Lily, and Jacob. Lilith, Vic and Jef's daughter, also spends a lot of time there, since she is dating Owen. Haven is the youngest. Leslie's son Songbear, Tuna's son Jon, Chris's daughter Caitlin, Evangeline's son and daughter Aurora and Julian, have also been central to the FLC. This group also blurs at the edges. Several of them have become active in land projects. Lilith took over the "black bag" for a while—collecting fees from campers and festival goers—and helps with registration, mailings, and bank deposits, as does Owen. Owen, Lily, and Jacob help clear trails, and Owen and his friends help with trash and recycling collections after festivals as well as with some of the hard physical labor on the land, such as tree clearing and fence building.

There are lots of children and teenagers at festivals, and they provide a good wait staff at meal times. It is also common at festivals for small children to approach adults with cookies or lemonade to sell. I love watching the younger children dance around the festival fire in the evening, because they are so free and seem to enjoy the occasions so much. Sometimes they dress up. At Elf Fest in 2007 a seven-year-old boy named Eric, wearing horns, said that he was "a midget troll." At Lammas in 2005, a group of children were dressed as hobbits.

Lilith, who is Vic and Jef's daughter, described to me her introduction to the Land Kids at the Wild Magick Festival in 2001 when she was ten years old:

> Lily . . . took me under her wing and dragged me along to these excursions in the woods . . . I was always the younger one. I was shy. I didn't really talk much. I didn't really feel like I fit in with them, but apparently I did because they kept wanting me to hang out with them, and I'm still hanging out with them now. (Lilith, 2009)

Michael's comments about his children growing up at Lothlorien point to the juxtaposition of freedom and shelter that he feels they have been able to

An Unreal Estate

experience on this land. It is interesting in his comments that he refers to the "normal" world (which is quite familiar to him, since he works there five or six days a week) as the unsafe and "weird" place, while Lothlorien—where they have exposure to a variety of lifestyles and behaviors (that would often be censored or regarded as unsafe and unsuitable for kids by the mainstream)—is the safe, grounding place:

> My kids love this place. Well, they all help. They all work here. And this is their home. This is their safety and their security and this is what makes it real for them. And even though I realize that three hundred feet down the driveway the world is what is it, and just 'cause we live three hundred feet away from it, the world doesn't go away, they are safer here, they're safer here than perhaps living in Indianapolis, in the middle of the streets.
>
> You know they're going to experience things here that are quite a bit different than what they would have in a city life, let's say . . . We're pretty open here; we allow a lot of things, we see a lot of things. People really push their parameters a lot. And I give my kids a tremendous amount of freedom to experience it. Because if they don't have the experience and they don't understand the difference between "Yes" and "No" and "Why" and "Why not?" just telling them "Because I said so" only makes you want to do it . . . So I always kind of take a more open approach with them . . . They're all going to have their own lives, you know, make their own choices, but here they will always have—they can come back to this. If it's too weird out there, come back, you know, get back on your feet. (Michael, 2006)

Safety for Michael, then, and for the kids, is not about living within a small range of lifestyles and mores, other than the ban on violence (which would result in removal from the land); nor is it about being kept at a distance from strangers, since new people come into Lothlorien frequently. It is about living in a tolerant and open environment.

Lothlorien is a physically challenging place compared to many camp sites in the industrialized world, partly because of its lack of commercial backing and resources—making gravel, for example, the material for most of the roads—and because of its policy of using only energy from sustainable sources in the public areas. Much of the work required for its maintenance is also physically challenging. Perhaps because of these factors, there are only a handful of severely disabled people who come regularly to Lothlorien. These include a

"The Land of Misfit Toys"

couple of merchants, one or two campers, and Andy, who was a Steward in 2006. But physical able-bodiedness for the rest of us is always temporary. Every person alive has been an infant and will at some point experience illness, injury, or old age—although there is a common tendency to forget this and to see disability rather than design as the problem when abilities and environments are misaligned (Oliver, 1990). Awareness has grown at Lothlorien, and participants have an intention to be inclusive. Some early design problems with the composting privies and showers have been gradually remedied, thanks to input from Andy and Ethan and work by Uncle Dan, Bonedaddy, Tuna, Shay, Rod, Cece, Paul F., and others. In 2007 a new wheelchair-accessible shower stall was built. The new composter was also built with wheelchair accessibility in mind.

In summary, there is an effort to be inclusive at Lothlorien, and this effort has been successful in most cases. Women are well represented on the Council and there is a balance of women and men among the Eldars. Recognition of the needs of disabled people is growing, with the newest structures being adapted to meet the needs of those in wheelchairs or on crutches. The few people of color I have met at Lothlorien also seem to be well integrated, although it must be a challenge for anyone who is part of a group that has historically been discriminated against to put themselves into a situation where they will be in such a small minority. There is a mix of class backgrounds. On the whole it is an accepting place for people from a variety of social strata, religions or identities, and with a variety of nonmainstream sexual orientations or lifestyle choices. Older people also seem well integrated with younger people, with a much greater level of cross-generational friendship than I have seen in most North American or English communities. The groups around campfires usually include a mix of ages.

Conclusions: Community and the Individual at Lothlorien

Earlier in this dissertation, I described the contrast between the religious and lifestyle values of Southern Indiana and the United States and those of Lothlorien participants as a whole. Lothlorien is a place that is accepting of Pagans, Goths, environmentalists, and people with nonheterosexual or nonmonogamous sexual orientations, as well as most other groups, and this may have contributed to some of its visitors being what Larry describes as "misfit toys" in the world at large. Regular volunteers are usually hard-working, skilled, and intelligent people and are not misfits in the sense of being lazy or irrational

An Unreal Estate

or antisocial. Rather they are often misaligned with mainstream culture for a variety of reasons.

A related theme from the interviews, which brings up a contrast between being inside and being outside the Lothlorien community, is the relative *ethical* alignment some participants experienced through being in a place that was trying to exemplify environmental and/or egalitarian ideals. In this case it was not so much that they came up against disapproval toward themselves in the outside world and experienced a new-found degree of acceptance and affirmation at Lothlorien as that they felt their own disapproval toward the world, and that they chose or endorsed Lothlorien by contrast. This was a less common explicit theme, but nonetheless one that was often implied. The two themes converge at the point where Lothlorien's level of acceptance and tolerance is itself understood as one of its ethical positions.

The accepting nature of Lothlorien's culture is more in evidence at festivals than at Council meetings, where the nitty-gritty of decision making is carried out. Pike (2001) describes festival space as something separate and marked off from everyday life. At festivals, people are on vacation, they are interacting with people they see only on these special occasions, they are attending rituals or drum circles around the fire, and they are away from home environments that remind them of chores or work obligations. Regular volunteers also see festivals as magical and special occasions for the most part, even though they may be working hard. Andrea says that people are at their best at festivals:

> At festivals it's different . . . Even those people who you may not associate with . . . they tend to be friendlier and not quite as off-ish, and they let go of those, like if they're cliquey, sometimes, they're *not* cliquey, and they're actually friendly, and they'll talk to you and they kind of forget about it. So, that's why festivals can be magical, because even people who don't get along or they've had bad past history tend to actually be really friendly and loving to each other. (Andrea, 2007)

Outside festivals, especially, there are plenty of exceptions to the ethic of agape and tolerance.

Yet in interviews, Lothlorien's role as a safe and accepting space came up more frequently than any other theme, and I regard this as a result of spontaneous experiences of communitas, of the cultivation of communitas through festivals and Bylaws, and of a more conscious adoption of agape, although these are not necessarily words used by participants. It also seems directly linked to a sense of freedom. Survey responses about people's first impressions of Lothlorien echoed this theme in interviews, including, "Wow, no judgment!" and "There is

"The Land of Misfit Toys"

nowhere else that I have ever felt so free." The ethic of acceptance encompasses a variety of lifestyles, temperaments, and social or environmental ideals. The fact that there is no single leader or single owner at Lothlorien is helpful here, since all views held by those actively involved have to be accommodated. There are a variety of religious, and nonreligious, outlooks to be accommodated too. Neo-Paganism is not the only belief system in the community, and there is no single worldview even *within* Neo-Paganism. Adjusting to the community, then, requires at least some level of tolerance.

In Carl Rogers's experience of successful therapy mentioned at the beginning of this chapter, a bottom line acceptance and appreciation of others—"unconditional positive regard"—was one of the factors that allowed for and enabled change. Within a culture with this kind of stance, participants at Lothlorien have access to personal or lifestyle changes as well as a sense of belonging. A culture of acceptance like this does not fix the individual into some reified form, nor define her, but enables growth and fluidity. At Lothlorien, then, it is easy to access a sense of community, which is further linked to the natural world, and at the same time there is also a cultural climate where people feel unusually free—free to come and go with minimal commitments, free to be creative or expressive and free to explore new sides of themselves.

To illustrate the way communitas at Lothlorien can work in practice, I will share a story that Laura told me about a difficult incident in her family life. She had brought her seventeen-year-old daughter, Jade, to Lammas in 2010, along with two of her friends, from Chicago and Bloomington. After a couple of days, Jade started to express reluctance to return home to the Chicago area, to her high school, where she had not been happy, to her Dad's house and to her normal routine. Several adults at Lothlorien talked to her about this and offered advice, trying to persuade her that it was important to hold out, to finish her last year of schooling before making a decision about her life. But as Laura said,

> It didn't really work . . . She got together with a friend and she tried to run away while we were all packing up . . . She packed up her stuff with a friend; she left the land. This is where it kind of relates back to tribe. We thought she'd gone for a walk in the woods, and when she didn't show up everybody started kind of thinking, "Well, something's kind of strange."
>
> [. . .] Braze gets up and starts looking and Conney goes out and starts looking and a whole bunch of people—Frank and Bryan and the Posthumas, and Lily got the fire department involved, and it was a big

humungous ordeal. But what I'm trying to get to, I guess, with this is the idea that had this happened to me at home it would have been a completely different situation. I wouldn't have known where to go, what to do, I would have had to do a lot of it on my own, and here I had this whole community of adults around me who were not only interested in trying to find Jade and get her back where she belonged, with the tribe, but they were there helping me out. It's just this sense of community, something has gone on with one of the children and everybody kind of steps up and steps forward, gets involved and says, "The children are important in the community, we need to take care of them, something has happened," and everybody just jumps to action.

It was hugely important, and in hindsight I look back at it and I'm thinking there was no better place, no matter what reason she did it for, there was no better place for her to try to cross that boundary and take that chance . . . In the end we had the Marshall Township fire department all out looking for her, we had two Lawrence County cops out looking for her, and Braze actually found her friend at Johnny Junctions. He's got mad tracking skills, I swear. But he was questioning people. We had some information from Jason. We had some information from Paul and Carmela, who had just recently seen them before Braze found him—found the boy. We probably didn't need to have involved all these exterior bureaucratic groups—it probably would have turned out okay. I'm glad that they were there.

Eventually a police dog finds her . . . and then Jade was released into my custody, and her friend ended up going to jail because his Mom wouldn't come get him. This was one of her friends from Bloomington . . . I think that kind of shows a . . . dichotomy—the difference between the world that we're choosing here at Lothlorien, too. His mother said, "No, he screwed up. I don't want anything to do with it. Take him off to jail." And the rest of us kind of wished that we could have hauled them both back, but we had no legal recourse.

Jade was encouraged to apologize to her younger sister and to the friend who had come with her from Chicago, both of whom had been worried. Then a group of people whom she knew well sat with her to talk about what had happened. Laura continued:

It was Scott Martin, who is my ex-boyfriend, and Braze, and a couple of other adults, and Jade, and her friend, and I, and we're sitting down in Healers' Circle and we're just talking with her after the fact, trying to

"The Land of Misfit Toys"

figure out what was going through her head. And there was no scream-ing, there was no yelling, there was no judging and throwing things and telling her she was stupid. She had a group of adults around her trying to talk to her. Her friend didn't get that benefit. That's a really huge example . . . And I think that happens on a much less dramatic level all the time.

The support she received in response to this incident also helped Laura to overcome some anxiety she had felt about communicating with Jade's father:

I came home on Monday and I worked, and I dropped Emmy off at home after camp, and I drove straight out to the town he lives in and I sent him a message on his phone: ". . . I could really use a friend and your thoughts, would you like to meet me for coffee?" and we sat down and we had a conversation like we hadn't had in years. And I think that encouraged him to step up more and talk to Jade himself. So weird things happen and I feel like I've matured and been able to actually deal with people on a more respectful level without being afraid so much. That's kind of a big deal for me. And part of it, I know, is this little person in the back of my head, this little voice that goes, "OK, you can come back home to the scary mundane world but there's a group of people who are out there, who care about you, who you can be in con-tact with, and who will support you and listen to you." Once again, kind of important. (Laura, 2010)

On the one hand this description shows a lot of community bonding and taking on of others' burdens—a "we" feeling among participants. It shows a recognition among many community members that the care involved, the work involved, in looking after children and teenagers is important and requires sup-port. On the other hand this bonding depends to some extent on respect for others' boundaries. Nobody takes overall charge and no one group or category of adults has more say than another. While it is understood that Jade, a minor, cannot be allowed to run away, there is advice rather than shaming or punish-ment for her. And the fact that Laura feels she can be listened to—in other words, that she can express herself freely without being judged—is part of what enhances her feeling of connectedness and confidence. It struck me throughout the interviews that community bonding and freedom were often juxtaposed. In Laura's narrative, as in many of the other interviews quoted throughout this chapter, communitas and individualism—in the sense of respect for individual autonomy—are not seen to be in conflict but as mutually supportive.

An Unreal Estate

This juxtaposition contradicts some recent writing in the social sciences on communitarianism. Clifford Christians, for example, quotes a communitarian point of view as arguing that "The total opposite of an ethics of individual autonomy is universal human solidarity . . . The primal sacredness of all, without exception, is the heart of the moral order" (2008: 206). I have no quarrel at all with the second of these sentences. (Nor, I suspect, would most advocates of individual rights.) Yet human solidarity, or group rights in Lothlorien's case, would be an empty phrase without recognition and respect for the choices and voices of each of its individuals. It is *because* it is acceptable to be, through choice or biology, a gay person, an atheist, Pagan, or Christian, a nudist, a woman, an environmentalist, a member of an ethnic minority, an elder, a polyamorist . . . rather than simply an "elf," as Lothlorien participants often call themselves, that people tend to feel such strong connections there. It is because people are free to come and go and because they feel free to make a range of lifestyle choices with a minimum of rules that they develop such deep loyalty to the place and people—to the extent that the land and festivals can be maintained entirely by volunteers. It is because they feel free that they can both take on each others' burdens at times and open up to be influenced by one another and to change. This is not to say that people do not feel this kind of loyalty and connection with less freedom or within more hierarchical social groups; clearly they often do. Submission to authority or a set of rules can be, in some cases, both emotionally fulfilling and a choice.[8] It *is* to say, however, that individual autonomy and solidarity can not only coexist but, at Lothlorien at least, seem to enhance one another.

From some points of view, the protection of individual freedom at Lothlorien might seem to associate it, place it within, a Euro-American modernist and free-market ideology. "Individualism" and "freedom" are terms that have often been muddled and muddied. They have been used by the political right, misleadingly, I would argue, as rallying cries for freedom from restrictions on corporations or even (in the United States) "freedom" from basic services like accessible health care or equitable education. Meanwhile on the left, scholars such as John Gray and Christians have come to regard individualism and even "human rights" as suspect—more attempted Western impositions on the rest of the world, masks for power. This too I see as misleading. Because of both these sets of associations, it is essential to separate out the idea of the kind of individual autonomy that is valued at Lothlorien (and elsewhere) from other current uses of this ideal.

On the one hand, as I argued in chapter 4, a free-market, social contract understanding offers inadequate explanations of decision making at Lothlorien

"The Land of Misfit Toys"

and elsewhere. Lothlorien is collectively owned, runs on volunteer labor and does not fit well into classical economic explanations. But in its descriptions of mainstream contexts, the social contract, free-market view, too, is often blinkered and partial. It tends to ignore the social realities in which many marginalized groups live, particularly those without easy access to resources, educational, economic, or otherwise, and those involved in the often invisible and unpaid work of caring. Martha Nussbaum points out, in *Frontiers of Justice* (2006), that since "work" after the Industrial Revolution has been defined in a narrow and specific way, the work of caring for people within (extended or nuclear) families and the work of caring for land and domestic spaces—beyond commercial purposes like tourism and food or lumber production—are erased from the picture, and those engaged in such activities, when they are visible at all, have hence come to look like "dependents" rather than like people making an essential social contribution. Meanwhile, those who require care—the very young, the very old, the sick, and those who have disabilities (in other words all of us at various stages of our lives)—are also rendered invisible in a classical social contract model.

Given these social contexts, it is not accidental that "individualism" as presented and mythologized in the popular media is often represented by a white, able-bodied male—the frontier cowboy or rogue policeman. He is someone who has both ready access to paid work and freedom from the work and time involved in caring for children or elders or caring for living spaces among family and friends. And, as in this case, while the networks of care that back up an individual are often invisible, so the network of life forms and environmental factors within which humans live also tend to be increasingly invisible or taken for granted, as most of us move, by necessity, from building to vehicle to building, and gather our information about the world through electronic screens or through print on paper. But these blind spots are neither inevitable nor essentially tied to the idea of individual freedom. Meaningful respect for autonomy can and should incorporate a recognition of the need for care as essential human work, a recognition of, and attempt to address, unequal access to resources, and a recognition of environmental contexts.

Western ideals of individualism, then, often render invisible our dependence on human and natural networks, and there is value in questioning and modifying oversimplified assumptions about what defines a person. However, arguments defining the individual as a (suspect) Western construct and the group, group rights, and group discourses as *primary* over the individual seem overstated. First, there are numerous examples of non-European societies (see for example Mann 2005 and Samson 2003, as well as other examples cited

An Unreal Estate

in chapter 8), which have great respect for individual autonomy, and many critiques of European and Euro-American societies are based precisely *on* the curtailment of individual freedom within them and on the ways this curtailment is disguised through terms such as "madness" (Foucault 1982). Second, relationships—in any but the most abstract, formal sense—presuppose agency. At Lothlorien this is especially clear since, in contrast to family membership, participants make a choice to be involved there. Lothlorien participants, like most human beings, also go and back and forth between different social contexts; in their case between the ElvinHOME community—with its clusters of alternative discourses like environmentalism and Paganism—and the mainstream world(s)—where many work or study or participate with families and friends. Thus each person is a part of several groups and networks rather than one, membership in any is temporary rather than permanent, and none of these groups have fixed boundaries.

Further, to take any network or group as primary over its individual members may also mask an inner hierarchy and silencing, even (perhaps especially) on the level of family. In pre-Revolutionary France, for example, the family was considered a singular entity, a sovereignty in miniature. Within this sovereignty the husband and father had a legal right to demand obedience from his wife and children. If he had enough money to pay for their keep there, and if they displeased him enough, he could have them confined to a convent or monastery indefinitely (Traer 1980). Some forms of free-market advocacy muddy the concept of autonomy in a similar way, by treating businesses and corporations as though they themselves were individuals, with "needs" of their own for unchecked expression, regardless of the enormous differentials in power and resources within them, and regardless of the fact that the vast majority of the people working for such corporations have no say in decision making. Entrenched inequalities like this tend to be overlooked when a community, culture, village, religion, family, or corporation is prioritized over its individuals, or when the whole concept of individuality is dismissed or blurred. The result is often a detrimental effect on the lives of the least powerful (Appiah 2005: 260.)

Some authors, notably Michel Foucault (1982), take the communitarian argument a step further than others, denying the reality of an essential subject or individual altogether. This creates a scenario where any social critique or assessment becomes meaningless. It is not possible to talk about social bodies, relationships, communities, *or* power without implying the existence of some kind of individual, at least in the sense of a locus of experience and intention. We each have a privileged access to our own sensations, emotions, perceptions, and desires that we could never have to anybody else's, and these experiences

"The Land of Misfit Toys"

and desires, while not fixed or static, must be assumed in any critique or un-masking of power, any concept at all of justice, solidarity, or human sacredness, or any rationale for social action. Individual agency and individual experience are implied in all of these.

The individual in this context of creative and personal freedom at Lothlo-rien is not regarded as a reified entity, but has access to a range of identities. I found people very reluctant to be pigeonholed, as in comments by Conney, Bonedaddy, Braze, Andrea, and others. Andrea's statement, "I'm not really anything," and Conney's "I tend to run from labels," are explicit examples. It is possible to acknowledge a self, and create the conditions for its individual freedom, without necessarily fixing or objectifying it and without denying re-lationships with, reliance on, or influences from others. The culture of accep-tance at Lothlorien tends to support people's senses of selves as fluid entities, free to change. Both individuals and social bodies (like the community itself) are continually contracting, expanding, and reconfiguring themselves as they interact with one another and the land.

The sense of "we" as well as "I," of "tribe" and belonging and "chosen fam-ily," is clear in the extraordinary amount of volunteer work some people are willing to do and in some common elements of the collective vision. This un-derlying ideal of acceptance—in its strong forms agape or communitas, and in its weaker forms tolerance—is complemented and sometimes reinforced by other forms of relationship, like philia, which is expressed through friendship and "chosen family," and eros (expressed through a variety of orientations). And it also aims to extend beyond the human community to nature: plants, animals, the elements.

All the forms of love or cooperation I have been discussing are reinforced at Lothlorien by rituals—rituals that make families, rituals that link people to the natural world, and rituals that add meaning to collective drumming and dancing around the central fire in the Thunder Dome. Rituals, then, will be the topic of the next chapter.

An Unreal Estate

A shrine set up in the Dome for Elf Fest 2008.

Courtesy of Christine Walsh-Newton

6

"Something Mystical and Fine"
Reimagining Ritual and Spiritual Experience

Something's going on in the universe; I don't know what it is.
I'm not going to say I can put a name on it, a face on it, or describe it.
Something's going on, don't know what it is; a beautiful thing.

Paul F., 2009

In a recent conversation, Scott made a distinction between "high drama" and "low drama" in human life, adding that he thought drama as a whole had an undeservedly bad name. As examples of high drama he referred to childbirth, first love, first humiliation, loss, and death. Ritual, he said, whether or not it is directly religious, reinforces high drama. Based on his associations with Lothlorien since the mid-1990s, he considered the group experiences of ritual there to have been vital to the community. At Lothlorien, ritual is one of the ways the community defines itself as a whole and distinguishes itself from the outside world. It is a formalized way to link participants to each other, to the natural world, and sometimes to a world of magic, myth, and fairy tales. It offers a different (but not necessarily competing) set of traditions both to mainstream Christianity and to more commercial celebrations. These traditions are drawn on creatively, and usually with a dose of humor. They use a lot of improvisation, drawing on imagery from a variety of sources.

I have already noted that, in conversations and interviews, Lothlorien members' religious definitions of themselves were varied and often idiosyncratic, rarely involving an exclusive faith. This also applied to the survey[1] participants who responded to the item "Religious affiliation/leanings, if any." A few described themselves as Pagans, about the same number called themselves open-minded Christians, and more made ambiguous entries such as "lots," "none," or "agnostic yet also personally devoted." If the community is defined as religious, then, it is not religious in a faith-based sense nor in any homogenous sense. But ritual is a core part of festival experience and of what draws people to the land.

In this chapter I shall describe a few of the rituals that I have participated in at Lothlorien. Some of these will relate to seasonal cycles, others to life transitions. I shall also look at some of the challenges of being openly Neo-Pagan in the United States. Finally, I will discuss the emphasis on experience rather than faith in spiritual life at Lothlorien. Several of the experiences that participants describe may seem familiar, while a couple of them are far out of the ordinary. Usually spiritual experiences were described to me by participants as personal and particular, rather than as forming part of a fixed metaphysical worldview that could (or should) be applied to other people.

Festivals, Rituals, and "Faerie Time"

One day Tuna and Braze put a sundial in the garden. At first there was an effort to get it facing in the right direction. After a while, though, Tuna said, "It doesn't matter, it's on Faerie time." I have heard this phrase used frequently to describe a different sense of time at Lothlorien. It is an aspect of being both away from *and* closer to "real life" there, away from the need for clocks and measurements, away from the "grid," but closer to natural time cycles. The phrase also refers to a sense of being in a place that is magical. And finally there is a humorous self-reference in the phrase. Certainly nothing happens very punctually. "Half past dark" or "dark-thirty" are other popular expressions—common beginning times for evening events.

The wider movement of Neo-Paganism seeks to restore a sense of time that honors the natural world and brings humans into a closer relationship with it. Hence, during the passage of a year, festivals and sometimes rituals at Lothlorien mark the seasons and the positions of the earth, moon, and sun. Stoeltje notes that many festivals around the world—not only Neo-Pagan festivals —are likely to follow the lunar or solar calendar, which predates the modern calendar. This has the effect of taking the festival celebration outside the realm of human agency: "Festival yokes the social group to this cyclic force, establishing contact with the cosmos and the eternal processes of time" (Stoeltje 1992: 268).

The Solstices—the longest and shortest days of the year—the Equinoxes, and the "Cross Quarter days" are celebrated, along with any known remnants of traditions that have been associated with these days. Thus in a Neo-Pagan

An Unreal Estate

year the Winter Solstice, which takes place around December 21, is celebrated as Yule (or the Long Night). The day between Yule and the Spring Equinox, a Cross Quarter day around February 1, is celebrated (or at least marked) as Imbolc or Candlemas or Saint Brigid's Day. The Spring Equinox, around March 21, is observed as Ostara (an Anglo-Saxon word from which Easter derives). The day between Ostara and the Summer Solstice, celebrated around May 1, is called Beltane, a Gaelic or Celtic word. Between the Summer Solstice (roughly June 21) and the Autumn Equinox (or Mabon) is Lammas or Lughnasad, around August 1. And between the Autumn Equinox and Yule is Samhain, or Hallowe'en. The four Cross Quarter days are Celtic and relate to Celtic festivals around those dates, such as May Day and Hallowe'en. The four Quarter days, the Solstices and Equinoxes, relate to German festivals and are also celebrated in many other cultures. Wicca originally began by celebrating only the Cross Quarter days and added in the Quarter days to have more opportunities for celebrations (Hutton 1999.) Collectively, these eight days are known as Sabbats. Vestiges of many of them (for example, Easter and Christmas) also remain in Christianity.

Michael relates the flow of life at Lothlorien, and its celebrations, to the rhythm of a traditional rural year:

> In the late part of winter to spring we start getting together and talking about projects, things we want to do, and who's going to do this and who's going to do that, as evidenced by that huge board that Jef did.[2] And that energy is so good coming out of winter, because you've got all those dreams and you've planted your seeds and you're kind of focusing on it; and then we get into spring and we work our butts off out here, and it's all in preparation to do the spring fest . . .
>
> On a magical level we really do pay attention to it. In spring you're planting, summer you're nurturing, and in the fall you're harvesting, and we sit and we eat and we feast and we spend time with one another and then comes winter and people go away. (Michael, 2006)

Currently the Lothlorien calendar of festivals and events is pragmatic as well as traditional. Elf Fest in May, the festival that attracts the largest number of visitors, falls on Memorial Day weekend, which is one of the more convenient times of year for people to get away from work. Beltane, the traditional date for a May festival, at the beginning of the month, always attracts a few extra visitors, who may celebrate around the Maypole or in the Thunder Dome, but is not as practical a date for most people. The other large festival—Wild Magick Gathering—is held around the time of the Autumn Equinox. Witches' Ball, which is

"Something Mystical and Fine"

related to Samhain, is held the weekend before the mainstream Hallowe'en to let people celebrate the other date with their families as well.

My first ritual that related to the wheel of the year, in 2006, was at Beltane, which is associated with springtime and fertility. About two hours after its pre-arranged beginning time, Jef announced a Maypole dance. I walked over to Lightning Shrine with Andy and Julie and sat on the grass with them and with Laura, who was already there, until it began. Twenty or so people were already grouped around the Maypole, with ten more around the edges. There were two or three men in Celtic clothes—capes or sarongs decorated with Celtic knots—and one wearing horns on his head. A couple of women wore velvet capes. Other women and men wore jeans and T-shirts. We all waited for Scott to come with his drum. Once he arrived and started a rhythm, Jef divided us into twos, back to back, so that half of us would be going in each direction. Each person took a piece of wool—on this occasion the colors were white or green—and circled around the pole, weaving alternately over and under the people we passed by until the strands became too short. There was a happy and also disorganized feel to the event. Some people danced or skipped their way around. By the time we finished, the Maypole was beautifully wrapped in green and white.

Maypole decoration and Maypole dancing have a long history in Sweden, Britain, Finland, Germany, and the Czech Republic, as well as other Western European countries. It is probably a pre-Christian practice and certainly a non-Christian one. Protestant authorities tended to view it warily and it was sporadically banned in parts of England. But the Cromwell government in the mid-1600s took this too far, banning it altogether throughout the nation along with most forms of dancing, music, and theater. When Cromwell was executed and Charles II was brought to the throne, the Maypole dance became one of the symbols of freedom from the Cromwell regime. The custom was revived enthusiastically, ironically regenerated by its former banned status. In the 1660s, Maypoles were erected at every crossing in London. In the nineteenth century, ribbon dances were developed as an addition to the Maypole tradition, like the dance described above.

The celebration continued on that Beltane evening with a fire and drumming at the Dome. On this occasion, Sarah had been clearing all the moldy or otherwise unusable books out of the library, so Chris threw them into the flames at intervals, with an ironic flourish, in a mock book burning. Later a man named Bill with a cape and headband sang a humorous song to the guitar about being a Pagan, to the tune of *I'm Proud to be an Okie from Muskogee*. It is called *Redneck Pagan,* and its refrain is as follows:

An Unreal Estate

The Maypole.

Courtesy of Christine Walsh-Newton

I think organized religion is just fine in its place
But you can keep all your opinions to yourself
Don't tell me my beliefs are wrong, and throw yours in my face
I go to the First Eclectic Paganism Church of God and Goddess Worship
And I believe in faeries, trolls, and elves . . . and dragons and gargoyles
   and frogs
And I'm proud to be a witch from West Virginia.

(Bill Reel)

Later in May—specifically the days before and after Memorial Day week-end—comes Elf Fest, which is the biggest and longest of the festivals, and in 2006 a few volunteers came to put in work hours as a barter for their festival fees, or just in order to help out. We had a Council meeting before it, with people volunteering for various tasks, but the mechanisms for many of the basics—collecting registration money, arranging parking, buying food—have fallen more or less into place over the years owing to the hard work of Eldars, Stewards and other volunteers. Festivals are a collective effort. People take on particular tasks, but those who have experience in running the festivals take on many other responsibilities as the need arises. Since I was unfamiliar with much of the background work that goes into Elf Fest's planning, it seemed miraculous to me that a festival for almost four hundred people could be pulled off with as little planning as I actually saw.

For camping and the small festivals and celebrations, people bring their own food, but at the two large festivals, Elf Fest and Wild Magick, breakfast and supper are cooked and served in the Long Hall. These are a couple of the only occasions where there is a dress code, but it is minimal. A sign reads "No sarong, no service." Cooking and clean up are two of the possible barter jobs that can be done in exchange for festival admission. The meals are inexpensive; they include sausages, eggs, pancakes, and home fries for breakfast, and burgers and assorted vegetables for the evening meal (along with other options, varying by the day). The kitchen barely breaks even, so meals are a service more than a business proposition. Children make up the wait staff, earning money, through tips, that they often spend at the vendors' stalls.

In some years, festival visitors complement the meals in the Long Hall by selling their own home-made meals or snacks. In 2006 and 2007, there was food for sale all day long at a vendor's stall called Jake's Greasy Spoon. This included donuts, fries, hot dogs, burgers, homemade sandwiches, coffee, and sodas. In 2009 and 2010, Paul N. (who was mentioned at the beginning of chapter 5) sold tea, coffee, and inexpensive food, and the campsite he shared with his friends was temporarily renamed Chez Paul.

An Unreal Estate

Vendors are concentrated in an area of Avalon called Merchantsville, on the south side of the camping circle, but if there are a large number of them they may spread all the way around. Some sell clothing—including Renaissance, bohemian, and Celtic styles—Pagan-themed and non–Pagan-themed jewelry, herbs, plants, candles, and ritual paraphernalia, cards, music, books (including lots of science fiction), ornaments, pipes, and snacks among other items. Many of the goods are handmade, and most are cheap. Some vendors follow a festival circuit and may also go to Renaissance fairs and events held by the Society for Creative Anachronism or other Pagan festivals. Others come only to Lothlorien.

In late May in Southern Indiana the weather tends to lurch from coolness and rain to heat and back unpredictably. In 2006 Elf Fest was very hot in the last couple of days. In other years it has had torrential rain. (One year's festival was nicknamed Aqua Fest because of this.) The festival is five or six days long, but merchants come before it starts to set up their tents, which is often an elaborate business.

The shrines receive more care than usual at festival times, especially in the Dome, and the elements—fire, water, air, and earth—are given prominence, as are mirrors. As mentioned in chapters 3 and 4, humor often plays into shrines, rituals, artifacts, and ornaments. The "book burning" and comic song, for example, went along with the more serious, trance-like atmosphere of drumming and firelight. As at the Maypole dance, ritual tends to involve playfulness.

Stoeltje describes festivals as occasions where group identity and heritage are expressed and reinforced (1992: 261). At Lothlorien, the cultural identities represented through festival clothing are an eclectic mix of Goth, Celtic, fairy tale, pirate, and hippie styles. Men and women both frequently wear sarongs and show tattoos and piercings. Celtic, Pagan, Norse, or Caballic symbolism are all represented among the tattoos, on jewelry, and in textile patterns. As noted in chapter 5, clothing tends toward femininity rather than masculinity, at least relative to mainstream culture. In cases where people dress up, at the Dome, for example, on Friday or Saturday nights, there are sometimes references to fairy tales—clothing reminiscent of witches, wizards, fairies, elves, or gnomes. Some men wear small horns on their heads as symbols of the Horned God. Some women or men dress elaborately, in long skirts and capes. Chris was apparently once painted green as a representation of the Green Man in a ritual designed by Terry. The tendency for most people at most festival times, however, is just as often to dress "down" as "up." Fewer clothes than normal are worn, depending on the weather. A few people (a tiny minority) go without clothes altogether. Men (frequently) and women (occasionally) go topless. Perhaps it is because some Neo-Pagans feel ridiculed, suspect, or weird in the outside world that they drop masks and extra clothes when they come to Lothlorien rather than add them.

It is difficult for me to find apt summarizing words for the group identities or group heritages expressed among all these images at festivals. "Pagan" is a possibility, because it is such a broad term. European themes from folk literature and ceremonial magic are others. References to various different periods in history blend with contemporary countercultural markers, like the piercings and tattoos. Pirate symbolism combines these two. Pirates are beyond the law. "It's pirate" is a phrase I have heard on several occasions by volunteers, talking of any aspect of the informal culture that is beyond the jurisdiction of the Council or other authorities. The Trollbar was an example of something referred to as "pirate." The implication was that it should be left alone.

Some of my other lasting impressions of the first Elf Fest I attended were of crowds, heat, mud, mosquitoes, exhaustion, and allergies. There was a smell of wood smoke and of food cooking. We did another Maypole ritual, with more people than the first time, more colors among the strands of wool and more chaos (partly contributed by myself and my dance partner, Haven, who was three years old at the time). There were musical performances on Friday and Saturday. In 2006 these were mostly in a folk roots style, with ballads. In 2007 a heavy metal Viking rock band, called Black Stone Ritual and fronted by a long time Lothlorien sponsor named Chucky, played in Lightning Shrine, raising the energy level and persuading some elves to get up and dance. Also there were a few workshops—on wild plants, by Lisa, on Celtic Wicca, and on belly dancing.

Nighttime is the core of festivals, and a time when some people experience shifts in consciousness:

> What we do on the festival field . . . it's wild magic for real, you know.
> The experience of a festival—you can go to a festival and have many
> different experiences. But there's this time, this harmonic chord that
> strikes the collective consciousness of enough people at a festival and at
> night that can create a moment where it is like Faerie. (Braze, 2006)

Activities at the Thunder Dome begin after dark, usually with a collective ritual, sometimes led by Jef, sometimes Vic, sometimes Lisa, sometimes Andrea and Katina, sometimes (recently) PJ, and sometimes others. At Wild Magick in 2008, for example, Andrea constructed a seven-foot wax tree to burn in the central fire pit, with leaves made of paper colored yellow and red—Fall colors—on which festival visitors had written down things that they wanted

PJ and friends working on a sand mandala
for Summer Solstice Reunion 2009.
Courtesy of Scott Martin

to be free of in the coming year. The tree was burned as about ten drummers began establishing a rhythm. The first dancers, about five men and five
women, wore antlers or autumn wreaths on their heads respectively. After a
few minutes the rest of the two hundred or so people in the Dome joined in
the dancing. Bread and water were passed around to all participants along
with the phrases "May you never hunger" and "May you never thirst." The
sharing of harvest foods was thus symbolically acknowledged, along with the
arrival of a new season. Another ritual, at Elf Fest in 2010, planned by Cece
and Brooks with help from Andrea, aimed to connect people with the cosmos,
with beautiful handmade planets and stars circling around the central fire,
which represented the sun.

In the past, especially before 1996 when many of the trolls left, rituals were
often strikingly theatrical. Terry and PJ were two of the key creators. Brooks
described PJ as the "resident wise woman" of the early 1990s (her role in his
experience of "Brigadoon" was noted in the last chapter). At the Summer Sol-

"Something Mystical and Fine"

Another (more mysterious) sand mandala, in blue and green,
designed by PJ for Summer Solstice in 2010.
Courtesy of Scott Martin

stices in 2009 and 2010, I had a chance to experience rituals that she and a
few other former trolls had designed. On both occasions they made huge sand
mandalas in the Thunder Dome. The first was in the shape of a lotus in blue,
white, green, lavender, and pink colors, and the stones around the edge of the
circle were also decorated with small white lotuses. Once the ritual was under
way, four women carried in giant lotus petals and opened and closed them in
unison. The second sand mandala was more mysterious, with abstract swirls of
blue on green and smaller circles within circles in green and blue and pink.
At the first ritual, there were invocations to the four directions and acknowl-
edgement of many spiritual paths around the globe; at the second there was a
suggestion to the people present to imagine their future selves looking in on
their present selves. Then the mandalas were danced away.

The definition of "ritual" in the context of Lothlorien is broad and not always
religious in any recognizable sense. The children and teenagers have often created wonderful, spooky, "Haunted Walks" through the woods at Witches' Ball.

An Unreal Estate

At Witches' Ball in 2006, Lily, Lilith, Jake and Owen, Chris's daughter Caitlin, Tuna's son Jon, and others had marked out a path with blood-spattered lanterns and gruesome sights. At intervals Owen (in a black mask) would pull someone from the line and they would scream in a blood-curdling way. Lily and Caitlin had staged a scene along the way in which Caitlin lay on a platform covered in blood (ketchup) and intestines (spaghetti) and Lily, with a face also covered in ketchup, pretended to be eating Caitlin's insides. It looked quite gruesome.

At Witches' Ball in 2009, there were hay rides, with horses, for the children and, later, two candy-filled piñatas made by Andrea. A table covered in black was set up in the Long Hall with a huge mummy, made by Vic and Andrea, lying on the top in the center. The room was decorated with pumpkins. There was a feast, after which Jason and Andrea set up a disco with green lights, a smoke machine, a disco ball, and a fire in the fireplace. People danced until midnight. At this point the mummy was carried down to the Dome to be burned with mock ceremony. At the last minute suggestions were called out for its name. "Toot an' Common" was one possibility, but "Bubba Ho-Tep"[3] was the final decision.

Neo-Paganism, Social Ostracism, and the Law

Neo-Pagan religions have not always been protected by the law in the United States in practice, although Wicca was legally recognized as a religion in 1985. At least two interview subjects affiliated with Lothlorien told me that they had had their Pagan associations used against them in courts of law—in divorce cases. Along with formal difficulties with the law, misinformation and prejudice about Neo-Paganism have been rife on an informal level in the United States and Europe. Braze describes being a Neo-Pagan as a high schooler in the 1980s:

> It was still very underground, very secret, very openly persecuted. You wore your pentacle on the inside of your shirt, you didn't talk about it. The groups were very small, they were very isolated and they were very close. (Braze, 2006)

And Teal describes a working experience:

> I remember when I took the first job I had, well, mind you, I was working in Burger King . . . and I had one girl that I was talking to about it and she seemed to be really excited about [Neo-Paganism], "Ah, that's interesting!" And I brought a book to work and I had it back in the coat

"Something Mystical and Fine"

room . . . and one of the bosses made me take it and put it back in my car. She was like, "We won't have that shit in here!" And in fact after that I worked from a different shift because she refused to work with me. (Teal, 2007)

Ronald Hutton often finds himself in the position, as an "expert" on Neo-Paganism in Britain, of dealing with the difficulties that arise from misinformation:

> Many Pagans, and especially witches, faced with a potential loss of homes, jobs or custody of children because of prejudices against their religion, called on me . . . More often, however, the call came from the other side, from members of the police forces, the caring services, the prison service, the hospital service, local government bodies, head teachers, school governors or the legal profession, and employers and landlords or landladies . . . In many cases the prejudices I was being asked to dispel, and the anxieties I was being asked to allay, were so ill-founded and so dangerous that the value of the exercise seemed beyond doubt. (Hutton 2003: 292)

Even when mainstream wariness of Neo-Paganism is not overt or legally damaging, it can lead to practitioners being ostracized or treated with suspicion. As an African American Pagan living in a small Indiana town, Janet has learned to be cautious about expressing her views:

> Outside of here I've learned to be more reserved, because sometimes the more people get to know about you the more they can use things against you. Some people are like that, right? I try to be careful who I'm hanging out with simply because of that reason. I don't want to go through all that . . . It is especially noticeable in small towns because people have less to do . . . People are more close-knit in smaller communities and a lot of times they don't . . . share your religious views . . . So you kind of learn to keep some of your religious stuff guarded because you don't want to offend, you don't want to cause a ruckus or anything . . . especially if you're different you learn that. (Janet, 2009)

More than half of the regular Lothlorien participants live in Bloomington or Indianapolis or Chicago rather than in Lawrence County itself—towns that are more tolerant, or have pockets of tolerance, of diverse religious practice. Tolerance of Neo-Paganism has also increased over the last three decades. Yet still there is a level of discomfort in public expressions that fall outside of the Judeo-Christian religions. Vic says that this is something she values about having access to a separate space:

There can be rites of passage, weddings . . . Out here in Mundania, sure, there's a park, but you're going to get people staring and open to remarks, but [Lothlorien] is a space that you can go and do that and not have to even worry about it. (Vic, 2006)

As a result not just of the contrast—for example in clothing, ritual, environmental ideals, and in some cases sexual mores—but of the predominance and "common sense" certainty of the former set of values and the lack of accurate information about the latter, Neo-Pagans have in many cases experienced ostracism, threats, suspicion, ridicule, and legal problems. At the least they have usually become accustomed to being thought of as strange when being open about their religious affiliation. Lilith, Vic and Jef's daughter, grew up in Ohio and learned at a very young age to keep her family's Neo-Pagan traditions hidden:

I've been doing Pagan-y type celebrations since I was little. Since I was tiny, tiny. I've been doing rituals with my parents, celebrating Samhain and Yule and the Solstice. We used to do it annually, just my family . . . I want to get back into it. I guess it's a form of meditation, if you want to look at it that way. Or therapy . . . That's my religion. I call myself Pagan. I didn't tell anybody growing up. (Lilith, 2009)

In Bloomington at the age of ten, Lilith had some of her first experiences of feeling free to talk about her practices in a public setting. She visited the alternative school where the Freese-Posthuma children were studying. A girl approached Lily (the third child in the Freese-Posthuma family) and said, "Sorry I missed the ritual." Lilith was amazed:

Oh my God, she talked about that in school! That's the coolest thing I've ever seen! And them being completely okay . . . It caught me off guard . . . "I'm allowed to say I'm a Pagan." I remember saying the Pledge of Allegiance in school every day and I would skip the word "God" or say "in Goddess we trust" when I was little. [In third grade] something slipped out . . . I told a kid I had magic or was magic. They made fun of it. [It felt bad] knowing they're making fun of exactly what my parents and I believed.

I'm pretty sure my grandmother, my other family, realize we don't really believe in God, but they definitely don't really understand what we believe, what we practice. We didn't really have giant Pentagrams or anything like that. We just really kept it to ourselves because I know that some people would think outrageous things.

"Something Mystical and Fine"

When I came to Lothlorien there were so many people. There were so many people dancing around the fire you couldn't even squeeze in . . . Lothlorien made my personal world a thousand times better because there were so many people I could talk to about rituals. (Lilith, 2009)

One of the reasons, then, that Lothlorien's founders wanted to find their own land was, like many of the communities described in chapter 2, to escape from distrust and misinterpretation, mainly because of their Neo-Pagan associations, although, as noted above, not all participants are Pagans. This distrust need not necessarily be overt or directly hostile, but the festival goers and volunteers still express a sense of relief at the chance to be in a place where they can express their religious identity without being in a small minority, and without, as Jef puts it

being thought of as a weirdo, or put down, or told you can't do it here. That was something I was impressed with as a camper; there is no one way, and nobody was saying there was one way to believe. (Jef, 2006)

Four Weddings, a "Wiccaning," and a Funeral

Ritual does not just passively reflect social relations but actively enacts, alters, creates, enhances, and negotiates them. Stoeltje (1996) points out that rituals are often conservative—that is they are literally ways to conserve social relationships. To illustrate this, as well as convey something of the feel of smaller rituals at Lothlorien, I shall briefly describe a few rituals I attended at Lothlorien which were linked to various stages in the life cycle and which served to shore up and expand family and "chosen family" connections on the land.

Choosing "Fairy Godparents"

One evening at Elf Fest in 2007, I was wandering toward the drumming in Thunder Dome and saw a large group of people near the turning for Heart Tree Circle. I was not sure whether this was an accidental grouping or whether something was happening there. It was dark, with small candles lighting the pathways, and a little difficult at first to distinguish who was in the crowd. Glacier, who was at the back, turned to me and asked, "Do you want to be a fairy godparent?" I had no idea what he was talking about but said "Yes" anyway.

The group moved down the short path to Heart Tree Circle, a cleared space surrounded by trees and with a small group of trees and a shrine at its center.

An Unreal Estate

We stood in a circle. There were perhaps twenty people. Jef began to lead a ritual. He stood next to a young couple with a newborn baby. The parents were called Christofer (Tofer for short) and Angie, and the baby's name was Jamison.

Jef said, "We're going to make a birthday cake." He had a bag of candles. He gave the bag to the couple and asked them to pick out thirteen godparents and to give each one a candle. When they were given their candles they were to make wishes for the baby. Angie held Jamison while Tofer went around picking out people. Tofer is an extroverted, cheerful young man with long hair and abundant tattoos. He handed short candles to the older people, long ones to the younger people (because they were going to be around longer.) He was joking with everyone as he did this.

Each time Tofer picked a godparent he said something about the role that person would play in Jamison's life. For example, when he came to Chris, he said that he would be someone to say, "Shut up and listen!" When he gave candles to Lyn and Glacier, who were expecting their own baby at that time, he talked about their child growing up to play with Jamison. To Conney, he said that she would be the one to say, "Come on in, the door's open," and he said that Michael would be the one to let the child sit by him at the computer and talk to him. Tofer said that Vic would be the person who would tell Jamison, "Don't worry, just come to the festival and we'll work it out." There was good natured laughter after many of these comments, laughter about the familiar words to be heard from familiar people.

Each of those chosen went to touch the baby and make their wish. Many of them did this silently. One of them, Rod, made some affectionate comments to the whole family, telling them how much he loved them.

When all thirteen godparents had been picked, Jef said, "This is a birthday cake, so we're going to blow out the candles now and think of our wishes for the baby." Then the candles were blown out and the ceremony was over.

In some aspects—the consolidation of community responsibility for a child, for instance—this ceremony was similar to a Christian baptism. It was not a formal or fixed gateway into a religious path, however. There were a lot of jokes and also a lot of affection among this group of people, who had known each other for years. And as far as I know, Jef made up the ritual himself, although elements of it came from fairy tales, like the references to "fairy godparents," and from Wicca. In fact, this kind of ceremony is often called a "wiccaning." The number thirteen is significant for several different reasons. It is the number of moons in a year and it is (in Wiccan ideology) the ideal number of members of a coven. The birthday cake is a more modern reference point. Jef and Vic both tend to

"Something Mystical and Fine"

mix modern and mundane symbols into their rituals. These two also tend to play down their own leadership. Tofer was the one who got the chance to do most of the talking and joking in this ceremony, while Jef played the role of facilitator.

Handfastings and Weddings

Coincidentally, Janet has been responsible for pulling me into three of the "handfastings," or Pagan weddings, I have attended, which are also ways of making and cementing community and families. Janet is a delightful, kind lady whose ebullience is infectious. I did not know the people involved in the first ceremony—in April 2006—and was still rather unsure about my role at Lothlorien and whether to go in to Radiance Hall. I said, "I haven't been invited," and, even though she had known me less than an hour, she replied, "I'm inviting you." Nobody seemed to mind. In fact I was not sure whether most of us in the room were there by chance or by design. Julie, Andy, Janet, and I were present, and a young man called Danny, who had come to volunteer in the garden, and who did in fact know one of the men to be married. A few members of the Freese-Posthuma family were there as "real" guests, as was an elderly man, perhaps a grandparent of one of the spouses-to-be.

This ceremony was for two very young couples (one already with a baby) dressed in beautiful, homemade medieval clothes. One young woman, the one with the baby, was wearing a long black dress with a headband and no make-up. Her fiancé wore a flowing white collarless shirt with long black leather cuffs or armbands and baggy black pants. The other young man wore an embroidered blue vest over a white shirt and pants. His fiancée wore a long white dress, partly satin. These two wandered in and out of the hall. The mother of one of the young men was to conduct the ceremony. She told me she had made the clothes for the young people herself. She was dressed in a blue velvet cape and blue clothes.

Once both couples were settled in the hall, the lady in the blue cape said that anyone who wanted to be in the circle should move forward. She added that the purpose of the circle is to hold in positive energy. Julie, Janet, and I happened to be sitting the closest and got drawn in. Danny joined the circle too. Acorn said, "Lucy's been very positive," perhaps to justify my presence since I was the newcomer to the group. The Freese-Posthumas and the elderly man stayed on the outside.

Acorn helped officiate. She began by purifying those of us who were to be inside the circle. She held a bunch of smoldering sage in her hand and drew a crosswise shape in front of each of us with it. When this was done, she "drew a circle" around all of us who were involved. With a small ritual knife in her hand

An Unreal Estate

she faced each direction of the compass in turn. From the north she called for blessings for the handfastings from the spirits of the earth, from the east from spirits of the air, from the south from spirits of fire, and from the west from the spirits of water. This is a way of creating a sacred space in many Neo-Pagan rituals, especially indoor ones. The Higginbothams, in their introduction to Neo-Paganism (2004) describe this as creating a "portable church." Calling on the elements reflects the belief that divinity is immanent in the elements of the natural world.

Once the circle was drawn, the lady in the cape began the ceremony, taking each couple in turn. She appealed to the elements again—earth, air, fire, and water—to support the marriages. She then had the couple join their right hands. She told them to be warm and affectionate with each other, to make love often, to be patient. The couples looked at each other while she was saying these words. One of the young women—the one without the baby—said "Yes!" when the older woman told the couple to make love often. Then they exchanged rings and vows, each member of each couple being asked if they accepted the other. At intervals in her speech, she said, "So mote it be," in a similar way to saying "Amen" at intervals in a Christian ceremony, and we who were part of the circle echoed the words. At the end of the speeches we echoed, "Blessed be" after her. (The first of these phrases, meaning "So must it be" was used in guild or ceremonial magic in Britain from the sixteenth century onward. Both are often used in Neo-Pagan ritual.)

I treated this ceremony rather solemnly. I had been used to Church of England services and to meditative yoga, which both tend to be reverential and quiet. My instinct was to close my eyes and concentrate on the words and the atmosphere. Janet and Julie, however, seemed more inclined to laugh (quietly) and whisper comments, not disrespectfully but jovially. A cup of blackberry wine was passed around for each person in the circle to sip. Each of us was asked to say a few words at this point. Janet said something about being patient with one another. Danny said that they should not give up on one another. I said I felt honored and appreciative to be included, that it was my first handfasting and that the young men looked handsome and the young women beautiful. Acorn then closed the circle by turning to each of the four directions again.

The elderly relative may have said something disparaging or skeptical shortly after the handfastings, because I noticed the lady in blue turning to him and telling him that the ceremony was legal, that there were witnesses.

Andy and Julie were handfasted in Grandmother's Garden on a warm, sunny Saturday at Elf Fest in May 2006. Grandmother's Garden is a grassy area on the

"Something Mystical and Fine"

South Road, just before one reaches the Long Hall. It is surrounded on three sides by trees and separated from the road by a small wooden fence. There is a flower bed in one corner, containing a gnome. Heart Tree Circle, at the west of the festival field, is a more common place for handfastings, but Grandmother's Garden is more accessible.

Lyn conducted this ceremony, with the help of Andrea, Glacier, Janet, and a friend of Julie's. The bride and groom wore handmade clothes with a lot of purple and silver, combining a medieval and Space Age look. They also wore and exchanged wreaths of purple flowers.

A few of the other guests were also dressed up. Andrea and another young woman had on purple dresses to match Julie and Andy's clothes. Lyn was wearing a low-cut medieval dress. One long-haired young man wore pirate-like clothes: baggy black pants, tall, old-fashioned boots, a white puffy-sleeved shirt, and an eye patch. Glacier also wore a white puffy shirt, but he told me that he didn't like his costume—he was only wearing it for the wedding. Among others, Acorn, Ethan, Jake, and a woman Julie and Andy were calling "Mother" were attending, as well as a lady in a wheelchair called Shining Fairy and her husband or boyfriend.

Because there were more attendants at this handfasting than the one I had attended earlier in the year, four guests marked the four directions. Andrea stood to the north, Glacier to the east, Janet to the west, and a young woman in a purple dress to the east. Lyn was conducting the ceremony and Mother was giving Julie away. Acorn began by playing "Greensleeves" on the violin. Then the people in each direction called to the spirits of the air, fire, water, and earth to bless the handfasting. After each of these invocations the speaker said "Blessed be" and we all repeated it. Lyn asked each of the couple to make promises of love and support, "as long as love shall last." They exchanged rings and kissed. Ethan took photographs.

I found out that Mother was not actually Julie's mother but a woman who is like a mother to lots of people in the Louisville Pagan community. Andy had known her for a long time. Julie and Mother got to know each other through Andy and came to like each other. Andy's real mother tolerates his Paganism, but neither of the couple's parents attended the ceremony. Andy's family is Catholic:

> They accept it, they don't condone it, they're just kind of "You're Pagan, okay," and go along with it. My mother is more accepting of it . . . My mom made [Julie] a dress; my mom is helping doing the planning, she made the clothes that I'm gonna be wearing, but my dad had nothing to do with it. (Andy, 2006)

An Unreal Estate

Julie's parents, especially her mother, worried about her associations both with Neo-Paganism and with Andy:

> Everybody else was Christian, they were Baptist and that was always the first question that came out of my mother's mouth. Has to be Christian, has to be a good little Southern boy—who I was supposed to marry . . . My mom—they all thought that he was controlling me and I was under some sort of satanic spell. They thought I was involved in a cult . . . Everything I was doing I was being made to do and nothing I was doing was on my own free will. (Julie, 2006)

Hence, at the handfasting, Andy and Julie were surrounded by an adopted family of friends rather than their blood family.

Janet speaks highly of both of them. I noticed that somebody pointed out to her that she had forgotten to say "Blessed be" for her part in the ceremony, but she shrugged this off. As at the first wedding, she was ready to laugh at any opportunity. And in fact her willingness to laugh and relative lack of concern over details seem to me as much a part of what makes Neo-Pagan ceremonies different from other religious ceremonies I have attended in England or the United States as the symbolism and the casting of the circle. As for other significant differences, the replacement of "Till death do us part" with "As long as love shall last" was indicative of a less stringent definition of marriage than the Christian one. Yet through the handfastings the couples were formally recognized by their communities, and drawn into a network of people, the elements, and the supernatural world.

At this point, fairly early in my research, I was still unfamiliar with handfastings and uncertain about what was expected of guests, even though I knew and liked Andy and Julie. I gave them a wedding present—a wooden salad bowl with a serving spoon and fork—but doubted the appropriateness of this right away. Was it an overly materialistic gesture? I did not see evidence of other presents at any of the ceremonies and am still not sure of all the details of Neo-Pagan wedding etiquette.

Joe described a more idiosyncratic Lothlorien wedding ceremony to me, dating back to the early 2000s. This involved his friend Hakan, who

> decided he wanted to get married naked in a tree. There were all these people who showed up who had never been on a trail before or ever been in the woods before. He wanted to climb the tree. Get married *in* the tree.

"Something Mystical and Fine"

So we went all the way down to the creek through Faerie. Took a right at the creek. And I was right behind this lady who had high heels on and it was muddy and we had to go through all these little tributaries and I literally had to push her up by the ass to get her up the hill.

He wanted everyone to be naked, right? He found this perfect tree that was surrounded by a field. The field was all stinging nettles and poison ivy and it was full of mosquitoes. As soon as you touched a blade of grass about a hundred mosquitoes would fly out . . . It turned out great. It really didn't dampen the spirits at all but it was pretty intense. (Joe, 2010)

Remembering Bob

Bob died of kidney failure in 2009. He had been a longtime festival participant and helper at Lothlorien, Jef's best friend since childhood, Vic's brother-in-law, and part of the Circle of 42. Jef considered Bob as much a brother as a friend, and was devastated by the loss. Two memorials were held for Bob. I will describe the second, which was attended by friends from the land, by blood family members who had come just for the ceremony, and by all the festival visitors.

Around the time of the first ceremony, Shay and Scott had made a wooden chair for Bob, in a style they thought he would particularly like. Anyone who wanted to had been encouraged to write a note to him on the chair, expressing words of goodbye or appreciation. It was put into a little shrine in Healers,' along with photos and other mementos. The central photo showed Bob on the swing in the Thunder Dome.

For Saturday night of 2009's Wild Magick gathering, Andrea had made another large wax tree, with Jason's help. Its trunk was cardboard, its branches were tree branches, there was a nicely carved wooden base and, again, there were cut-out paper leaves. This time the leaves were white, and earlier in the evening people had been invited to decorate them in autumn colors and with anything they chose to write: wishes, or aspects of their life they wanted to let go of.

At "half past dark" fireworks began at Upper Boom, and then Frank, Spencer, Jason and Scott brought some large, round slabs of wood and set them in the central fire pit in the Thunder Dome. They lit these and set the tree on top, with sparklers in its branches. Then somebody brought Bob's chair and set it under the tree. The tableau was perfect, a comfortable-looking wooden chair under a tree, both beginning to burn, with light from the sparklers, all against the background of darkness.

An Unreal Estate

A white bird, hand-made from paper or papier-mâché, was released near the fire, lifted by a paper lantern with a candle inside. It went all the way up to the top of the Dome, caught for a few seconds in the metal scaffolding, got free and then kept going up. Led by Jef, people began to chant, "Bob! Bob! Bob!" and to circle the fire pit, dancing. One of the fireworks was a rocket containing Bob's ashes, and there were cheers when it exploded.

Spirituality, Faith, and Direct Experience

Terry, who had instigated a lot of rituals in Lothlorien's early years, did not see these in terms of religion, saying, "I'm basically a Christian, but I don't like religion at all." In the words of Paul also, and several other people I interviewed, the purpose of rituals like those described above was not necessarily to effect "magic" or express faith but rather to enhance community and create enjoyable experiences.

> I always thought the rituals were fun whether they meant or did anything at all, just because people would gather and there would be some sense of community action. Fun playing with stuff like that even if it is only theater. (Paul F., 2009)

The bottom line of these rituals for most participants, and indeed in many of the more formal Neo-Pagan traditions, is experience. A range of types of out-of-the-ordinary experience are accessible at Lothlorien. Some members are moved by time alone in the woods, others by collective rituals. Some, like Jason, draw on the pulsing energy of the Thunder Dome. And for a few years at festivals, Dan V. has created labyrinths marked out by candles around the Lightning Shrine, which create (psychological and literal) space for meditation and quiet introspection as one weaves silently between the lights in toward the center and out again.

Unusual experiences were often described by people I interviewed in emotional or physical terms rather than religious terms. If I was offered mystical or metaphysical explanations for experiences, these were almost always interpreted tentatively, as their perspectives, rather than presented as certainties.

Jason, for example, one of the core Dome rats, talks about his time there in ways that are grounded in his personal feelings and sense impressions. He once described to me a night at Lothlorien when the moon was full and the leaves on the trees were lit up so that they looked like flowers. Here is another description, of the Thunder Dome, and while he is talking about "magic," he is talking about it in terms of sensations rather than in terms of a belief system:

"Something Mystical and Fine"

The Thunder Dome on a festival night.
Courtesy of Christine Walsh-Newton

. . . You can feel the magic when you walk in, when the dome is cranking on Friday night or Saturday night, or sometimes even on Thursday
night. When it's cranking, you know, you can feel your body, just in
your body. You can walk into that space and feel a change. You can feel
the power of the dancers and the power of the musicians all contribut-
ing, and just rotating around this hub of a big fire, a big ball of energy
right there that's hot, that's bright, that is right there in front of everybody. It's a powerful experience. . . . I remember going down my first
night in 2001 at Wild Magick, and I just sat there with my jaw down. I
was like, "Wow, this is big stuff. This is really powerful." And it was, and
it still is. And, I am so glad that over the years, I've been gifted to share
a part of that magic making . . . (Jason, 2008)

He describes his fire dancing with a whip in terms of inspiration and a flow of
energy:

I enjoy inspiring people. I enjoy being inspired by people, by other dancers, other drummers. And it's change, it's allowing energy, it's allowing things to flow through you. Both receiving and giving. (Jason, 2008)

Finally he sums up his Dome experiences in very straightforward terms:

I'm just myself down there . . . It brings out a happier side of me. (Jason, 2008)

In interviews, people described experiences of Lothlorien that ranged from those relating to internal states of mind, sensations, or insights at one end of a continuum, to strikingly unusual perceptions of the external world at the other. I saw no reason to doubt any of these experiences, since I trust the integrity and intelligence of all the interviewees involved, nor did I see a reason to regard one type of experience as more or less "spiritual" than another.

Joe and some of his friends, for example, enjoyed drumming and socializing and appreciated the beauty of the land, but stayed away from anything that smacked of religion, belief, or "magic":

The whole ritual thing I avoided completely . . . there were several of us who were there for drumming and having fun and camping with our friends. (Joe, 2010)

Yet Joe also had experiences he described as connected with spirituality, although he is hesitant to use this word. "Spirituality," in this context, is not something metaphysical but something internal and grounded:

At one point I just sat down in Lightning and I closed my eyes and I was really meditating, for lack of a better word, and I was really struggling with "What in the world do I want to do with my life?" And I have this clear memory of feeling like something in my head . . . was telling me that I was going to be a teacher after all . . . I didn't involve myself in a lot of the rituals and stuff, but I really did feel . . . ever since I first went there, this strong connection to the place and also spirituality, for lack of a better word, like here was a place you could get some grounding. That was actually the point where I told Pam that I needed to move to Chicago. (Joe, 2010)

Further along this continuum are experiences like Janet's. Janet describes herself as an empath; she is very sensitive to the feelings of others. This makes a city environment uncomfortable and overwhelming to her at times, and the relative calm of the community at Lothlorien is a relief to her by contrast:

"Something Mystical and Fine"

I'm sensitive to all that . . . People can show one emotion outwardly and I can feel what's really going on—a lot of the time—sometimes not so much. Sometimes I just turn it off. I don't even want to deal with all that. But here it doesn't matter. There's so much here that regulates it. It's never overpowering for me. (Janet, 2009)

She goes on to explain this:

When people are in a place periodically, they leave an imprint. They leave an imprint of energy on places. Depending on how much emotion is involved . . . I mean there is always a trace somewhere, on a stone or on a rock. And I also notice that when people get very energetic or angry and they're on this land, it doesn't really change things. It recycles . . . It goes away when people learn from it. When people learn, it becomes information. People just get more receptive information when they're meditating out here or whatever, because of the imprint that people have left here, and because they're closer to nature. (Janet, 2009)

Still further out of the range of "everyday" experience, and combining inner and outer perception, Brooks, at the time when he lived at Lothlorien, frequently had intuitions that defied commonsense notions of reality:

I had a *déjà vu* several times a day. The veil between worlds is thin; you can see outside of our narrow mindset of how we describe ourselves, that science and religion fall so short of. Things made sense out there. (Brooks, 2009)

Finally a few people described experiences to me that seemed almost impossible to explain. Paul F., for example, told the following story:

I just had one notable experience here, that—well I didn't believe what I was seeing. We did some ritual that one of the Eldars at the time led, and it was addressing each of the eight major directions and each corresponding shrine, which were to be noted as fairy shrines . . . And each one had its own sound in turn, with which we would be able to call the fairies. Well, the ritual ended after great length with a good amount of mirth. We all went our ways, and as I was headed with some friends toward our camp over there . . . I saw fairies—Disney-sized, frigging, glowing fairies. And I've never seen a firefly two to three inches long move maybe twenty-five miles an hour and stay lighted the entire time.

An Unreal Estate

And there were many of them . . . At that point one actually hovered not too far from me and I could hear its wings. And that's when I realized the unreality of what I was seeing . . . I could see a general form . . . I could hear its wings beating . . . It was just really strange—really, really strange.

We wanted the fairies to feel safe to come out, and to do so we had to not only call them but to be joyful and mirthful; and we were, because it was silly and fun. (Paul F., 2009)

Brooks also told me of an extraordinary experience. A lady who was visiting the land had decided to do an Artemis ritual. It was a wet night and she was having difficulty in lighting a fire. She asked Brooks to help, and offered to let him watch the ritual afterward. Part of this involved unveiling a bust of Artemis, which had been draped in a dark cloth:

She laid out the Olympus Tarot. It's a beautiful tarot . . . every card has a figure of history or Greek mythology, with Artemis the peak of it. She went to bed . . . Cedar, my dog, and I were, as usual, up at three in the morning and heard all these dogs coming. I didn't know Artemis had hounds. And it was a moonlit night; it was cloudy and the drizzle had petered out and, you know, when it's a full moon it lights up everything. All the clouds had opened up, it was totally illuminated. These dogs come running up right outside the bus . . . These dogs go streaming by us, absolutely invisible—nothing there, just noises—and Cedar takes off, chases them. I'm like, "No, Cedar, no!" I didn't know what they were, but I knew they were invisible dogs, running real fast, barking . . . So I went and grabbed him and brought him back. She brought Artemis back to the land, invoked Artemis. And she had slept through it. (Brooks, 2009)

In spite of having had these experiences, neither Brooks nor Paul approach religion or spirituality in a faith-based way, and neither talk much in terms of metaphysics, at least to me. Paul appreciates what he sees as Lothlorien's open-mindedness, and this was one of its original attractions for him:

I don't particularly subscribe to anybody's particular notions of theology or anything. And that's what I like about it. Because nobody else really does either. (Paul F., 2009)

He also seems to take almost a postmodern or approach to reality, a kind of radical skepticism:

"Something Mystical and Fine"

A lot of people come seeking what's behind the veil . . . Maybe some of them have their own fantasies about that—a self constructed fantasy world. I suppose we all do really. It's only a collective reality we're agreeing upon. Personal reality is that list of perceptions that only we can describe. (Paul F., 2009)

Brooks too seems wary of specific forms of religion. For him, it is "that light in their eyes" that legitimates a belief system, not the beliefs themselves:

All gods are God. Everyone has pretty much got it wrong, but that initial impulse at the start of the religion—there's something mystical and fine. That's what I want . . .

I like people who have these funny religious beliefs, as long as they've got that light in their eyes. (Brooks, 2010)

Conclusions

There are people who subscribe to specific beliefs at Lothlorien; forms of Paganism in some cases, Christianity in others, Buddhism or Taoism in others, combinations in others. But almost of necessity in such a pluralistic community, other paths have to be acknowledged. Taken as a whole, the religious climate at Lothlorien is somewhat like that of parts of precontact (or early contact) Native North America, or of India (Bonvillain 2001; Stewart 2004), in that the existence of multiple beliefs and practices is seen as given, and in that these do not necessarily contradict or even exclude one another. A very popular film I saw in Delhi in 1988, called *Amal, Akbar, Anthony,* told a story of three brothers separated from their mother and from each other at birth. The mother was a disciple of the sage Sai Baba, while each of the sons grew up in the folds of a different religion. Amal was Hindu, Akbar was Muslim, and Anthony was Christian. The film showed each brother, and the mother, experiencing miracles through their particular paths. The mother recovered her sight and the brothers all received divine help from their respective traditions in pursuing three different romances. In this movie the religions were presented as equally powerful and valid rather than pitted against one another.

A similar eclecticism and tolerance is in evidence at Lothlorien. It is a place where a variety of rituals are enacted on a regular basis, some of which enhance the links between humans and nature, marking the seasons, while some honor shifts in major life transitions—birth, marriage, death—"high drama," to use Scott's phrase. Most are legitimated by experience rather than by faith. It is a safe space for nonmainstream religious expressions and for those who have

An Unreal Estate

experienced subtle or overt discrimination for their religious affiliations in the outside world. It is also a place where unusual spiritual experiences are acknowledged and supported.

Lothlorien has absorbed influences both from loosely Neo-Pagan traditions and from some aspects of modernity. Improvisation—drawing on the present and future as well as the past—is an essential part of ritual there. Most people are comfortable with rationality and science, and with criticisms of or questions around their beliefs. (At this point I am using the word "rationality" in the sense of the capacity for self-reflection and recognition of a range of points of view, rather than Weber's (1904) definition of instrumental rationality.) As I noted in chapter 3, Lothlorien's culture in most cases involves a choice to cultivate enchantment or community, and a general openness to spiritual experience as one of many other kinds of experience. I noted in the same chapter that neither a sense of connection with, nor a sense of disconnection from, nature is inherently rational or irrational. Rather they are interpretive or experiential positions, which can inform and expand rationality.

Bonedaddy's words from the first chapter, for example, "I believe in the earth because I'm standing on it. I believe in my friends and the people I love. I believe in my emotions," Braze's, "Planting things in the earth is the real magic," and Conney's, "Nature includes rocks and dirt and us . . . People are at the core animals" offer a view of the world where there is less of an experiential break between humans on the one hand and nature, sensation, and emotion on the other than is usual in the United States or Europe. This follows in part from more optimistic assumptions about both nature and human nature—an original innocence replacing the idea of original sin. This cluster of ideas can be as much *de*mystifying as mystifying and could form the basis for a different and broader rationality.

"Something Mystical and Fine"

The Maypole in winter.
Courtesy of Scott Martin

7

"A Gypsy Community"

Cycling, Learning, and Moving On

> . . . Not a cradle,
> a magic Eden without clocks,
> and not a windowless grave, but a place
> I may go both in and out of.
>
> *W. H. Auden, 1965, from "Thanksgiving for a Habitat"*

I was struck by the transience of Lothlorien's community during my first year. A festival evening at the Thunder Shrine would feel strange to me if there was no one dancing or drumming whom I knew well. Memories of people I had seen in previous festivals and people I had hoped to see again were a part of the experience, along with the unknown and familiar people who were actually there. Absences became almost as much a part of the way I saw the land and the festivals as presences. But my sense of transience during this period was partly a result of the relatively brief time of my involvement. Vic's more long-term perspective shows continuity among participants:

> Some of these folks you might only see twice a year and you make really good friends, some people might come back every five years or whatever, but . . . people come back. (Vic, 2006)

Brown (2002), Wallace (1956), and Zablocki (1980) examine the history of intentional communities in search of cycles that may offer predictions about them. These three authors argue that the beginnings of such movements are responses to individual or societal stress. Zablocki takes an especially broad view of history—looking across the centuries—and correlates times of high levels of conflict with times when communes of one kind or another tend to emerge. Wallace looks at stress on both personal and societal levels as the crucial first factor in the origins of "revitalization movements," including intentional communities. Next comes a period, he argues, of "cultural distortion," when inconsistencies in the culture are apparent and its stated aims or values are out of alignment with its actual processes. Then comes "mazeway reformulation," a reconfiguration of existing cultural themes, often resulting from an individual's revelations, where new cultural systems are envisioned. This is followed by organization, by cultural transformation, by routinization and by a new steady state.

Based on his extensive historical research, Donald Pitzer (1997: 3–13) notes that utopian communities tend to have similar life cycles, with a communal phase in the early years, often as a matter of necessity in a group that is struggling with social ostracism or economic crisis. This is then succeeded by a time when a community continues but takes up private ownership. In other words it makes more sense, in this view, to look at communalism as one phase in the development of a community's existence rather than as a discrete entity in itself with a distinct beginning and ending.

Andelsen (2002) also breaks with many writers on intentional communities, in this case by theorizing about them primarily in terms of the positive factors that pull people in. He acknowledges explicitly the utopian factors involved in envisioning alternative communities and sees their formation in terms of "coming together" (131–148) rather than "breaking apart" from the mainstream. He adds a typology of communal beginnings. Most intentional communities, he argues, form either through the inspiration of a charismatic leader, through a shared ideology, through affinity groups who wish to intensify their friendships, or through a combination of these elements. (It is refreshing that he does not claim that *all* of them fit one of these types.)

Among Andelsen's three typologies, Lothlorien fits most easily with the shared ideology model. As for the beginnings of the community and festival site, these came, based on Michael and Terry's narratives, from revelation, and in fact from visions. After a shared Tarot card reading, both had closed their eyes. Michael had a sensation of being immersed in the consciousness of the foliage around the globe. Terry had a vision of elves. Both felt inspired to begin a nature sanctuary as a result of these experiences. This last point also ties in with Wallace's model, since he argues that revelation is often part of an early stage in revitalization movements.

Internal transience, ironically, is one of the keys to Lothlorien's longevity and stability. It falls into a category of its own because it combines its land-based

An Unreal Estate

community with a festival site. Stewardship, land ownership, and festival planning are collective, but most people do not rely on the land to meet their basic necessities, or only in a limited way (as a place to stay or live in a structure that must be either portable or belong to the organization as a whole). Tuna said, in an interview, "This is a gypsy community." He pointed out that nobody is tied to Lothlorien by obligation or need. People drift in and out. Lothlorien combines its relative longevity as an intentional community and festival site with a great deal of fluctuation both on a daily and a yearly level. Most active volunteers live away from the land. Even the long-term residents have jobs in Bloomington or nearby. The bulk of Lothlorien's sponsors come in only for festivals, which they may do, however, over the course of many years. Because of this fluidity it is difficult to fit Lothlorien into any of the existing schemes or theories about the life cycles of communities.

The features of Lothlorien that one could consider to have carried on from its beginnings are the land itself and a community connected with the land, its festivals and the collection of ideals on which it was established. Of this community, Conney, Michael, and their children, Hedwig, and one or two other founding members still live or spend a significant amount of time at Lothlorien. Also a sizeable proportion of the active volunteers, Eldars, and Stewards have been involved on some level for ten, fifteen years, or more. This is quite unusual among purely residential intentional communities. Lothlorien is shored up, also, by a much larger community network in the Midwest as a whole with a certain stability of its own. This includes people who are sympathetic to Neo-Paganism or environmentalism and friendship groups who have camped together over the years. Facebook has consolidated and expanded these networks. At Elf Fest in 2010, Bonedaddy made a point to ask first-time visitors how they had heard about Lothlorien. "Facebook" was the most common response.

Kuhlmann notes the high turnover of community membership at Twin Oaks, which is a more typical sedentary intentional community. The average length of stay there is four or five years (Kinkade 1994; Kuhlmann 2005). In the first years, she maintains, members look at their experiences and their work in the context of the wider society from which they have recently come and are energized, appreciating the difference in lifestyle. But after a few years, their focus is more inward, on the community. Without the wider context, internal flaws are easier to see.

At Lothlorien people maintain contact with the outside world, so the contrast between the two environments is always apparent. There is also great flexibility because of the variety of levels of involvement. Even a person who is having

"A Gypsy Community"

problems with other members of the community or with the way it is being run may visit for long enough to do a particular volunteer task or attend part of a festival to see a friend. Turnover at Lothlorien is less than at Twin Oaks because involvement with the former is usually much looser. In terms of transience, Twin Oaks and Lothlorien provide an interesting contrast. Lothlorien appears to be in constant flux as people come in and go out, but in fact has the more underlying communal stability of the two.

"Lessons Rained On Me": Learning and Other Gifts

In chapter 5, I noted that the nonjudgmental culture of the community seemed to encourage increased confidence, self-acceptance, and the capacity for self-exploration, an idea many interviewees expressed. Lothlorien, because of its many differences from the outside world, can also profoundly alter people's philosophical perspectives. A few long-term participants who had lived on the land at one time or another told me that Lothlorien had helped them to make significant changes. These seemed often to relate to extensive time in natural surroundings, and to a sense of reconnection. Braze considered that he had experienced more growth in the years he spent living at Lothlorien, even in the relatively isolated winters, than in all the years of his adult life before that time. He found new insights:

> You spend some time in your own head. Isolation is a great aid in that. And you get a much clearer picture . . . It's a different isolation. Because when you set up a camp in the middle of the forest and start tuning in with what's going on around you, you realize—you truly bring into your soul the richness and the amount of depth that life adds around us and if you go into places like the forest in large enough areas . . . you end up with just observing the multitude of species that are perfectly doing their thing all around together, independently, and you look at your own DNA and you look at your roots and you go, "Wow, man, my DNA was part of this tapestry of DNA and so, why am I . . . isolated and cut off by my own society?" and so I started questioning that. (Braze, 2006)

Learning about building shelters and about edible plants on the land also enabled him to let go of a layer of anxiety related to economic survival:

> I can walk out into that wilderness and survive forever. It's really hard. But that's what gives me a sense of security . . . Because unless our spe-

cies figures out how to destroy and sterilize every last shred of life on this planet, I can go make a living. That is the only place where I've really found true security. You know, biosecurity. Bio-survival security. So that allowed me to de-invest all of the bio-survival anxiety that is tied to monetary units and, "Am I doing well in my job, am I making my bills, what does my credit score look like?" (Braze, 2006)

Like Braze, Laura sees her learning in terms of experiencing connections between herself and the natural world, and also between herself and other people. For her, this is a return to sensations she remembers as a child:

This whole path has shifted me into a more healthy space psychologically, and it wasn't instantaneous, it's a lot more work than I thought it would be, and I'm still working on it, but . . . having that broader worldview that everything is connected, and . . . I think about empathizing with people instead of controlling them or avoiding them, and trying to be compassionate and . . . trying to hear what's going on around me in nature and the land. And I'm outside right now listening to crickets and tree frogs and trying to remember how to feel like I'm a part of that, like I did when I was four. And then doing that and crossing it over and doing that with people. (Laura, 2010)

Her learning also has a practical aspect:

I've kind of figured out a path that I really appreciate and can dig into and love learning about, and it has to do with the earth and sustainability and being able to support yourself and your family and your tribe . . . Lothlorien then becomes my research ground, because I'm working with natural resources. It becomes my training ground for teaching, because they're always looking for people to come out and teach things to the people who are out there . . . I feel like I've grown up since I've started going there. (Laura, 2010)

Brooks's time of living in the white bus in the late 1990s led to improvements in his health; the migraine headaches he had suffered from while working as a paralegal stopped. More striking still in his narrative was the process of letting go of some of the traumas from his time in combat, and the way he saw this transformation reflected in the responses of people he interacted with. My impression of Brooks was in line with his description—he exudes good will—and I was surprised to hear that that had not always been the case:

"A Gypsy Community"

Pan overgrown.
Courtesy of Braze T. Smith

I could never go back. I was so charged up from what happened there. Lessons rained on me. I did a couple of thousand hours out there . . . I've been charged up ever since . . . Just the way people look at me and smile, light up instantly. Instead of going, like, "Oh, honey, get the kids, lock the door, lock the window!" Like the Neo-Platonists—when you see God you become god, when you see beauty you become beautiful, when you see art you become artful. I went to combat, saw some horrific things and kind of carried that with me . . . I've seen lots of hurt . . . There was definitely a transformation, and I assume it happened from being out there. Just living in the woods, on a mundane aspect, was terrific for me. (Brooks, 2010)

For all three, putting themselves in a natural environment proved healing, and this involved removing some of the distance between themselves and the natural world—observing it, working for and with it, remembering their own links with it. In the last chapter, I noted that experiencing such links could as

An Unreal Estate

easily be seen as demystifying, as mystifying. They may also provide keys to psychological health. In Laura's view, separation from nature, attempts to control nature, are at the root of human mental problems and unhappiness:

> We've all been taught that it's good and right to have dominion . . . I have a distinct feeling that that kind of ideology is what causes a lot of conflict in people . . . I think it conflicts with the individual inner psychology of any one given person. It causes conflict, it seems, if you're pushing against this world that you're born into, if you're trying to fight it and control it. I think that causes rifts in your logic and your reasoning. (Laura, 2010)

Moving On

Romantic breakups have kept a couple of formerly active volunteers away in the four and a half years since I have been visiting Lothlorien. Janie also notes a burnout factor in people who become very actively involved. She does not see this as a bad thing:

> The tides of change work well in a lot of ways. I remember someone kind of referring to it as a spiraling in and spiraling out. People come in and then they squeeze up so tight and then they end up spinning out, you know, because I think they just wrap themselves up so tight . . . and they kind of weed themselves out . . . And sometimes I find that's good because some of those people, you know—because it's such an open society you have just a wide range of people that come in and out of there. Some people get really involved and kind of maybe take almost too much of a personal ownership of things and not keep that community sense, and so then that starts to cause some turmoil. (Janie, 2007)

But the most common factor that drives people away has been interpersonal conflict within the community. Sarah, Lyn, and Glacier left for this reason. Terry still finds his rift with Lothlorien very painful, saying, "The wizard of Lothlorien is in exile from the place he created for everyone." He added, later in the interview, "I'm just hurt by all of this—all the friends, all the time, all the energy, all the work."

Moving away from Lothlorien, sporadically or permanently, need not necessarily represent a break with its ideals however. Sometimes it provides inspiration for, or stepping stones to, other communities. Scott saw his stretches of

"A Gypsy Community"

living full time at Lothlorien as temporary, describing the place as "a test kitchen for ideas." Many people I interviewed expressed personal dreams of the next place after Lothlorien—of some day having either their own communities or pieces of land with lakes or rivers. Andrea's is one of the most ambitious and is thought out in detail. Since this book began with one of her early and most idealistic visions of Lothlorien, it is interesting to see how time on the land engendered further perspectives on her future:

> What I want in my future is I want a technology-based commune where everything is solar, and it is a modern, convenient kind of lifestyle with being ecofriendly and healthy in general. I want to be an example for other people. I mean my dream if I had all the money in the world that I could want, or you know, just enough, is I would like to start communities that are networked throughout the country and so that you could produce certain foods and then it would trade and it would just have a system of maybe a few rules or maybe it would depend on the people that are running that particular part of the community in whatever part of the country, you know. Through barter . . . And maybe sell some things too. I mean there's always things like land taxes and I don't think I would ever go nonprofit because there's a level of that with the government involvement that kind of frightens me when you have to . . . If you dissolve it you have to sell it to a preexisting 501(c)(3) and I don't know that I would, I don't think I would go for that . . .
>
> I always thought that it would be kind of neat if I had my own community to have like a bunch of, a dome city, basically, or domes, because domes are the most heat and cool efficient . . . You could build domes where they could be added on with other rooms and stuff but you could have ones that were there for people who wanted to travel between the communities and were only temporary. So you would have work that was, like, for temporary people, and so you can still have that temporary community and then you can have the people that want to stay for a long period of time . . . I would like something like Lothlorien but without the festivals, basically. I think the festivals are great but I think it kind of deters from the idea of a stable community. (Andrea, 2006)

Obviously, this vision has some points in common with Lothlorien and some points of difference, such as the dome city, the greater level of stability, and the avoidance of both festivals and nonprofit status. In spite of her enchantment with Lothlorien in the beginning, Andrea seems not to have expected it to prove an ideal residence on a long-term basis. Instead she refers to it as a "training ground":

> I've never had the intention of living at Lothlorien with the expectations that it was going to turn into what I want. I know that it is a training ground to kind of be able to experiment with it, but there are people who have been there for a long time who expected it to turn into more of a stable, intentional community, but it's not founded on that because it was never financed by doing large agricultural projects. It's been financed by festivals, and I think it's nice. I would come back and visit for the rest of my life as long as it's open for festivals. But I just want to live somewhere that's more stable. (Andrea, 2006)

Andrea's dream of a stable intentional community is shared by a few other people currently involved as well. She also sees wider implications for her dream, looking to an alternative economy for mainstream society as a further ideal:

> Our economy's set up where there's always going to be poor, middle-class, and rich people, and if the economy switched to people living where they are completely self-sufficiently supporting themselves except for some barter, because of course, people can't grow certain foods in certain areas and . . . I don't want to say communist, because that's the wrong word for it, but it would be—I'm not very good at political jargon, so, everyone would be equal, everyone would have the same amount of things. Everyone would only have to work for what they need for their survival and nobody would be footing more of the bill than anybody else, and so the people on top, they don't want that. The people in the middle, they want to be up on top because they're almost there, and the poor people are the ones working for minimum wage and doing the most work. (Andrea, 2006)

Several people who used to be involved at Lothlorien have gone on to form other communes or festival sites. Braze and his friend Hope bought farmland in Illinois, where Laura may eventually move also. They envision the farm as a place for practical, sustainable living, with Lothlorien as a kind of backup, a "community and sanctuary" for spiritual support. Rowan and her husband AJ have moved out of Chicago to grow plants and herbs in Southern Indiana. Jason and Andrea have plans, in 2011, to by a piece of land near Bedford. Ourhaven, a Pagan festival site in nearby French Lick, was started by a former Lothlorien member. Wildheart, in northern Indiana, was also started by Lothlorien members. Several people participate regularly in two or three of these

"A Gypsy Community"

communities. Tuna says, "Lothlorien is like an amoeba that grows and splits off." At Lothlorien, as elsewhere, people move on. This can be due to burnout or family pressures or relationship problems within the community. But often Lothlorien provides a stepping stone or new vantage point and they can move on toward a place they see as new and better—the next Utopia.

An Unreal Estate

8

"A Spontaneous Social Experiment"

I had time to stand in the driveway looking at the sparkling lights of
hundreds of candles, listening to laughter, voices, and music drifting
across the field on a beautiful early summer night and think,
"Look at what we've done. Look at what we've created."
. . . There were moments of revelation and moments of pure joy.
Listening to call and response rounds of "Yo Ho" (with harmonies!)
echoing between circles. Dancing with babies, having so many of "my" kids
together, meeting the beginnings of the third generation of elves. Acquiring
a new target for my smart-aleck remarks, playing Frisbee barefoot for hours
(black eye and all). Seeing so many people from the past and so many new
faces. Working side by side with folks who were new to Lothlórien a year ago.
. . . Feeling truly, perfectly HOME.

Conney, Facebook posting, 2010

I was moved, after Elf Fest in 2010, to read Conney's impressions, which she had
posted on Facebook. Like the other Eldars, Stewards, and long-time volunteers,
Conney usually spends her festival time working. She is often either in the
kitchen, organizing volunteers for essential tasks, or buying supplies for meals.
She has lived at the front gates of Lothlorien with her family since 1987 and has
experienced enough drama, conflict, mess, change, noise, loss, and hard work
there to develop a jaded view of alternative communities. This year, for the first
time in years, there were enough kitchen volunteers for her to participate fully
in the festival itself. She sounds, oddly, as starry-eyed as any first-time visitor.

Conney says, "Look at what we've created," and she has a right to be proud,
even a little disbelieving. Lothlorien is "unreal estate" in the sense that in many
ways it defies common sense and common expectations. In this concluding
chapter I will first sum up some of its unusual and defining features under two

broad categories: the reenchantment of the natural world and the juxtaposition of safety and freedom. Then I will go on to discuss the potential significance of this community in particular, and experimental, or antistructural communities as a whole, in the context of mainstream culture, and in the processes of cultural change.

The Reenchantment of the Natural World

Most regular participants at Lothlorien see the animal and plant worlds not only as alive but as conscious. When Braze gave a guest lecture for my class at Indiana University, he talked in detail about the many relationships between plant and insect species in the community garden. "Decoy" plants that distract destructive insects from other plants, insects that pollinate, and "companion" plants all help to make the garden closer to a self-sustaining ecosystem—a system that cares for itself and improves its soil with something akin to wisdom. Braze's level of respect for nature is shared by many (not all) environmentalists. Some participants go a step further than this. For many, respect for the elements—earth, fire, air, water—and for the planet and the nonhuman world has religious aspects to it. The elements, plants, animals, have power, and have something to teach on a spiritual level, while humans, as extensions of the natural world, have something to learn from them. Lothlorien itself is sometimes referred to as a conscious entity. Here the environment is reenchanted, thus countering the "disenchantment" that Weber described as part of the industrial worldview.

At Lothlorien, perhaps because participants have grown up and still spend much of their time in a modern state, the natural world is to a large extent consciously reenchanted rather than being *assumed* to be a magical, powerful place. It is reenchanted by people who are comfortable going back and forth between a scientific, skeptical point of view and a faith in the power of nature. And feeling reverence for the natural world, feeling connected to the natural world, are no less congruent with science than feeling oblivious to or in charge of or disconnected from it. A couple of interviewees, in fact, suggested the reverse:

> Western religion, the base of Western spirituality, is this idea that we are born into the world from outside, and it's a place where things have to be controlled and overcome. And it's just part of the mindset that we're raised with over here in the West . . . It's creating a false view, almost a hallucination. (Laura, 2010)

An Unreal Estate

A small shrine among the trees at Heart Tree Circle.
Courtesy of Michelle Chaney

Festivals and rituals at Lothlorien aim to reinforce the connections and reverence there—between people and one another, between people and land, between people and the worlds of imagination, between people and hidden aspects of themselves. This is often perceived as valuable for the land too. Jef suggests that participants' thoughts and images about Lothlorien, as much as their physical efforts, are what make the forest and community thrive. (It is characteristic of Jef that he expresses this as one possible position among many):

> In my personal opinion, since I've been doing lots of rituals at the land, I feel that the constant positive visualization of everybody out there has as much to do with the success as whatever work the handful of us that are doing the thing have to do with it. (Jef, 2006)

From this range of perspectives toward the natural world comes a desire to build, garden, and steward in ways that are respectful and sustainable. The composting privies, the Long Hall and the shower house represent innovative attempts to build so as to conserve energy and resources. The forest is left to itself as much as possible. Pollutants are avoided on the property.

At the same time the land at Lothlorien is literally, materially reenchanted, too, through art works, shrines, and decorations that add a magical feel to the landscape, through references to stories, and through the drumming, candle lights, music, and campfires. I have included many first impressions of Lothlorien in this book, but I will add one more here, from Frank, because it conveys just this feeling of enchantment. He arrived on a May evening in 2008:

> It was raining and misty so it was darkish but not really . . . People had started lighting candles and votives and laying them along the road and along the pathways and in the trees and on the little posts everywhere you went. And as you looked through the mist all you could see were these little tiny points of light everywhere, all throughout the woods, for ten acres. And wherever you looked there they were and they guided you around like little fairies, saying, "Here, come this way. This is the way to go. Welcome home." It was a little universe. (Frank, 2009)

Safety and Freedom at Lothlorien

Lothlorien is both a "sanctuary" and an open community, juxtaposing ideals of safety and freedom. It is transient partly because it is a festival site, a place where people come and go in the course of a year. No obligation binds one to staying. No conditions or behaviors, other than those that directly threaten

An Unreal Estate

other humans or the natural world, exclude one. Decision making is democratic and happens at a grassroots level. Work is voluntary, required only of those who want to be able to participate in decision making, or to live there full time.

The English language sometimes equates safety with boundaries and walls, as if safety and freedom were a contrasting pair. We say "safe as houses." The related word "security" in legal or political discourse is almost synonymous with rules, penalties, weapons, and enforced exclusions. But there are different elements within the concept of safety. A sense of safety can be induced not only by walls, threats, or predictable rules, but through an accepting social environment. This is what Lothlorien strives for (often, but not always, successfully), both through its informal culture and through its Bylaws, which are based around guarantees for freedom of expression and religion. It imposes some behavioral limits—for example on violence, verbal threats, sexual harassment, tree cutting, use of pollutants, drug dealing, or public sexual activity—but its ideological boundaries are very broad.

Partly because of this breadth, there is frequent conflict at Lothlorien, especially around organizational decision making. Yet at the same time, people talked about feeling accepted at Lothlorien in a number of different contexts, some of which had to do with being part of marginalized identity groups in North American culture, particularly religious affiliations or sexual orientations, and more of which were about acceptance on a personal level. Further, acceptance does not seem to be regarded as an end point in itself for most of the people who talked about it, but to enable further changes and activities for them inside and outside the community. This theme came up again and again in interviews.

Safety in this context correlates with change and fluidity. This idea is the core of Carl Rogers' psychotherapeutic practice, where "unconditional positive regard" on the counselor's part is an important component of clients' ability to make changes in themselves. It is also reminiscent of Turner's observations about communitas emerging in liminal or antistructural contexts, where social life is in flux. Safety and belonging at Lothlorien are cultivated in these affective terms rather than in terms of protections from threats on the outside or inside. They are closely correlated with respect for individual freedom and autonomy, including freedom from interference for animal and plant species—a kind of grass roots (rather than corporate) liberalism that extends beyond humans.

Lothlorien's particular approach to autonomy and creative and religious freedom avoids two positions that have been detrimental to many marginalized groups. The first position is the social contract view of the individual as an isolated and fixed entity who acts on self-interest, who takes an instrumental

"A Spontaneous Social Experiment"

approach to resources, to the natural world, and to other people, and who can survive independently at all times. The second position takes individuals and individual autonomy as Western cultural constructs with no real substance and is wary of arguments or policies aimed at personal freedom or human rights, since these involve an individualistic rather than relational view of human beings.

In response to the second position, it is important to note that respect for autonomy is not intrinsically a capitalist ideal, nor is it mainly a European or Euro-American ideal. To pick a few Native North American examples in the realm of political participation and the recognition of human rights, Charles Mann (2005) makes a convincing argument that the ideals of individual autonomy and democracy in the United States were inspired in large part by the Haudenosaunee and other Native nations from eastern North America (see also Johansen 1982). Sally Roesch Wagner (2001) makes similar points about the influence of Native Americans on American feminism, which involves agency and autonomy for women. Reading any part of the *Jesuit Relations* makes it clear that the Hurons and Algonkians had a much greater respect for individual autonomy and choice (including autonomy and choice for women, children, and the elderly) than did the French in the early years of colonization (Lawn and Salvucci, eds., 2003; Leacock 1954). And Samson (2003; see also Bonvillain 2001) notes the very high levels of respect for autonomy relative to mainstream Canadian culture among the present-day Innu nation in Canada. Yet all of these cultures had a collective approach to property and land ownership.

Meanwhile, in an African context, Kwame Anthony Appiah argues that Asante influences were crucial, along with a critical response to British colonialism, in the development of his father's political convictions: "Two things, in particular, strike me about the local character of the source of my father's increasing commitment to individual rights: first, that it grew out of experience of illiberal government; second, that it depended on a sense of his own dignity and the dignity of his fellow citizens that was the product of Asante conceptions" (Appiah 2005: 269).

Turning to non-Western examples of respect for autonomy in the realm of religion, many Asian spiritual paths—Buddhism, Hinduism, and Sufism for example—have had long histories of being oriented more toward individual inspiration, practice, devotion, and experience than toward faith, with an understanding that there are many possible approaches to connection with the Divine, and that these do not need to exclude or discount one another. Further, the gradual introduction of religious ideas to the West from Asia over the last two hundred years or so has had a liberalizing effect on religion here, mak-

An Unreal Estate

ing it more common to approach spirituality through practice and individual experience and to draw ideas from many paths.[1]

The type of autonomy cultivated through the Bylaws, among the governing Council and in the informal culture at Lothlorien, is broad, aiming to include women, those of minority ethnic groups, religious groups, sexual orientations, or levels of physical ability, and plant and animal life. It is empowering in that it enables people to value and express and explore new sides of themselves (as in Lunis's and others' comments in chapter 5) and to take on a wider range of points of view or behaviors (as in Teal's comments in the same chapter). Lothlorien strives to be a safe and accepting social environment that opens up options rather than closing them off. The individual in this context creates freely, but in relative anonymity and as part of an unpredictable and cumulative mix of other creators. Individuals are also changeable and fluid, and in the context of the community, can play with identities and ideas. A range of options is embodied in the variety of religious symbols and lifestyles that are acceptable and that exist side by side. And there is also the context of communal responsibility and sharing, of Keeping Each Other Alive.

At Lothlorien, efforts to allow for individual autonomy are combined with recognition of the need for care, with a loose but generally supportive collective culture, and with a shifting patchwork of group cultures. In most cases, respect for lifestyle freedom enhances the sense of belonging. The latter translates, on an organizational level, into shared ownership of the land and shared decision making. It translates in informal culture into the cultivation of agape and the development of "chosen families." Belonging and connectedness also expand out and encompass the natural world. And connections are enacted, further defined and reinforced through rituals and through the festivals.

Safety and freedom at Lothlorien, then, and potentially elsewhere, are mutually supportive rather than antagonistic. Paradoxically, people often feel most at home in the places they can leave at will.

Lothlorien, Living Experiments, and Social Change

Over the course of history utopian visions have changed. It is as if each place and time period is a patch of ground in some hilly and forested terrain, and from each of these patches of ground only certain other places are visible. Or to put it more pedantically, the vantage point of each time, place, and circumstance is associated with its particular power relations, social norms, problems, values, conflicts, blind spots, and technological possibilities, and inspires particular questions and desires that the vision attempts to resolve. While Plato and

"A Spontaneous Social Experiment"

other Greek philosophers from the upper strata of their societies concerned themselves with ideal systems of law and government, English medieval utopian visions were often chiefly preoccupied with food (Claeys and Sargent 1999.)

There are times when a new direction can only be conceived imaginatively, through fiction or art, in different worlds or future or past times, or even after death. At other times experimentation is possible on a small scale. Sometimes fiction inspires experimentation, or vice versa. Many of the utopian communes discussed in chapter 2 were inspired by fiction, and many also attempted to deal with specific contemporary issues—segregation, inequality, the alienating effects of the Industrial Revolution.

Lothlorien has drawn on images and symbols that owe much to Romantic literature and to Neo-Paganism. Some of its key cultural, philosophical, and economic features, environmentalism, collective ownership, religious pluralism, offer interesting imaginative possibilities in their turn. While it has its share of flaws and conflicts, the community presents an alternative model of values and practices that are antistructural (to use Turner's term) in the context of the United States and much of the industrialized world. In particular its approaches to waste disposal, building, forest stewardship, and sustainable camping on a minimal budget are impressive. And Lothlorien has already made a difference to some individuals even as an isolated and unusual example. The following quote from Andrea illustrates this:

> It was a place that it was possible to make a transition . . . It gave me
> a lot of hope that it could actually happen and I could do it, because
> other people had. (Andrea, 2007)

Appiah (2006) points out that shifts in behavioral norms rarely come about through reasoned argument (although reasoned argument plays a part in their origins). Rather, people tend to become habituated to sets of behaviors and relationships and to base their sense of what is desirable on what they are used to seeing. He calls this "the primacy of practice." As examples he offers the processes of gradual habituation that led to a shift away from binding women's feet in China and the recent growing recognition of gay and lesbian couples by families, the media, and the law in the industrialized West.

Each time a group of people try a mode of life that is unusual, given its social context, they create the likelihood of it at first being seen as possible and eventually being seen as "normal"—at least one option among others. This does not mean that eventually everyone will adopt it, but it does mean that it may come to be considered an acceptable way of life. And Lothlorien is genuinely unusual, economically, politically, environmentally, and culturally.

An Unreal Estate

A "Green Man" and a red and yellow wreath.
Photo by Lucinda Carspecken

Bonedaddy says that he has looked around at other communities and come to this conclusion:

> Nowhere in the country is a place set up like this one. It's a kind of spontaneous social experiment. (Bonedaddy, 2006)

I noted in chapter 2 that intentional communities tend to inspire strong responses, especially in their early years, from observers and participants alike. These run the gamut from ridicule to suspicion, to disgust, to passionate advocacy, especially in cases where their values or norms are at odds with the cultures of which they are a part. An alternative way of living is an attempt at disproof of the commonsense assumptions of its time and place about desirable and feasible ways to live. And to the extent that it creates familiarity with new social formations, this is an effective disproof. Every social experiment, if it is sustained for any length of time, expands the range of lifestyle choices for people in the society beyond it and can thus be perceived as a threat or as a dream, as can any force for change.

In its role as a sanctuary, secluded from the mainstream for pockets of time, Lothlorien also provides the setting for individual exploration. Not only intentional communities but other nonconformist or marginalized spaces within large states—ghettos, prisons, minority religious groups, guilds, speakeasies, street corners—have often unwittingly provided the breeding grounds for new cultural forms, new expressions of opposition, and new thought. What Lothlorien provides is not perfection by any measure but it is a distinctive, chosen form of sanctuary, where participants change, grow, and in some cases develop further utopian visions of their own.

"When Humanity lands there, it looks out, and seeing a better country, sets sail. Progress is the realisation of Utopias" (Oscar Wilde 1891).

An Unreal Estate

Notes

1. "That Dose of Unreality"

1. James C. Scott's *Seeing Like a State: How Certain Schemes to Improve the Human Condition Have Failed* (1998) describes some disastrous examples of state-run attempts to impose utopian blueprints from above.

2. ACT UP NY, "Rev. Jerry Falwell (with Rev. Pat Robertson) blames pagans, abortionists, feminists & gays and lesbians for bringing on the terrorist attacks in New York and Washington," partial transcript of comments from the September 13, 2001, telecast of the 700 Club, on ACT UP AIDS Coalition to Unleash Power, at http://www.actupny.org/YELL/falwell.html.

3. Wild Magick Gathering is one of Lothlorien's two largest annual festivals, and is held around the time of the Fall Equinox.

4. See chapter 4.

5. See chapter 3. "Faerie" is the name of the forested part of Lothlorien.

6. *Brigadoon*, a 1954 film musical produced by MGM and directed by Vincent Minnelli, depicted a magical village in Scotland that emerges from the mist for one day every one hundred years. It was based on a nineteenth-century German story by Friedrich Gerstacker.

2. "Dream Flowers"

1. Bonewits, Isaac. 2005. "How Many 'Pagans' Are There?" Version 3.0. At *Isaac Bonewits' Cyberhenge*, http://www.neopagan.net/HowManyPagans.html.

2. See, for example, Goodison and Morris, eds., 1999, and King, ed., 1997.

3. Peter Bramwell has written a fascinating account of the way Neo-Pagan ideas are contested, expanded, and changed through children's literature in his 2009 book *Pagan Themes in Modern Children's Fiction: Green Man, Shamanism, Earth Mysteries*.

4. See chapter 5 for a definition of polyamory.

3. Faerie and Avalon

1. *Never Again the Burning Times* is the name both of a song sung in Pagan circles and of Loretta Orion's book about Neo-Paganism (1995).

2. Black Madonnas are found in various parts of Europe, date back many centuries, and possibly relate to pre-Christian traditions originating in Africa. For a discussion of their origins and prevalence see Moss and Cappannari, 1982, "In Quest of the Black Virgin: She is Black Because She is Black."

3. "Forty-two" is given in this novel as the answer to the question of "Life, the Universe, and everything."

4. *The Blair Witch Project* was a horror movie produced in 1999 by Haxan Films.

5. Sometimes parallel and strikingly similar practices originate in different places. Calling to the elements from the four directions of the compass, for example, or "casting a circle" of sacred space, is a tradition that dates both to early Christianity and to ancient Greek ritual, was revived in Renaissance Europe, was practiced in Masonic rituals in Europe from the sixteenth century onward. It became part of Wicca and subsequently the broader Neo-Pagan movement from the mid–twentieth century. Many American Indian cultures, drawing on their own separate long-standing traditions, also call on the four directions, and this has occasionally led to misunderstandings. Magliocco cites an incident from the 1993 Parliament of World Religions where Lakota elders also attending took offence at this practice, seeing it as cultural appropriation, until members the Covenant of the Goddess, a Pagan group, approached them and described the parallel tradition in the Old World. The two groups then held a public ceremony together as an indication of their mutual understanding (2004: 216).

4. "A Loose-Knit Anarchy"

1. See, for example, Richard Conniff's *The Ape in the Corner Office*.

2. Tasks include (but are not limited to) pre-Festival promotion, mowing campsites and public areas, dispensing wood at all the stations, putting new bags in recycle bins, gathering and disposing of trash and recyclables, cleaning the Long Hall, Dome showers, and stage, raking and maintaining the composters, cleaning the boiler and hauling and stacking wood to heat it, bagging ice and washing buckets for the ice house, mowing and marking parking spaces, organizing parking, collecting registration and pre-registration fees, lighting the paths and the Dome with candles, buying food and planning meals, cooking, washing dishes, bookkeeping, maintaining roads and paths, helping campers, cleaning fire pits and checking fire pit safety, responding to email and mail, setting up the sound system for the stage, organizing volunteers and barters, making announcements, and leading workshops and rituals.

3. In 2006, event revenues (not including Witches' Ball) came to $22,634.32. This included over $11,000.00 for Elf Fest and just under $8,000.00 for Wild Magick Gathering. Membership dues came to $1,906.00, and contributions and miscellaneous income came to just under $1,800.00. The biggest expenses were property taxes, at over $4,000.00 for the year as a whole; maintenance, at $3,914.30; utilities (including water, gas for the kitchen stove, and trash removal), at around $2,800.00; supplies, at $2,106.54; liability insurance, at $1,835.25; construction, at $1,572.88; printing for promotional materials, at $1,339.25; and firewood (this is provided for festival participants), at $1,150.00.

4. See chapter 3.

5. See Pike (2001: 209–210) for an example of an incident at a Lothlorien festival where this did not happen and the issue was not resolved.

5. "The Land of Misfit Toys"

1. Pitzer's edited book *America's Communal Utopias* (1997) brings together some excellent examples of historical studies. Others have been cited in chapter 2.

2. Susan Love Brown's edited collection *Intentional Community* (2002) offers a new direction here, approaching contemporary communes (and some historical ones) from an anthropological perspective.

3. William Smith, another sociologist, also gives attention to affective factors in his large (1999) study of families within communes.

4. C. S. Lewis (1960), and also Hillery, added a fourth category by separating affection and friendship, but in my discussion I shall include these in the same general category.

5. It is still common in many countries, however, for parents to make decisions for sons and (more commonly) daughters concerning the person they may have a sexual relationship or marriage with, and in many cases erotic love grows or emerges within an arranged marriage.

6. The "complex marriage" arrangements practiced at Oneida (see chapter 2) and the similar system of "polyfidelity," smaller-scale group marriages consisting of families of six to eighteen or so people, which was practiced at the Kerista commune in San Francisco from 1971 to 1991, could be said to be forms of polyamory but are not typical, since these two cases involved large numbers of people and less individual choice.

7. The flag has three horizontal colored stripes. The top one is blue, to signify openness and honesty. The middle is red, to signify passion and romance. The bottom band is black to signify solidarity. In the center is a *pi* sign relating to the first letter of "polyamory."

8. See Hillery for a discussion of freedom and community in the monastery—a very different context—and also Appiah (2006: 9–13.)

6. "Something Mystical and Fine"

1. See chapter 1. Since I ended up with fewer completed surveys than full-length interviews, I did not establish a basis for solid statistical analyses.

2. Jef had set up a board in Radiance Hall with all the tasks around Lothlorien written on it, so that people could add their names to what they planned to do.

3. The name Bubba Ho-Tep came from a comedy horror film of the same name, produced in 2002 by Jason Savage and directed by Don Coscarelli.

8. "A Spontaneous Social Experiment"

1. Examples of this, from India alone, include Emerson translating the Bhagavad Gita in the late nineteenth century as he was conceiving his Transcendentalist philosophy, Indian spiritual ideas in the works of early twentieth-century novelists

like E. M. Forster, Somerset Maugham, and Francis Hodgson Burnett, and later influential authors like Aldous Huxley and Ram Dass, the hippie movement's fascination with Indian spiritual traditions, and, finally, ideas about meditation, visualization, immanent divinity and the value of all paths that have seeped into general dialogue since the mid–twentieth century.

Bibliography

Ackroyd, Peter. 1997. *Blake: A Biography.* London: Ballantine Books.

Adams, Douglas. 1979. *The Hitchhiker's Guide to the Galaxy.* London: Pan Books.

Adams, Richard. 1972. *Watership Down.* London: Rex Collings.

Adler, Margot. 1986 (1979). *Drawing Down The Moon: Witches, Druids, Goddess Worshippers and Other Pagans In America Today.* New York: Penguin Compass.

Andelsen, Jonathan. 2002. "Coming Together and Breaking Apart." In Brown, ed., *Intentional Community.*

Appiah, Kwame Anthony. 2005. *The Ethics of Identity.* Princeton, N.J.: Princeton University Press.

———. 2006. *Cosmopolitanism.* Princeton, N.J.: Princeton University Press.

Arndt, Karl. 1997. "George Rapp's Harmony Society." In Pitzer, ed., *America's Communal Utopias.*

Auden, W. H. 1965. *About the House.* New York: Random House.

Bartelt, Pearl W. 1997. "American Jewish Agricultural Colonies." In Pitzer, ed., *America's Communal Utopias.*

Bauer, Jacqui, Burnell Fischer, Gustavo Garcia-Lopez, Robert Holahan, Prakash Kashwan, Elinor Ostrom, and Brian Steed. 2006. *Revisiting Elvin H.O.M.E. Inc. and the Lothlorien Forest.* IFRI Y773 Report.

Behar, Ruth. 1997. *The Vulnerable Observer: Anthropology That Breaks Your Heart.* New York: Beacon Press.

Bellamy, Edward. 1996 (1888). *Looking Backward.* New York: Dover.

Berger, Helen. 1999. *A Community of Witches.* Columbia: University of South Carolina Press.

Berger, Helen, Evan Leach, and Leigh Shaffer. 2003. *Voices From the Pagan Census.* Columbia: University of South Carolina Press.

Berlin, Isaiah. 1990. *The Crooked Timber of Humanity.* Princeton, N.J.: Princeton University Press.

Boas, Franz. 1940. "The Limitations of the Comparative Method of Anthropology." In *Race, Language and Culture.* New York: Macmillan.

Bonvillain, Nancy. 2001. *Native Nations.* Upper Saddle River, N.J.: Prentice and Hall.

Bramwell, Peter. 2009. *Pagan Themes in Modern Children's Fiction: Green Man, Shamanism, Earth Mysteries*. Basingstoke, UK: Palgrave Macmillan.

Brewer, Priscilla. 1997. "The Shakers of Mother Ann Lee." In Pitzer, ed., *America's Communal Utopias*.

Brown, Susan Love. 2002. "Community as Cultural Critique." In Brown, ed., *Intentional Community*.

———, ed. 2002. *Intentional Community: An Anthropological Perspective*. Albany: State University of New York Press.

Bruner, Edward. 1986. "Ethnography as Narrative." In Turner and Bruner, eds., *The Anthropology of Experience*.

Butler, Marilyn. 1985. *Romantics, Rebels and Reactionaries: English Literature and Its Background, 1760–1830*. Oxford: Oxford University Press.

Cabet, Etienne. 2003. *Travels in Icaria*. Syracuse, N.Y.: Syracuse University Press.

Campbell, Joseph. 1949. *The Hero With A Thousand Faces*. Princeton, N.J.: Bollingen.

Castoriadis, Cornelius. 1998 (1975). *The Imaginary Institution of Society*. Cambridge, Mass.: Massachusetts Institute of Technology Press.

Charles, Matthew. 2010. *Utopia and Its Discontents: Dreams of Catastrophe and the End of the "End of History."* Rev. paper presented at Utopia, Dystopia, and Critical Theory, SSPT conference, May 2010.

Christians, Clifford. 2008. "Ethics and Politics in Qualitative Research." In Norman Denzin and Yvonna Lincoln, eds., *The Landscape of Qualitative Research*. Vol. 3. Los Angeles: Sage Publications.

Claeys, Gregory, and Lyman Tower Sargent. 1999. "The Land of Cockaigne" (excerpt). In Claeys and Sargent, eds., *The Utopia Reader*. New York: New York University Press.

Clifford, James. 1986. "Introduction: Partial Truths." In James Clifford and George Marcus, eds., *Writing Culture: The Poetics and Politics of Ethnography*. Berkeley: University of California Press.

Clifton, Chas. 2006. *Her Hidden Children: The Rise of Wicca and Paganism in America*. Lanham, Md.: AltaMira Press.

Conniff, Richard. 2005. *The Ape in the Corner Office: How to Make Friends, Win Fights, and Work Smarter by Understanding Human Nature*. New York: Crown Business.

Cuzzort, R. P., and E. W. King. 1989. *Twentieth-Century Social Thought*. Chicago: Holt, Rinehart, and Winston.

Das, Dilip, and Arvind Verma. 2005. *Police Mission*. Lanham, Md.: Scarecrow Press.

Davy, Barbara Jane. 2006. *Introduction to Pagan Studies*. Lanham, Md.: AltaMira Press.

Delano, Sterling. 2004. *Brook Farm: The Dark Side of Utopia*. Cambridge, Mass.: Belknap Press.

Dettwyler, Katherine. 1994. *Dancing Skeletons*. Long Grove, Ill.: Waveland.

Douglas, Mary. 1966. *Purity and Danger: An Analysis of the Concepts of Pollution and Taboo*. London: Routledge.

DuBois, W. E. B. 1995 (1928). *Dark Princess*. Jackson: University of Mississippi Press.

————. 2004 (1911). *The Quest of the Silver Fleece.* New York: Harlem Moon.

Durnbaugh, Donald. 1997. "Communitarian Societies in Colonial America." In Pitzer, ed., *America's Communal Utopias.*

Emerson, Ralph Waldo. 2010. *Emerson's Essays.* New York: Harper and Row.

Ferrucci, Katherine. 2004. *Limestone Lives.* Bloomington: Indiana University Press.

Fike, Rupert, ed. 1998. *Voices From the Farm.* Summertown, Tenn.: The Book Publishing Co.

Foster, Lawrence. 1997. "Free Love and Community." In Pitzer, ed., *America's Communal Utopias.*

Foucault, Michel. 1982. "The Subject and Power." In *Beyond Structuralism and Hermeneutics.* Chicago: University of Chicago Press.

Frazer, James. 1922. *The Golden Bough.* New York: Macmillan.

Funke, Cornelia. 2005 (2003). *Inkheart.* New York: Scholastic.

Gage, Matilda Jocelyn. 2010 (1893). *Woman, Church and State: A Historical Account of the Status of Woman Through the Christian Ages, With Reminiscences of the Matriarchate.* New York: Forgotten Books.

Gardner, Gerald. 1999 (1949). *High Magic's Aid.* New York: Pentacle Enterprises.

————. 2004 (1954). *Witchcraft Today.* New York: Citadel.

Gay, Peter. 1995 (1966). *The Enlightenment: The Rise of Modern Paganism.* New York: W. W. Norton.

Geertz, Clifford. 1973. "Thick Description: Toward an Interpretive Theory of Culture." In *The Interpretation of Cultures.* New York: Basic Books.

Gimbutas, Maria. 1982. *Goddesses and Gods of Old Europe.* London: Thames and Hudson.

Goldstein, Herman. 1990. *Problem Oriented Policing.* Philadelphia: Temple University Press.

Goodison, Lucy, and Christine Morris, eds. 1999. *Ancient Goddesses: The Myths and the Evidence.* Madison: University of Wisconsin Press.

Gottman, J. M. 1994. *What Predicts Divorce? The Relationship between Marital Processes and Marital Outcomes.* Hillsdale, N.J.: Erlbaum.

Grahame, Kenneth. 1995 (1908). *The Wind in the Willows.* London: St. Martin's Press.

Graves, Robert. 1948. *The White Goddess.* London: Farrar, Straus, and Giroux.

Gray, John. 1996. *Mill on Liberty: A Defense.* New York: Routledge.

Greenwood, Susan. 2000. *Magic, Witchcraft and the Otherworld: An Anthropology.* Oxford: Berg.

Gudeman, Stephen. 1999. *Economic Anthropology.* Northampton, Mass.: Edward Elgar.

Guinee, William. 1987. "Satanism in Yellowwood Forest: The Interdependence of Antagonistic World Views." *Indiana Folklore and Oral History* 16(1): 1–30.

Guthrie, James. 1984. *A Quarter Century in Lawrence County, Indiana, 1917–1941.* Bedford, Ind.: Lawrence County Historical and Genealogical Society.

Harvey, Graham. 2000. *Contemporary Paganism: Listening People, Speaking Earth.* New York: New York University Press.

Heinlein, Robert A. 1992 (1961). *Stranger in a Strange Land.* New York: Ace/Putnam.

Hemenway, Toby. 2000. *Gaia's Garden.* White River Junction, Vt.: Chelsea Green.

Heselton, Philip. 2003. *Gerald Gardner and the Cauldron of Inspiration.* Sequim, Wash.: Holmes Publishing Group.

Higginbotham, Joyce, and River Higginbotham. 2004. *Paganism: An Introduction to Earth Centered Religions.* St Paul, Minn.: Llewellyn.

Hillery, George. 1992. *The Monastery.* Westport, Conn.: Praeger.

Holden, Anthony. 2005. *The Wit in the Dungeon: The Remarkable Life of Leigh Hunt.* Boston: Little, Brown.

Holmes, Richard. 2010. *The Age of Wonder: The Romantic Generation and the Discovery of the Beauty and Terror of Science.* New York: Vintage.

Hopkins, Pauline. 2004 (1903). *Of One Blood.* New York: Washington Square Press.

Hutton, Ronald. 1999. *The Triumph of the Moon: A History of Modern Pagan Witchcraft.* Oxford: Oxford University Press.

————. 2003. *Witches, Druids, and King Arthur.* London: Hambledon Continuum.

Huxley, Aldous. 1932. *Brave New World.* London: Chatto and Windus.

Iwanska, Alicja. 2006 (1971). "Purgatory and Utopia: A Mazahua Indian Village of Mexico." In Norman Denzin, ed., *Sociological Methods.* New Brunswick, N.J.: Transaction Books.

Jacobs, Sue-Ellen, Wesley Thomas, and Sabine Lang, eds. 1997. *Two Spirit People.* Urbana: University of Illinois Press.

Johansen, Bruce. 1982. *Forgotten Founders.* Ipswich, Conn.: Gambit.

Jordan, Brigitte. 1978. *Birth in Four Cultures.* Prospect Heights, Ill.: Waveland.

Kamau, Lucy. 2002. "Liminality, Communitas and Charisma." In Brown, ed., *Intentional Community.*

Kanter, Rosabeth Moss. 1972. *Commitment and Community.* Cambridge, Mass.: Harvard University Press.

Kelly, Aidan. 1991. *Crafting the Art of Magic: A History of Modern Witchcraft.* St. Paul, Minn.: Llewellyn.

King, Karen L., ed. 1997. "Women and Goddess Traditions." In *Antiquity and Today.* Minneapolis: Fortress Press.

Kinkade, Kat. 1994. *Is It Utopia Yet?* Louisa, Va.: Twin Oaks Publishing.

Kipling, Rudyard. 1906. *Puck of Pook's Hill.* London: Macmillan.

Kitch, Sally. 1989. *Chaste Liberation.* Urbana: University of Illinois Press.

Kok, Terry. 1985a. *Elf Lights.* Self-published.

————. 1985b. *Faerie Wyzdry.* Self-published.

Kramer, Heinrich and Jacob Sprenger. 1487. *Malleus Maleficarum.* http://www.malle usmaleficarum.org/.

Kuhlmann, Hilke. 2005. *Living Walden II.* Urbana: University of Illinois Press.

Kuman, Krishan. 1991. *Utopianism.* Buckingham: Open University Press.

Kumar, Krishan, and Stephen Bann, eds. 1993. *Utopias and the Millennium.* London: Reaktion Books.

Lacan, Jacques. 2007. (1936) *Ecrits.* New York: W. W. Norton and Company.

Lamb, Sarah. 2000. *White Saris and Sweet Mangoes: Aging, Gender, and Body in North India.* Berkeley: University of California Press.

Lang, Sabine. 1998. *Men as Women, Women as Men.* Austin: University of Texas Press.

Lawn, Katherine, and Claudio Salvucci, eds. 2003. *Women in New France: Extracts from The Jesuit Relations.* Merchantsville, N.J.: Evolution Publishing.

Le Guin, Ursula. 1994. *The Dispossessed.* New York: Harper Prism.

Leacock, Eleanor Burke. 1954. "The Montagnais 'Hunting Territory' and the Fur Trade." American Anthropologist Memoir 78.

Leland, Charles. 2009 (1899). *Aradia: The Gospel of the Witches.* Sioux Falls, S.D.: EZreads Publications.

Lewis, C. S. 2004. *The Chronicles of Narnia.* London: Harper Collins.

Losada, Marcial, and Emily Heaphy. 2004. "The Role of Positivity and Connectivity in the Performance of Business Teams: A Nonlinear Dynamics Model." *American Behavioral Scientist* 47, no. 6: 740–765.

Luhrmann, Tanya. 1989. *Persuasions of the Witch's Craft,* Cambridge, Mass.: Harvard University Press.

Magliocco, Sabina. 2004. *Witching Culture: Folklore and Neopaganism in America.* Philadelphia: University of Pennsylvania Press.

Mankiller, Wilma, and Michael Wallis. 1993. *Mankiller: A Chief and Her People.* New York: St. Martin's Griffin.

Mann, Charles. 2005. *1491.* New York: Vintage.

Mannheim, Karl. 1955 (1936). *Ideology and Utopia: An Introduction to the Sociology of Knowledge.* San Diego, Calif.: Harcourt.

Marcus, G. E., and D. Cushman. 1982. "Ethnographies as Texts." *Annual Review of Anthropology* 11: 25–69.

Marcus, G. E., and Michael Fischer. 1986. *Anthropology as Cultural Critique.* Chicago: University of Chicago Press.

May, Dean L. 1997. "One Heart and Mind: Communal Life and Values Among the Mormons." In Pitzer, ed., *America's Communal Utopias.*

Mead, Margaret. 1928. *Coming of Age in Samoa.* New York: Morrow Quill.

———. 1949. *Male and Female: The Classic Study of the Sexes.* New York: Morrow Quill.

Mill, John Stewart. 2009. *The Basic Writings of John Stuart Mill: On Liberty, The Subjugation of Women and Utilitarianism.* New York: Classic Books America.

Miller, Timothy. 1998. *The Quest for Utopia.* Syracuse, N.Y.: Syracuse University Press.

———. 1999. *The Sixties Communes.* Syracuse, N.Y.: Syracuse University Press.

More, Thomas. 2001 (1516). *Utopia.* Newark, N.J.: Yale University Press.

Morgan, Lewis Henry. 2000 (1877). "Ethnical Periods" and "The Ancient Family." In *Ancient Society, or Researches in the Lines of Human Progress from Savagery through Barbarism to Civilization.* New Brunswick, N.J.: Transaction Publishers.

Morris, William. 1891. *News from Nowhere.* London: Reeves and Turner.

Moss, Leonard, and Stephen Cappannari. 2010. "In Quest of the Black Virgin: She Is Black Because She Is Black." In James Preston, ed., *Mother Worship: Theme and Variations.* Chapel Hill: University of North Carolina Press.

Murray, Margaret. 1921. *The Witch Cult in Western Europe*. Oxford: Clarendon Press.

————. 1933. *The God of the Witches*. Oxford: Oxford University Press.

Myerhoff, Barbara. 1986. "Life, Not Death in Venice." In Turner and Bruner, eds., *The Anthropology of Experience*.

Nation, Richard. 2005. *At Home in the Hoosier Hills*. Bloomington: Indiana University Press.

Niman, Michael. 1997. *People of the Rainbow*. Knoxville: University of Tennessee Press.

Nussbaum, Martha. 2001. *Upheavals of Thought: The Intelligence of Emotions*. Cambridge, UK: Cambridge University Press.

————. 2006. *Frontiers of Justice*. Cambridge, Mass.: Belknap.

Oakes, Richard. 1993 (1972). "Remnants," excerpted in Mankiller and Wallis, *Mankiller: A Chief and Her People*.

Oliver, Michael. 1990. "Disability Definitions: The Politics of Meaning." In *The Politics of Disablement: A Sociological Approach*. Basingstoke, UK: Palgrave MacMillan.

Orion, Loretta. 1995. *Never Again the Burning Times*. Prospect Hill, Ill.: Waveland Press.

Orwell, George. 1945. *Animal Farm, a Fairy Story*. London: Secker and Warburg.

————. 1949. *Nineteen Eighty-Four, a Novel*. London: Secker and Warburg.

Ostrom, Elinor, and Harini Nagendra. 2006. "Insights on linking forests, trees, and people from the air, on the ground, and in the laboratory." *PNAS online*, http://www.pnas.org/content/103/51/19224/F3.expansion.html.

Paine, Tom. 2003. *Common Sense, The Rights of Man and Other Essential Writings*. New York: Signet Classic.

Peters, Thomas J., and Robert H. Waterman. 1982. *In Search of Organizational Excellence*. New York: Harper and Row.

Pike, Sarah. 2001. *Earthly Bodies, Magical Selves*. Berkeley: University of California Press.

————. 2004. *New Age and Neopagan Religions in America*. New York: Columbia University Press.

Pilon, Juliana Geron. 2007. "Utopia and Its Discontents." *The National Interest* (March–April)

Pitzer, Donald E. "Introduction." In Pitzer, ed. *America's Communal Utopias*.

————, ed. 1997. *America's Communal Utopias*. Chapel Hill: University of North Carolina Press.

Popper, Karl. 1962. *The Open Society and its Enemies*. Princeton, N.J.: Princeton University Press.

Rafert, Stewart. 1996. *The Miami Indians of Indiana*. Indianapolis, Ind.: Indiana Historical Society Press.

Ravenhearts, Morning Glory Zell, and Otter. 2006. "Frequently Asked Questions re: Polyamory." Quoted in *Wikipedia*, "Polyamory."

Rexroth, Kenneth. 1974. *Communalism: From its Origins to the Twentieth Century*. New York: Seabury Press.

Robert, Gen. Henry M. 1876. *Robert's Rules of Order*. Available at www.robertsrules.com/.

Roe, Nicholas. 2005. *Fiery Heart: The First Life of Leigh Hunt*. London: Pimlico.

Rogers, Carl. 1980. *A Way of Being*. Boston: Houghton Mifflin.

Rothstein, Edward. 2003. "Utopia and Its Discontents." In Edward Rothstein, Herbert Muschamp, and Martin Marty, eds., *Visions of Utopia*. New York: Oxford University Press.

Salomonsen, Jone. 2002. *Enchanted Feminism: The Reclaiming Witches of San Francisco*. London: Routledge.

Samson, Colin. 2003. *A Way of Life That Does Not Exist*. London: Verso.

Sargisson, Lucy. 1996. *Contemporary Feminist Utopianism*. London: Routledge.

Scott, James C. 1998. *Seeing Like a State: How Certain Schemes to Improve the Human Condition Have Failed*. New Haven, Conn.: Yale University Press.

Sen, Amartya. 1999. *Democracy as a Universal Value*. New Delhi: Lecture.

Shea, Robert, and Robert Anton Wilson. 1975. *The Illuminatus! Trilogy*. New York: Dell.

Shelley, Mary. 2010. *Frankenstein*. New York: Oxford University Press.

Shelley, Percy Bysshe. 1994. *The Complete Poems of Percy Bysshe Shelley*. New York: Modern Library.

Simecka, Milan. 1984. "A World With Utopias or Without Them?" In Peter Alexander and Roger Gill, eds., *Utopias*. London: Gerald Duckworth.

Skinner, B. F. 1948. *Walden II*. Indianapolis, Ind.: Hackett Publishing.

Slacek, Brleck, and Hancic Turnsek. 2010. "Utopia and Its Discontents: How Young People Are Making Sense of the Public Sphere," *International Journal of Learning and Media* 2(1) (Winter): 25–37.

Smith, William L., 1999. *Families and Communities*. Thousand Oaks, Calif.: Sage.

Spiro, Melford. 2004. "Utopia and Its Discontents: The Kibbutz and Its Historical Vicissitudes," *American Anthropologist* 106, no. 3: 556–568.

St. Clair, William. 1989. *The Godwins and the Shelleys: A Biography of a Family*. New York: W. W. Norton.

Starhawk. 1993. *The Fifth Sacred Thing*. New York: Bantam.

———. 1999 (1979). *The Spiral Dance*. New York: Harper San Francisco.

Stewart, Tony. 2004. *Fabulous Females and Peerless Pirs: a Tale of Mad Adventure in Old Bengal*. New York: Oxford University Press.

Stoeltje, Beverly. 1992. "Festival." In Richard Bauman, ed., *Folklore, Cultural Performances, and Popular Entertainments*. New York: Oxford University Press.

———. 1996. "The Snake Charmer Queen." In Colleen Cohen, Richard Wilk, and Beverly Stoeltje, eds. *Beauty Queens on the Global Stage*. New York: Routledge.

Stoeltje, Beverly, Christie Fox, and Stephen Olbrys. 1999. "The Self in 'Fieldwork': A Methodological Concern." *Journal of American Folklore* 112, no. 444: 158–182.

Sutcliffe, K. M., and T. J. Vogus. 2003. "Organizing for Resilience." In K. Cameron, J. E. Dutton, and R. E. Quinn, eds., *Positive Organizational Scholarship*. San Francisco: Berrett-Koehler.

Sutton, Robert P. 1997. "An American Elysium: The Icaren Communities." In Pitzer, ed., *America's Communal Utopias*.

Bibliography

Thoreau, Henry David. 1993 (1849). *Civil Disobedience*. New York: Dover.

———. 2005 (1854). *Walden*. Available at http://www.archive.org/stream/walden 01thor#page/n7/mode/2up.

Tolkien, J. R. R. 1987 (1954). *The Lord Of The Rings*. Boston: Houghton Mifflin.

Tonnies, Ferdinand. 2005 (1887). *Gemeinschaft und Gesellschaft*. Darmstadt: Wissen-schaftliche Buchgesellschaft.

Traer, James. 1980. *Marriage and the Family in Eighteenth-Century France*. Ithaca, N.Y.: Cornell University Press.

Turner, Victor. 1995 (1969). *The Ritual Process: Structure and Anti-Structure*. Chicago: Aldine Transaction.

Turner, Victor, and Edward Bruner, eds. *The Anthropology of Experience*. Urbana: University of Illinois Press.

Tylor, Edward B. 1958 (1871). "The Science of Culture" and "The Development of Culture." In *Primitive Culture*. New York: Harper and Row.

Valiente, Doreen, and Evan John Jones. 1990. *Witchcraft: A Tradition Renewed*. Seattle: Phoenix Publishing.

Versluis, Arthur. 1993. *American Transcendentalism and Asian Religions*. New York: Oxford University Press.

Victor, Jeffrey. 1993. *Satanic Panic: The Creation of a Contemporary Legend*. Chicago: Open Court.

Wagner, Sally Roesch. 2001. *Sisters in Spirit: Haudenosaunee (Iroquois) Influences on Early American Feminists*. Summertown, Tenn.: The Book Publishing Co.

Wallace, Anthony. 1956. "Revitalization Movements: Some Theoretical Consider-ations for Their Comparative Study." *American Anthropologist* 58, no. 2: 264–281.

Weber, Max. 1958 (1904). *The Protestant Work Ethic and the Spirit of Capitalism*. New York: Charles Scribner's Sons.

Wegner, Phillip. 2002. *Imaginary Communities*. Berkeley: University of California Press.

Weisbrot, Robert. 1997. "Father Divine and the Peace Mission." In Pitzer, ed., *America's Communal Utopias*.

White, Lynn Jr. 1967. "The Historical Roots of Our Ecological Crisis." *Science* 155(3767):1203–1207.

Whitman, Walt. 2006 (1891). *Song of Myself*. Available at http://openlibrary.org/ search?sort=new&subject_facet=Accessible+book&publisher_facet=Digireads .com.

Wilde, Oscar. 1891. "The Soul of Man Under Socialism." *Fortnightly Review* (Feb. 1891).

Williams, Raymond. 1977. "Hegemony." In *Marxism and Literature*. Oxford: Oxford University Press.

Wilson, James, and George Kelling. 1982. "Broken Windows." *The Atlantic Monthly* (March 1982).

Wolf, M. 1992. *A Thrice-Told Tale: Feminism, Postmodernism, and Ethnographic Respon-sibility*. Stanford, Calif.: Stanford University Press.

Wright, Frances. 1822. *A Few Days in Athens*. London: Longman, Hurst, Rees, Orme, and Brown.

Yeats, William Butler. 2004. *The Celtic Twilight: Faerie and Folklore*. New York: Dover.

Zablocki, Benjamin. 1980. *Alienation and Charisma: A Study of Contemporary American Communes*. New York: The Free Press.

Zamyatin, Yevgeny. 1952 (1924). *We*. London: Dutton.

Zell, Morning Glory. 1990. "A Bouquet of Lovers," *Green Egg*, #89, Beltane. Available at http://original.caw.org/articles/bouquet.html.

Index

Brook Farm, 49, 57

Brown, Susan Love, 46, 58, 215, 237n5:2

Brown County Democrat, 11

Building, 22, 70, 81, 98, 118, 174; and budgeting, 72, 232; and residences, 112–114; and sustainability, 62, 63, 90, 92, 93, 97, 99, 129, 130–131, 134, 143, 152, 218, 222, 228

Butler, Marilyn, 31–34

Bylaws, 75, 93, 108, 117, 123, 125, 133, 138, 139, 141, 147, 149, 177, 229, 231

Byron, Lord George, 32, 33, 34, 35

Cabet, Etienne, 49

Calvinism, 46, 107

Campsites, 4, 5, 12, 13, *60,* 70, 71–75, 116, 142, 175, 236n4:2

Care, 107, 182; of children, 51, 107, 137, 170, 152, 179; of community, 24–25, 128, 149, 180, 231; of land, 6, 13, 27, 63, 71, 117; and polyamory, 173. *See also* Work

Children, 4, 86, 98, 107, 137, 170, 179–180, 182, 192, 196–197, 198, 235n2:3; and autonomy, 230; and communes, 48, 51, 55; and community networks, 154, 155; and connection with nature, 219; in family hierarchy, 183; growing up at Lothlorien, 174–175; and Neo-paganism, 198, 199–200; and Wiccaning, 200–204

Church of All Worlds, 29, 172

Class, 9, 19, 53, 57, 77, 147, 151, 153–154, 162, 176, 223

Coleridge, Samuel, 32, 77, 82

Collective ownership, 2, 17, 61–62, 71–72, 75, 100, 104, 134, 182, 217; and communes, 46–52; in fiction, 55, 232; and freedom, 103, 142, 149; and Native Americans, 9, 230. *See also* Communes

Communes, 2, 10–11,12, 19, 27, 55, 58, 77, 99, 118, 132, 143, 146, 153, 156,

222, 223, 234, 237n5:2; and commitments, 156–157; history of, 45–53; and inspiration from fiction, 54–55; and leadership styles, 120–122; and nuclear families, 157, 237n5:3; and social cycles, 156, 215–216, 217. *See also* Utopianism

Communitarianism, 149, 181, 182–184, 231

Communitas, 2, 144, 146–149, 161, 163, 168, 177, 178, 180, 184, 229; and love, 156–157

Composting privies, 71, 72, 75, 76, 77, 91–93, 105, 112, 118, 125, 135, 146, 153, 176, 228, 236n4:2

Conflict, 4, 79, 81, 85, 89, 90, 98, 106, 115, 129, 132–136, 141, 149, 157, 221, 229, 231, 232; conflict resolution, 108, 136–139, 140; inner conflict, 221; in religious traditions, 38

Consensus, 108, 109, 117

Creative freedom, 2, 72, 75–79, 80, 97, 98, 106, 141, 143, 149, 178, 184, 229

Crowley, Aleister, 29, 39, 41, 88

Darwin, Charles, 37

Darwin, Erasmus, 33, 37

Das, 124–125, 141

Davy, Barbara Jane, 30

Davy, Humphrey, 32, 34

Democracy, 17, 37, 39, 49, 54, 57, 72, 108, 109, 118–122, 137–142, 143, 229, 230

Demographics, 150–154

Dianic witches, 29

Diggers, 31

Discordians, 29, 89

Dissenters, 31

Druids, 28, 29, 114

Drumming, 5, 16, 22, 44, 82, 84, 86, 87, 90, 122, 123, 129, 184, 190, 193, 195, 209, 228; conflict over, 133–134

DuBois, W. E. B., 55

Index

Earth Liberation Front, 7

Economics, 107, 148; and Anthropology, 57, 106; among communes, 47, 48, 50, 51, 216, 223; at Lothlorien, 2, 71–72, 98, 103–106, 107, 111, 112, 113–115, 119, 125–132, 142, 143–144, 182, 218, 232. *See also* Work

Economy, 47

Egalitarianism, 9, 37, 39, 41, 52, 106, 119–122, 134, 143, 163, 177

Eldars, 55, 108, 109, 111, 115, 119, 120, 124, 127, 138, 139, 151, 169, 176, 192, 210, 217, 225; Eldar contract, 116–118. *See also* Hierarchy; Leadership

Elf Lights, 8

Elf Lore Family, 7, 68

ElvinHOME, 8, 64, 104, 106, 108, 121, 123, 125, 137, 141, 143, 144, 146, 151; and economics, 126–127; mailing list, 150

Emerson, Ralph Waldo, 36, 77, 237n8:1

Engels, Frederich, 37

Enlightenment, 28, 30–35, 37, 39, 40, 107

Environmentalism, 2, 6, 13, 15, 17, 62, 65, 93–97, 99, 106, 128, 129, 131, 135, 143, 153, 176, 177, 178, 181, 183, 217, 226–228, 232; and individualism, 182; and Neo-paganism, 42, 43, 45; and organization, 104–105, 140; range of perspectives on, 63–64; and rationality, 69–70, 182, 226

Eros, 156–161, 184

Faerie, 15, 61, 64–70, 73, 76, 80, 188, 194, 206, 235n5

Faerie Wyzdry, 66

Fairy tales, 3, 28, 35, 36, 59, 65, 86, 187, 193, 201. *See also* Fiction

Falwell, Jerry, 11

Families, 147, 154–155, 157, 162, 170, 171, 178, 184, 199, 224, 232, 237n5:3;

"chosen family," 25, 156–161, 231; on The Farm, 51, 157; and individualism, 182–183; among Keristans, 51; among nineteenth century settlers in Southern Indiana, 9, 10; and polyamory, 172–173; and rituals, 200–207; among Shakers, 47; and social contract, 182; and ties between Romantic and Enlightenment thinkers, 34

The Farm, 51, 121, 157

Father Divine's Peace Missions, 50, 52, 120

Fellowship of Intentional Communities, 50

Festivals, 1–2, 8, 11, 12, 13, 14, 18, 20, 45, 59, 63, 64, 70, 76, 98, 135; and camp sites, 72–75; and children, 174; and communitas, 147, 158–161, 177, 228, 231; demographics of, 150–151; and gender, 170–171; individually run, 134; and organization, 105–106, 122–123, 126–127, 133, 181, 217, 225; and race, 168–169; and ritual, 188–197, 200–202, 203–204, 206–207, 208; and Thunder Dome, 82–90; and transience, 215, 217, 228; and "unreality," 21–22; and yearly calendar, 71, 235n1:3. *See also* Policing; Rituals

Fiction, 2, 3, 12, 23–27, 58–59, 62, 74, 76, 82, 193; and ethnography, 53–54, 57–58; and Neo-Paganism, 29, 40, 41, 42, 54, 235n2:3; utopian fiction, 2, 3–4, 49, 54–55, 56, 58, 232. *See also* Fairy tales; Mythology

Forest management, 8, 63, 65, 99, 104, 140, 141, 228, 232

Foucault, Michel, 183

Fourier, Charles, 48–49

Frazier, James, 54

Freedom. *See* Acceptance; Autonomy; Creative freedom; Individualism

Freemasons, 39, 41

Index

Revolution, 182; and networks, 155; as outside employment, 152–153, 162, 175, 183, 197–198; and volunteering, 72, 82, 105, 106, 126–127, 128–132, 140, 184, 229. *See also* Building; Economics; Gardening; Protestant work ethic

LUCINDA CARSPECKEN teaches qualitative research methods and anthropology at Indiana University. Her research interests include the anthropology of literature, environmental anthropology, and Neo-Pagan Studies.